Learning the Arts in an Age of Uncertainty

Walter Pitman

Copyright © Arts Education Council of Ontario, 1998

CANADIAN CATALOGUING IN PUBLICATION DATA
Pitman, Walter, 1929–
Learning the Arts in an Age of Uncertainty

ISBN 0-9684672-0-2

Cover design by Sheila Britton
Author photo by Jim Parr

Edited by Stuart Ross
Designed by Paul Mergler

Printed in Canada by Aylmer Express Limited, Aylmer, Ontario

Arts Education Council of Ontario
Oakburn Centre, 15 Oakburn Crescent
North York, ON M2N 2T5

Phone:
416-229-6384

Published by the Arts Education Council of Ontario.

Acknowledgements

One can never adequately thank all those who have over many months provided assistance and support in the writing of such a volume.

A few of those who have helped: Louis Applebaum, Stephen Campbell, Fran Cohen, Judith Fine, Tony Ketchum, Jon Mergler, Jim Parr, Rae Perigoe, my daughter Anne Pitman-Davidson, Paul Schafer, Barbara Soren, Alan Thompson, and especially my wife Ida, whose patience and understanding is infinite.

⌘　⌘　⌘

The publication of this book would have been impossible without the generous assistance of the Laidlaw Foundation, the Samuel and Saidye Bronfman Family Foundation, and the Ontario Arts Council.

To Zoë, our granddaughter.

Pray summon up now if you will, the play time of your youth;
Young limb, sweet song, a childhood game, adventures impromptu.
When play was natural as breath. When play was given due.
When all pretend, and all far-fetched was simple to make true.

But some of us in growing up, have lost, or set adrift,
Or given up, forgot, or worse; been beaten from that "gift"
By tyrant brutal. Bully cold. Who threatens to punish swift
Any and all who dare to play and celebrate that gift.

Now if by chance you find yourself oppressed in some employ,
We pray you'll not forget the gift no bully can destroy.
For play is more than childhood game, much more than fancy's toy.
It is a way to find a way, to heal, release, bring joy.

Tom Wood, "Claptrap,"
© Dundurn Press, 1997

Contents

Introduction
The Day School Came Alive 1

Chapter 1
The Arts and the World Our Children Face 14

Chapter 2
The Arts in our Schools: Their Presence and Possibility 44

Chapter 3
The Arts and the Process of Learning 62

Chapter 4
The Arts — Living Together and Learning a Living 90

Chapter 5
Assessment and Excellence 115

Chapter 6
The Arts and Being Canadian 132

Chapter 7
The Arts and the Abundant Life 163

Chapter 8
Integrating The Arts — Integrating the Curriculum 194

Chapter 9
Artists and Teachers, Parents and Community 218

Chapter 10
Strategies for Change 242

Epilogue 260

Appendix A
Not a Frill: The Centrality of the Arts in the
Education of the Future A-1

Appendix B
Keynote Address by Robin Phillips B-1

Appendix C
Philadelphia Resolution C-1

Appendix D
Ontario Arts Education Accord D-1

The Day School Came Alive

We have to regard it as our sacred responsibility to unfold and develop each individual's creative ability, as dim as the spark may be, and kindle it to whatever flame it may conceivably develop.

Victor Lowenfeld

Throughout our lives, we are influenced in our attitude to learning by the personal experiences we recall in the educational setting which dominated our early years. The strongest memories of our past are built around schools, classrooms, teachers, and playgrounds. These venues held possibilities for the truly transformational experiences of our childhood to take place.

Yet during childhood and particularly adolescence, it was expected that we refer to school as a place associated with boredom, humiliation, and even pain. Only after a mind-numbing part-time job had dulled our lives or the never-ending days of holiday idleness had lost their initial excitement, were we able to compare life experiences and find the generosity of spirit to concede that school could be a pleasurable source of companionship and joyful activity.

The modern school as an institution is a product of the Industrial Revolution and it was meant to be a space for striving and achieving, for accomplishing what the law and society had decided every child must master. Indeed, the concept of the school as learning factory has never been completely abandoned, even in our own century. The institution was originally designed to be a place where youth would learn to arrive on time, behave with suitable deference to adults, and would work — yes, work — at whatever drudgery had been assigned. In spite of all the new classroom technology, brightly illustrated textbooks, and the more intellectually stimulating extracurricular activities such as sports, debating, and science clubs that have found their place in the timetable of the neighbourhood school, the negative connotations of the institution have never been overcome and badmouthing school has ever been a popular sport of the young and old. Much of the criticism endured by schools is merely a playing out of this ancient game.

However, at least for many of us, on a day we long remembered, something magical happened. A theatre group arrived in the gymnasium, a fresh, bright collection of actors who dramatized our concerns — finding relationships which mattered, facing the pain of a home life fraught with violence, confronting the sense of inadequacy which children and adolescents of every generation must bear – and we were touched. In days past, the play might have been about alcohol abuse — today it is more likely about drugs and the dangers of indiscriminate sex. The specific message of the presentation on that special day may have disappeared from our minds, but we know that at that moment learning meant something.

Or perhaps we made our way to art class and found a different person at the front of the room — a focussed individual who was anxious that we mold a piece of clay or create a puppet using our experience of the world we had grown to know. Perhaps for the first time we felt our meagre expression was important to somebody who had expertise and commitment and cared about what we did. We worked with purpose and concentration, not just for marks on a report card but for some other reason which at the time we were not sure of. That contact with the arts somehow spoke of a world that went beyond the fragmented experience of different subjects, topics, and skills that seemed to be the sum total of the schools' capacity to address the scope of our experience outside the classroom. We found ourselves *transformed*, even though this was a word we hadn't yet encountered.

Or perhaps it was a trip to a museum or an art gallery that seemed to symbolize a unity of knowledge that we may later have realized was the cultural dimension of our life, what Paul Schafer has called "the way in which people visualize and interpret the world, organize themselves, conduct their affairs, elevate and embellish life, and position themselves in the world."[1] The romp through a Greek gallery said all we could have imagined about the literature, the mathematics and science, the sculpture and architecture, the games and drama of the ancient world without isolating any single one of these elements. Indeed, we found that the integration of these seemingly disparate items gave new relevance and insight to everything we had gathered from the textbook. We discovered, for example, that a depiction of a runner on an exquisite vase could tell us something about the role of the Olympic Games in the ancient world, the importance to the Greeks of both body and mind, the relationship of master and slave, the attitudes toward male and female gender roles, the essential factors that led to the development of a culture which ultimately contributed to the creation of a political system we have defined as "democracy."

Without knowing the word, we were viewing *holistically* a slice of humanity's story, and we may have understood for a moment that it was the only way we could clearly understand the mysteries of human existence and the interdependency of everything around us. If the 19th and 20th centuries have stressed increased specialization, then the 21st century will demand greater integration of all the disciplines that help us comprehend the complexity and vulnerability of our environment. Herman Daly and John Cobb outline the educational problem for the university community, but it is equally relevant to elementary and secondary schools:

> [T]he organization of knowledge in the university is such as to work against its contribution to the broad human need for understanding. This does not prevent bits and pieces of the information it supplies in one form to enter into another organization of knowledge that does promote understanding. It does not prevent members of the university faculties themselves using knowledge in ways that promote understanding. But it does work toward minimizing rather than maximizing these contributions. The more successful and exclusive are disciplinary goals, the less the contribution of the discipline to our understanding. The result is an "information age" but little comprehension of our real condition.[2]

The reality is that the way knowledge is perceived and purveyed by the university has its effect all the way down to the kindergarten teacher.

Teacher education is in the hands of the university. Thus, the measure of success, certainly at the secondary school level, is the percentage of students who are accepted by the university and proceed to do well there. Yet the survival of the species may depend on the success we have in educating generalists who can take the latest knowledge from a host of disciplines and provide new strategies for saving the planet. That experience in the museum or gallery may have been our first contact with the intellectual comprehensiveness that will be the way of the future in the schooling of our young.

Sometimes the magic moment in the school timetable did not involve the intervention of new voices and bodies, or even transportation to another venue, but merely the excitement of a teacher who wanted to produce a play or a musical and was calling for a commitment of time and energy quite beyond the ordinary. Suddenly school was more than enforced attendance, a series of static meetings, the inevitable homework assignment, the pressure of yet another test. It was an opportunity to be a part of a process that involved the heart and mind of every participant. There were lines to be learned if the play was to go on, and most of all there was a sense of purpose to be shared. There was much to be experienced — endless rehearsals of texts and exits and entrances, long periods of waiting to perform, late-night hours of frantic repetition. Most of all there were hours with new friends and companions, in some cases developing relationships that lasted a lifetime. We shared, perhaps for the first time, an objective that mattered, even if it was only the presentation of a single performance of a one-act play written by student colleagues.

Surprisingly, communication with the teacher became one of informality based on a common cause. No longer was that person, at best, an instructor in things seemingly irrelevant to our lives and being; at worst, a keeper of order in an otherwise unruly classroom. Rather there was a sharing of frustration, exhaustion, and excitement. The relationship had less to do with power and subservience roles than with a common purpose. In place of external goals — the curriculum imposed by forces beyond our understanding — there was an inner intensity that defied description. In short, there was learning that had relevance, learning inextricably connected with something we wanted to achieve.

As well there was the consciousness of the moment, an ecstasy of activity that filled every thought. We had come to resent the fact that most of schooling is about the future, a preparation for being a good citizen, a productive worker. Much of the stress we experienced then came from the memory of past failure and inadequacy as well as the fear of impending personal tragedy and societal disintegration made all the more devastating because we understood so little and had not developed the defences that adults ultimately find to make life tolerable, even acceptable. Engaging in an artistic activity — whether it be the rehearsing of a play or the preparation for a concert — taught us that the only point of experience over which we can have any control is the present. It is then that we can experience the exultation of taking risks and overcoming our fears. We can only celebrate life in the now. We came to realize that real artists, as they create, compose, or perform, find their happiness in the release of the moment as well as in any hope that their artistic product might have lasting significance.

However, it was not just the realization that learning could be manifestly joyful and immediately fulfilling, it was the burst of insight that told us that what we had spent our time mastering was important, not to get marks in order to pass the grade, but for living our lives more effectively. We discovered we could write something that nobody had written before and that someone else would want to read and enjoy. We found that the conflict resolution that occurred in the play we were rehearsing related to our own personal struggles. We had the "aha" experience of a composer who has successfully expressed her joy and sorrow, her fear and courage, in her music. Learning could be connected to our immediate need to know and respond. Little did we realize that these hours of intense association with artistic matters were training us for the very purpose that society most valued but least recognized as outcomes of these experiences. Whether it be the Conference Board of Canada or the local Chamber of Commerce, the educational expectations of the business community — the ability to think clearly, critically, and logically, the capacity to work together in teams effectively, the practice of self-discipline, the enhancement of imagination and creativity, the achievement of self-confidence, the capacity to articulate ideas with style and clarity, the commitment to excellence — are the very ones emphasized in these moments of artistic effort, enhancing the child's abilities to be a contributor to society either as an employee or volunteer. But being a worker is only one role that the school prepares children to assume — and it may become increasingly less important as "the end of work" is gloomily predicted by many observers. One hopes that the educational experience will prepare children to enjoy what philosophers have called "the good life." The study of philosophy has been consigned to the university, yet discovering the values upon which behaviour throughout a lifetime are to be based is surely the central purpose of the educational experience.

The arts facilitate joyful learning as no other process can, simply because they build on the innate individual and collective desire to express profound ideas and feelings in dance, song, story, or picture. This can be seen by any observer of children as they play, either alone or with others, dramatizing events they have witnessed, singing their own original songs and moving as though choreographed by the divine impulse within. But do the arts encourage thoughtful contemplation on matters of eternal significance? Would an arts-based curriculum, focussed on the belief that knowledge of the world through all disciplines could be effectively approached and grasped, establish the understanding of the good life as the truly central purpose of all learning?

The question of content and its implications arises. The child sitting in the traditional classroom is bombarded with messages — this is history, this is science, this is mathematics. . . . From this melange of information the child must find a philosophy of life that will make sense of the universe. The arts, in their emphasis on connectedness, the transient nature of beauty, and the forms and patterns of sound, fibre, stone, and colour, have engaged the finest minds of the past that focussed on the issues of ethics and morality. The stuff of the arts must be those things which our society will leave to future generations to ponder and evaluate. The arts encourage loyalty and commitment to those institutions and ways of doing things that have served the past well, but demand a critical examination of those things that no longer serve us effectively in the present.

An integrated arts-based program would ensure that young people were prepared to confront their futures through a process of self-examination based on the greatest art, music, dance, and drama that has analyzed the human condition in past ages. To understand the nuclear age or the post-nuclear age as mere fragments of scientific, historic, literary, and mathematical development without binding these elements in an intellectual and emotional unity is to deprive children of the most basic tools whereby they can understand themselves and the world. Such a shift in the curriculum and teaching practice — away from the vocational emphasis — modifies, at the most appropriate time, the obsessive expectation that has been imposed on the school — that of providing the skills and essential information for the workplace. In the context of this integrated learning, the first priority must be that of self-understanding and the second that of grasping the societal context within which the good life is to be lived. Only then can schools prepare young people for making a contribution to the new global workplace.

In spite of intense recollections of great moments in the arts that stand out clearly in our memories, it was obvious that schools did not regard the arts as very important. The "real" work of the school took place during mathematics or science classes, or, at the secondary school level, in the machine shop or business practice room. It was never categorically stated that the arts were not the real work of the school, it was simply that the triumphs on stage or at the easel were never evaluated with rigour for a mark on a report card, and it could only be assumed that the mark would not have mattered much anyway. Unlike in the case of English or mathematics marks, one's future well-being was not perceived to be at stake when it came to the arts.

Even today, the mindset that led Cromwell and his Puritan forces to abolish the theatre in England remains embedded in the psyche of the descendants who found their way to the New World. The general opinion that the arts represent mere entertainment is strengthened by the usually unexpressed opinion that the arts are a danger and may indeed erode strength of character and moral fervour. In the case of males, the arts are seen as a feminizing influence undermining the mental and emotional rigour that produces competitive and entrepreneurial individuals for the business world.

It may seem self-evident to the enthusiast that the arts communicate a set of values, an understanding of the human condition, and a belief in the way in which people learn, develop, and behave, preparing us to compete in the new global arena. However, in the minds of many, thankfully decreasing in numbers, the arts represent the human propensity for the bizarre, the revolutionary, the dangerous, the violent, and the mindless.

On the other hand, George Grant makes the case that the arts have been placed on the periphery of our modern society precisely because they are presumed to be essentially benign — they have no power to "make history":

> This exaltâtion of activism can be seen in its negative side in the way it has inhibited these activities, such as daydreaming, sensuality, art, prayer, theoretical science, and philosophy, which do not directly challenge the world, and that therefore have been linked together in contradistinction to the practical, under that exalted term leisure. . . . Historically, the artist, the historian, the mystic have béen outsiders in our Protestant civilization.[3]

Yet if there has been any trend in recent years it has been the lonely mission of the arts to reverse this perception and drive us in the direction of making judgments about the inhumane, selfish, destructive forces this society has unleashed in the name of progress, efficiency, and productivity. This explains the reason for rejection of the arts, as evidenced by the current decade's reduction in funding to arts councils and the CBC, indeed, the minimizing of support anywhere that artists can be found rejecting the truth as politicians conceive it. The conflict goes far beyond our children's classrooms.

We live in a world dominated by economics: profit is the obsession of our society. This explains the main educational trends of the '80s and '90s. North America has shifted the emphasis in the curriculum of its schools, colleges, and universities in the direction that will best serve the global market and at the same time provide comfort to a populace overwhelmed by the speed of change and wanting to be assured that their schools are returning to the perceived values of the past. This dichotomy surfaces in every discussion of education, whether around questions of curriculum or teaching methods.

The debate has many faces, sometimes becoming a struggle over the recognition of individual difference in contrast to perceived legitimate societal expectations, the role of testing practices, and the place of the school in sorting out elites who can compete in the global economy. Howard Gardner of Harvard University, in his book *Multiple Intelligences*, describes the present state of mind in educational circles in the United States:

> As I see it, American education is at a turning point. There are considerable pressures to move very sharply in the direction of "uniform schooling," there is also the possibility that our educational system can embrace "individual-centered schooling." A struggle is under way at this moment about the probable direction in which schools will veer. My own analysis of the scientific evidence indicates that we should as a polity move in the direction of individual-centred schooling. . . . At present the most vocal contributors to the debate are calling for "uniform" schools. Stripped to the essentials, their argument goes as follows. There is a basic set of competencies, and a core body of knowledge, which every individual in our society should master. Some individuals are more able than others, and can be expected to master this knowledge more rapidly. Schools should be set up in such a way to ensure that the most gifted can move to the top and that the greatest number of individuals will achieve basic knowledge as efficiently as possible. For that reason, there should be the same curriculum for all students, the same methods of teaching, and the same "standardized" methods of assessment. Students, teachers, administrators, school districts, states, and even the whole nation should be judged in terms of the efficiency and effectiveness with which these common standards are achieved. Paying attention to individual differences is at best a luxury, at worst a dangerous deviation from the essential educational priorities.[4]

In 1995, a Royal Commission on Learning in Ontario recommended a provincially produced common curriculum, a regimen for testing students in language literacy and numeracy, a process of re-certifying teachers every five years — in short, a schooling system responding to the desires of politicians, parents, and newspaper editors for easy solutions to the complex reality that every learning life is different and must be individually accommodated. Behind the "uniformity" alternative is the faith that such schooling will make our children and young people competitive. Ironically, it may do much to ensure that they are less so if individual imagination and creativity are crippled.

Even our democratic system of government is at risk in this rush toward globalization and trivialization of individual difference. More involvement of parents and interested members of the community at the neighbourhood school level (as presently promised in the creation of school advisory councils) will not reverse the effect of a central control system based on a common curriculum devoted to economic progress and enforced by centralized assessment procedures. If the capacity of our students to cope with future political challenges has anything to do with their creative thought and their willingness to use the democratic system to solve collective problems, then the commitment to freedom and choice which infuses the arts must have a significant place in their learning lives. At present, that is not the case, but it should be if we value the strides we have made toward the democratic ideals espoused throughout the 20th century.

The arts have vigorously fought the imposition of political control over the creative impulse. That is why, in the best of all possible worlds, government funding to artists and arts organizations has come through arm's-length arts councils and has been based on peer evaluation rather than political considerations. That has always been the preference of the artist, often at great economic sacrifice when a more "friendly" response that flattered the party in power might have brought more generous support.

The issue of arts in our schools and the argument for integrated arts-based learning becomes much more than a mere curriculum-scheduling problem in our schools. It concerns the very essence of education and learning. It has to do with the nature of the preparation of young people for the world they will face. It concerns the values which will sustain them in both their personal lives and in their roles as members of a community and a society. Thus the magic of the arts in the lives of children and adolescents becomes inextricably tangled with the kind of classrooms we have in our schools and the way teachers and students feel about themselves and the educational process.

The challenge is that of making the school, particularly at the elementary and secondary level, come alive with relevance and excitement every moment of the child's learning life. That day in our children's experience — when the arts intervened and made the classroom come alive — could be a pattern for constant and continuing education, so much so that the term "drop-out" disappears from the educational jargon of our time, and children and youth see the school as a place where life and learning become joyfully and meaningfully one.

NOTES

1. D. Paul Schafer, *Canadian Culture: Key To Canada's Future Development* (Toronto: World Culture Project, 1995), p. 12.
2. Herman E. Daly and John B. Cobb, Jr., *For the Common Good: Redirecting the Economy Toward Community, the Environment, and a Sustainable Future* (Boston: Beacon Press, 1989), p. 125.
3. George Grant, *Philosophy in a Mass Age* (Toronto: University of Toronto Press, 1995; originally published by the Copp Clark Publishing Company, 1959), p. 71.
4. Howard Gardner, *Multiple Intelligences: The Theory in Practice* (New York: BasicBooks, 1993), pp. 68-69.

Chapter 1   The Arts and the World Our Children Face

The arts live consciously and they live literally by faith; their nature and their uses survive unchanged in all that matters through times of interruption, diminishment, neglect; they outlive governments and societies, even the very civilizations that produced them. They cannot be destroyed altogether because they represent the substance of faith and the only reality. They are what we find again when the ruins are cleared away.

Katherine Anne Porter

A school curriculum that fails to address the individual needs of children and young people is unthinkable. A learning program that fails to take into account the nature of the society surrounding the classroom would be laughable. Any changes in the learning patterns proposed for our children must be approached with sensitivity for, and understanding of, the societal context within which the schools must serve students, their parents, and society as a whole.

There can be no greater contrast than that between the confidence with which our forefathers greeted the arrival of the 20th century and the relative despair that engulfs those who have the courage to contemplate the coming of the 21st century. Those living at the end of the 19th century were enamoured of the idea of progress. New inventions and discoveries had brought greater opportunity for travel and more leisure in the home. There was every reason to believe the new century would see these technological wonders benefit the lives of people of all classes and conditions. The worst phase of the Industrial Revolution, with its exploitation of women and children, and its horrendous conditions in the new factory cities, was over. War, which had certainly been an element of the early 19th-century years of Napoleon and French imperialism, had now been contained, and although lesser conflicts provided excitement — the Franco-Prussian War, the Crimean War, and the struggle of Japan and Russia — the phenomenon of large-scale conflict was thought to be a relic of the past. This belief flourished in spite of, and perhaps because of, the extraordinary development of weapons of war in the last half of the century. Although there were tensions around the policies of the great powers to acquire resource-rich colonies to feed their industrial machines, few expected the conflagration of 1914 and its continuation in 1939, which, of course, became the central events of the 20th century. In the 1890s, however, there was every reason to believe that an increased knowledge of the universe's forces would result in more technological development, bringing peace and prosperity to the masses.

Today, few look on the coming of a new century with anything but consternation. The final decade of this century has been one of increasing discontent over the intransigence of a host of societal problems. If we were to seek a descriptive term to characterize this decade of the '90s, we might use words such as *greedy, violent, mean-spirited,* or *uncaring.* It has been a decade of uncertainty heavily laced with irony. The uncertainty comes from the apparent loss of any values and behaviours which could give some expectation of pattern and form to human affairs, thereby promising a level of predictability and reassurance.

John Kenneth Galbraith, in a book of collected notes for his 1973 television series *Age of Uncertainty*, points out why he and his colleagues chose the program's title — reasons that relate as well to this volume a quarter-century later:

> We settled early on the title *Age of Uncertainty* for the series. It sounded well; it did not confine thought; and it suggested the basic theme: we would contrast the great certainties in economic thought in the last century with the great uncertainty with which problems are faced in our time. In the last century capitalists were certain of the success of capitalism, socialists of socialism, imperialists of colonialism, and the ruling classes knew they were meant to rule. Little of this certainty now survives. Given the dismaying complexity of the problems mankind now faces, it would surely be odd if it did.[1]

However, in our present age, irony prevails along with uncertainty. Allan Bloom points out that "Irony flourishes on the disposition between the way things are and the way they should be, while accepting the necessity of this disproportion."[2] Reinhold Niebuhr was convinced that history was not tragic or pathetic, but ironic. Things simply did not turn out the way they should have. The main point at this juncture in human affairs is that we have no confidence that we can predict with any accuracy the directions of the coming century and we have a sense of powerlessness in the face of massive and seemingly unsolvable problems in a spectrum of areas — urban planning, population control, environmental deterioration, crime, war, and violence, to mention only an obvious few. As well, we know things are not "the way they should be" and we have less confidence in our ability to set them right than at any time in human history.

It is banal to say we are going through a period of transition. That could be said of every decade in this century. But a large element of the uncertainty we feel revolves around the sense that the triumph of the free-market economy and the fall of state socialism or communism has taken us only halfway across a deep chasm and that we must now focus on the creation of a new economy in which to nurture a more egalitarian society and a healthier environment. The irony of the present is that the fall of the Berlin Wall — the symbol of the decay and destruction of one ideology based on a materialist theory of humankind's motivation — may also augur the fall of its competitor, traditional capitalism, based on a similar philosophy of the pre-eminence of things economic.

David C. Korten writes, in *When Corporations Rule the World*:

> In the quest for economic growth, free-market ideology has been embraced around the world with the fervor of a fundamentalist religious faith. Money is its sole measure of value, and its practice is advancing policies that are deepening social and environmental disintegration everywhere. The economics profession serves as its priesthood. It champions values that demean the human spirit, it assumes an imaginary world divorced from reality, and it is restructuring our institutions of governance in ways that make our most fundamental problems more difficult to resolve. Yet to question its doctrine has become virtual heresy, invoking risk of professional censure and damage to one's career in most institutions of business, government, and academia.[3]

In this aura of confusion and helplessness, it may appear bizarre to place on the public agenda a strengthened role for the arts in our schools. It has all the elements of the ludicrous, the fighting of a forest fire with a spoonful of water. Yet the arts, particularly when one discipline finds increased power through connection with other forms of expression, thrive on both irony and uncertainty. Every public performance is an exercise in uncertainty, indeed, glories in the risk of the "happening." It is a rare occurrence when things turns out as expected. An intense and continuing experience with the arts allows children to become accustomed to the new, the innovative, the unexpected — surely learning that is more relevant than lessons filled with clear definitions and structured linear responses.

There are those who would feel more comfortable if our time were defined simply as an age of technology. The curriculum response could then logically centre on computer skills. Curiously, the term *technology* raises more questions than it answers. Langdon Winner points out that every period of history could be termed an age of technology, that the meaning of the term has become "amorphous," that one could say that "technology is everything."[4] Ursula Franklin amplifies this point of view:

> Technology is not the sum of the artifacts, of the wheels and gears, of the rails and electronic transmitters. Technology is a system. It entails far more than its individual material components. Technology involves organization, procedures, symbols, new words, equations, and, most of all, a mindset.[5]

Although the word *technology* covers much, it fails to define the age. Yet the attitude toward the future is very much the result of the understandings we have of its nature and capabilities. The early confidence of experts that all the energy needs and agricultural productivity of the planet could be solved by some trick of technology still influences many citizens. Even in mid-century there was still some faith that it was only a matter of time before the mysteries of poverty and disease could be explained and overcome. Today, our experience with the AIDS epidemic and the long struggle to find cures for cancer has convinced humankind that the perception of the world as a complex but completely explainable, logical mechanism needs revising.

Stephanie Pace Marshall, executive director of the Illinois Mathematics and Science Academy, finds hope in the new perceptions of reality in terms of the role of the school:

> Discoveries in modern physics have caused the scientists' description of the universe to change from the metaphor of a clock to the metaphor of a kaleidoscope and this metaphor and all it suggests holds great promise for transforming our schools into authentic learning communities. . . . Deriving our insight from Newtonian physics, we behaved as if we believed that by studying the parts we could understand the whole, and that analysis inevitably leads to synthesis. But this shouldn't surprise us. After all, isn't that the way a predictable and clockwork universe works?[6]

Marshall points out how this perception influenced our classrooms and the learning that went on within them:

> By design we have constructed and operated our schools as we have understood our world, and these constructions have produced learning-disabled institutions, students, and staff, including us, who have suppressed creativity and potential to survive. This efficient, orderly, and linear design of schooling no longer makes any sense.[7]

For those who believe the arts have a special role in developing creativity, these are welcome words indeed. Particularly telling is the linking of this characteristic with the concept of survival, for in this age of ironic uncertainty, that is indeed the ultimate test of relevance.

With doubt cast on these formerly assured touchstones of objective truth, those who believe in the arts and their power in the learning process no longer have to face the charge that their preoccupations are subjective and transitory while those pursuing mathematics and science are dealing with the objective and the eternal. No longer can it be claimed that to propose an integrated arts-based curriculum is an exercise in mixing apples and oranges — associating the "soft" knowledge of creative literature, music, drama, and visual arts with the "hard" lessons to be mastered in the maths and science classrooms. In spite of the enormous extensions of our knowledge it has brought, the 20th century has also forced us to realize that the more we discover, the more we recognize the limitations of our knowledge. This can be said of virtually every area of human observation and analysis. The arts, the social sciences, and the humanities are joined by virtually every discipline in confronting this humbling reality. This does not mean the study of science has become less important because it can no longer be counted on to deliver the solutions to every problem. Rather, it means that those whose interest and intelligence leads to a life of scientific enquiry can be encouraged to understand these limitations, that the web of knowledge creates a seamless cloak of many colours, woven from the threads of human study and experience, but subject to the limitations of our humanity and the boundaries of a short life on a small, impermanent planet.

Our daily lives reveal the extent of the irony we confront in every context and the need we have to bring more sophisticated understandings to our human predicament. In particular, we are forced to recognize that the discipline-based, vertical, linear approaches of the past can no longer help us cope with such problems as environmental issues. In 1994, I found myself faced with such a task. I was asked by the Province of Ontario to chair the board of an Interim Waste Authority responsible for finding landfill sites to cope with the mountain of garbage produced by Toronto and its surrounding region. The alternatives to landfill acquisition were either environmentally irresponsible or financially devastating. The studies to determine the best sites were carried out with efficiency and accuracy, using the most modern techniques and equipment.

However, understandably, such a process demands full disclosure to any citizens who might be affected. Long and complicated quasi-judicial hearings ensued and every opportunity was given to ensure that all those opposed would have their say. Months of work and an expenditure of $100-million resulted in the realization that nothing could be accomplished. The technical work was flawless, the findings incontrovertible, but the fury of those affected by the choice could not be contained. The process ended when a new government called off the unpopular search. But the solution to the waste problem continues to evade the community. Indeed, Toronto's waste is still sent to the US to landfills regulated in a less environmentally friendly fashion, or to air-polluting incinerators.

In the context of these procedures that were dominated by the litigious and the controversial, there was no place for the poetic or the visionary. There was no place for a discussion of the common good and the well-being of future generations. Only property rights of individuals close to selected sites and the distorted images of the affected

KATHRYN DAY'S REGAL ROAD SCHOOL MUSIC PROGRAM

Regal Road Elementary School sits on the lip of a prehistoric lake created by ancient glaciers in what is now downtown Toronto. Built in the last century, it has the high ceilings and wide halls that characterized the architecture of fine schools of that time. Now it is filled with children from every imaginable country and clime bringing with them a rich assortment of language and culture.

The music program is in the hands of an energetic young woman, Kathryn Day, who provides every child with a musical literacy to see them throughout their lives. They come to her in waves as the regular staff, taking preparation time for lessons as part of their contract with the school board, send their charges to Kathryn. First, a class of grades three and four, followed by an unusual combination of kindergarten and grade one. After recess a class of grades five and six arrive with more energy to burn. Thus, she meets every child in the school over the week and has the names of all 460 students stored in her memory bank.

The notation of rhythm is stressed here — clapping, body movement, repetitive sound patterns — but in the end students come to know how music "looks" and how it can be written down. These concepts demand concentration and constant reinforcement. A song about spring which includes the very rhythmic patterns just mastered follows, and then a few moments at the computer to see how modern technology provides a window on this most ancient of human joys, the celebration of the sound dynamic of the universe.

The next class is entranced by the selection of instruments which are to be used in creating a composition about the wind — xylophones, drums, streamers, and triangles appear from nooks in the room and music is magically produced, music that mirrors the experience of the children involved.

The final group of older students actually experiments with various combinations of instruments, writing out their own arrangements of sounds that can be reproduced in the future. The level of sound is overwhelming, but never mere noise. It is punctuated by the continued efforts of young people measuring the mystery of music and becoming comfortable with their own creativity in making it. The emphasis in every class is on intense participation, never mere passive listening. It is based on the concept of music literacy, not just appreciation.

A well-trained, capable teacher of enormous patience and monumental commitment, Kathryn Day has even developed a community choir of parents who meet to sing together, thereby sharing the learning experience of their own children. It is a step forward to-

communities had any place in the debate. It was clear that the learning experience of all participants was woefully inadequate to deal with such a question, one that will be a major agenda item for governments in the next century. This was a small fight in one small part of the world, but on a global level it has become crucial as the wastes of the well-to-do industrial nations are now dumped into the environments of poorer nations that can be bribed to accept them but have the least capacity to cope with the toxins involved. Such will be the problems of the future, to be comprehended in all their multidisciplinary complexity. Our schooling simply does not prepare young people for these kinds of questions, just as 19th-century education did not provide the skills of understanding, cooperation, negotiation, and diplomacy that might have given the 20th century a history different from that of one filled with violence, torture, and death. The integrated arts-based learning process is one strategy to deal with a host of problems which range across a spectrum of disciplines and have a horizontality that defies our traditional learning models.

Ironic uncertainty has to do with ambiguity and the presence of dichotomy, contradiction, and anomaly. Indeed it often concerns multiple choices, all of which are partly right and partly wrong. Contact with the arts shows us how many "right" answers there can be in the interpretation of a play

ward the ideal of making the arts important to the entire family, diverting its collective attention away from the ubiquitous television to the joyous business of making music.⌘

and how many "wrong" solutions there can be in expressing an idea or emotion using the medium of paint or plaster. An example from opera illustrates this well: Jon Vickers and Ben Heppner, two splendid Canadian tenors, have explored the complexities of the title role in Benjamin Britten's opera *Peter Grimes*. Vickers saw the hatred and violence of Grimes, and his drowning at sea in the final scene, forced on him by his neighbours, seems utterly just. Heppner, on the other hand, perceives Grimes as lonely and uncommunicative, thereby misunderstood by the villagers. His death reveals another aspect of the human condition but even more meaningfully explores the intolerance of the community. Both interpretations, as well as many others, are "right." They speak to the perception of human nature held by the artist and the message that seems relevant to the times of the performance. Such an arts experience opens our minds to a myriad of solutions that may have to be used concomitantly or in sequence in dealing with any life situation, be it a personal or collective challenge.

An understanding of ironic uncertainty can be drawn from the wonder of creativity, which aligns totally disparate ideas to find new answers. It is about wonder and awe, the completely unexplainable phenomena of a Shakespeare or a Mozart or a Picasso. Irony is a view of human affairs that celebrates flexibility and recognizes subjectivity. It is a state of mind that demands a holistic conception that can accommodate the reality of our personal experiences as well as the growing mountain of published data about every aspect of our surroundings. We discover that insight, common sense, and intuition can often reveal aspects of reality that scholarly analysis may obscure.

Irony has a close affinity to humour and the sense of the absurd which humans must possess if they are to survive the first newscast of the day, or the headlines in the local newspaper. It is the wonder of so many art forms that even when they address the most serious topics, they have the capacity to make us laugh. When David Earle, the normally serious founder of and choreographer for the Toronto Dance Theatre, can, in his piece "Furniture," mock the pretensions of the Western cowboy tradition, the well-heeled dilettante's "night out" in full regalia, and then examine the tale of Sleeping Beauty within a panorama that reveals criminal rather than romantic intent, then dance has achieved a new level of hilarity — and relevance. Arts-based learning must nurture humour and wit, an antidote to the studied seriousness and artless pomposity that so often make the solution to any problem impossible.

Not only have the events of the '80s and '90s shaken our faith in the objective truths of our earlier mind-set, but major philosophical movements have come upon us with frightening speed. Feminism has exposed the reality of patriarchy that has infused every institution, confronting with searing effectiveness the male preoccupation with power and violence. A recent production of *Rigoletto* by the Canadian Opera Company featured Canadian mezzo-soprano Jean Stillwell who, with a splendid interpretation of the role of Maddalena, revealed the degree to which male preoccupation with revenge and violence could result in savage brutality, thus speaking to the problem of violence against women with particular poignancy.

Environmentalism has highlighted the importance of a holistic perception of the planet and its needs if human survival is to be possible, and a new theology has captured the wisdom of native cultures in recognizing that humans are not masters of creation. Indeed, the issue of native land claims has been complicated by the unwillingness of the conqueror to accept the position of native people that ownership of nature — land, trees, and water — is an affront to the Creator. The concept of environmental stewardship as a religious point of view in both the Roman Catholic and Protestant faiths, as well as other great world faiths, takes on a unique application. Yet this revelation of co-creation and co-responsibility of human and divine has come at a time when church attendance has been declining and church influence diminishing (even though general interest in spirituality has apparently been increasing). The church is in a state of trauma over the intellectual shifts it is being forced to face, whether it be environmentalism, feminism, or any of the other assaults on long-held interpretations of Biblical truth. Our predominantly 19th-century institutions cannot function effectively without significant change. These institutions include massive corporate structures, beleaguered trade unions, both parliamentary and congressional governing systems, traditional church polities, and in this array of dysfunctional entities, one must include school systems, colleges, and universities.

On the environmental issue, ironic uncertainty is apparent to children in every classroom. Young people are very much aware that, in spite of the enormous potential of technological power, we are distant from any solution to the major problems we face. An obvious example is global warming, a phenomenon now conceded to be real after years of denial by the politically dominant sector of the scientific community. A visit to a school on any Environment Day will show that youth is far ahead of the adult world on this topic. These young people know what the greenhouse effect is all about, how the earth's surface will be affected, how the low-lying lands will be flooded, how millions of people will be made refugees, and the climatic implications for the very neighbour-hoods in which they live. They are aware that there can be no solution unless there is restraint by the developed northern-hemisphere nations, particularly in the matter of limiting CO_2 emissions. They are aware that the gasoline engine is the mainstay of the automotive industry, which is, in turn, the major driving force of the Western industrial economy. The failure of incredible technological capacity to cope with a problem threatening the very life of the species is an irony not lost on this generation.

The schools may have been unkind to the arts, but the sciences have thrived on the attention they receive in a technological society that sees scientific advance and discovery as the very basis of the new economy. As well, the sciences have thankfully seized on the environment as the undeniable link to relevance in the lives of students. Hundreds of young people are engaged in community clean-up days, transforming local rivers and streams from garbage-ridden embarrassments to beautiful neighbourhood assets. Thousands of trees have been planted by children determined that they will not grow up in wastelands predicted by the experts.

Young people know the planet is suffering. They have seen the mountain of waste our consumer society produces every day, and although their personal behaviour may not have caught up with their enthusiasm for the earth (pop cans and candy wrappers continue to litter the schoolyard), they know the present wasteful style of our communities must come to an end. Indeed, this incapacity to connect their own personal behaviour to the global crisis is an indication of the failure of the present fragmented approach to learning.

One day my grandson announced, to my horror, "By the time I grow up, there will be nothing left." I wish I could have assured him that his fears were exaggerated. But the Rio Conference on the Brundtland Report had just taken place, and Western industrial countries, led by US president George Bush, had decided to derail the proceedings. Only a commitment to restraint and a promise of appropriate technological assistance to developing countries could have saved the conference. But Mr. Bush had only one thing in mind — to be re-elected — and was prepared to take any action necessary to assure American voters that nothing which threatened American prosperity would be tolerated, no matter what the cost to the environment.

This generation, which has grown up with both the television and the computer, is not impressed with either as assured tools to salvation. Indeed, it will be this generation who will have the courage to ask very difficult questions about the efficacy of many technological developments that have done little to enrich our lives or improve our chances in the future. Yet only a comprehensive understanding of the interconnectedness of technological processes and the broader issues of ecological well-being can help them to formulate those questions. A curriculum that uses the arts to integrate the learning of young people is a place to begin. The question asks itself, "Are we prepared to provide them with the tools to bind up the wounds of this planet, save the remaining species, retain and restore the rain forests on which many of these insects and animals depend, reverse the preoccupation with mega-projects that have devastated millions of acres of arable land, and focus attention on the thin layer of topsoil on which we all depend for our continued sustenance but which is eroding with alarming speed?"

How can the integrated expressions of the arts be seen as a response to these massive challenges? The arts develop the creativity and imagination without which no amount of data, no commitment of resources, can hope to succeed. The arts channel the emotional commitment of a people and express their fears in a potentially positive manner. The arts provide the images which move us to both understanding and action. Communication in word, picture, form, colour, and texture is the ultimate challenge for every artist seeking to address these fundamental questions of ecological consequence.

Many years ago, Danny Grossman, a gifted young dancer and choreographer, was moved by the assault on both nature and the human condition that the environmental crisis represented. He produced "Endangered Species," a deeply evocative dance presentation that included terrifying expressions of outrage against the violent, militaristic, power-oriented behaviour encouraged by our culture. The brutal physicality, the inexorable waves of violent attack across the stage, and the sense of inevitable doom were all stated by the dancers with such visual eloquence that the audience was bombarded with the fact that human survival is problematic at best.

Besides making the continuity of the human species central, the arts point to an obvious truth. We can deal with these problems of ecology only on an interdisciplinary basis. Saving the planet is about chemistry and physics, but it is also about geography, anthropology, climatology, biology, and, yes, the arts. Grossman's performance involved the visual arts in the costumes and the set, the music as a driving accompaniment, and dance, of course, in the movement of the participants. The "dramatic" was revealed in the interaction of the forces of light and dark. An emotional climax overwhelmed every member of the audience. Yet all these elements were grounded in the presentation of an intense intellectual journey toward an understanding of an impending ecological and human disaster.

It has been many years since I first saw the ruin of Coventry Cathedral and experienced the emotion that came from hearing Benjamin

Britten's *War Requiem*, written on the occasion of the dedication of the new Cathedral built alongside. That composition, coming at a time, in 1961, when the great powers were girding themselves for a war to end war, brought that issue down to the personal pain of death and dismemberment, and did so through music that soared and a poetic text that moved to tears the thoughtful members of an entire generation. Even in the sanitized and security-obsessed gallery in Madrid, one cannot view Picasso's "Guernica" without a twinge of revulsion over the total negation of human values that characterizes modern warfare. There is reason to believe that half a century of artistic expressions of the horrors of war, admittedly along with the technical power that threatened humankind with total annihilation, have thankfully saved us from a nuclear holocaust. Music, paintings, and drama may seem benign interventions, but there is a power in the arts which enters the minds and spirits of men and women of different ideologies and national ambitions, reminding them of their common humanity.

I can remember being a part of an audience listening to the Red Army Chorus and Orchestra at the Canadian National Exhibition in the days when there was an artistic presence at that ancient institution. The singing was glorious. One was thrilled by the voices, but also by the love of country which had inspired so many of their selections. Here, in black boots and full uniform, was the Cold War enemy, demonized by politicians and press, making the sounds of angels. At the end of the performance, the crowd of thousands, who had struggled past anti-Soviet picketers to attend the concert, rose to cheer and applaud. The choristers, some in tears, applauded back. In those few moments it was hard to believe that the East and West could not find accommodation. A concert does not replace careful negotiation, but it reinforces the knowledge that hatred and distrust is not a basis for peace and coexistence.

These artistic events, taking place over many years, contributed to a context in which political leaders found it more difficult to dehumanize the perceived enemy, thus making accommodations in such areas as weapons control legitimate. To that degree, the arts was one of the elements of peace-building that went beyond the provision of peace-keeping forces when there was little peace to keep.

Learning through the arts is to expect inclusiveness of both style and subject. I watched the Canadian Opera Company visit an inner-city school and perform in a room filled with children's drawings of Cinderella (the production to be given that afternoon). The enthralled audience of children from six to 10 years old participated as the chorus, and were overwhelmed by the incredible skill of the designer who found a way to make a length of textile play the role of backdrop as well as costumes for the entire cast. They watched as conflicts were resolved, as characters were revealed and transformed. Even technology intervened as the local television station turned up with cameras at the ready. No discipline boxes (history, politics, literature, music, decorative arts) were left isolated and unconnected in that room — or in the minds of those students. It may seem a long leap from international war and ecological threat to a production of *Cinderella*, but the nature of conflict was revealed and the path to reconciliation examined in a way that the very young could easily comprehend. Incorporating such an experience into a curriculum seeking to examine relationships, whether individual or collective, could advance children's understanding of such concepts as tolerance, negotiation, and accommodation.

We are now entering a phase of conflict which could bring down all our efforts to contain the destructive effect of war. Having passed the decades when a conflict between the two major powers threatened us all with nuclear annihilation, we find that some 30,000 nuclear warheads remain, frighteningly available to the most irresponsible terrorists, while on the international front we are faced with dozens of "identity conflicts" involving peoples within nations who turn to brutal wars that kill thousands every year. Project Ploughshares, a prestigious peace organization centred in Conrad Grebel College in the University of Waterloo, has for many years been identifying the hot spots on the international front and proposing strategies to shift international policies in the direction of reconciliation. The organization's periodical, *Monitor*, points out that for most of the last half of the 20th century there have been 30 to 40 wars going on during any given year. Since 1980 there have been only three "country vs. country" wars — Britain against Argentina over the Falkland Islands, Iraq against Iran, and China against Vietnam over a border issue. Of course, the Middle East erupted, bringing upon Iraq a controversial police action that had as its stated aim the restoration of Kuwait as an independent state, but the fact remains that war has essentially been a matter of dissidents in existing states believing that their rights and economic opportunities have been violated, fighting for the only solution that can protect them — separate existence as an autonomous nation.

Peace can come only within the context of a recognition of those human rights and the wide range of discrimination and inequity which has brought on the violence and brutality, victimizing mainly women and children who are unfortunate enough to be in the way. Ironically, these solutions are more cultural than political, involving relationships rather than boundaries. Willingness to accept the realities that must be a part of either a multi-ethnic state or a community of ethnically oriented communities is a cultural decision, and the world of literature, music, and drama, both live and on film, have much to say about the state of mind and spirit which will bring that about.

The "horizontal" approach to knowledge and understanding is the only rational direction for an education that will prepare young people to face an age of irony and uncertainty and the issues before it. It must begin with an integrated, cross-disciplinary involvement of all the arts disciplines, along with a strategy to make the artistic approach available to enrich every facet of knowledge and understanding. That is the essence of an integrated arts-based curriculum.

All major modern problems are multi-faceted and multidisciplinary, whether it be the environment, international affairs, crime and punishment, urban planning, transportation, or immigration. All demand a spectrum of considered reflection that goes far beyond an isolated, single-disciplined approach. Most of these issues include a confrontation around basic values and demand a position on human rights, justice, equity, and equality. This is the stuff of the arts. This is what great literature and music is about, both prose and poetry, both classical and modern. This is what actors are engaged in expressing and what composers are writing music about. This is the subject matter of the dancer and the photographer and filmmaker. Whereas knowledge appears to be fragmented, indeed competitive, in the guise of a school timetable, the arts at their best in our society complement and mutually celebrate community and connectedness.

We believe that environmental and peace issues can be solved only in the context of democratic traditions. However, we approach the new century with flagging confidence in the various forms of governmental organization, be they parliamentary or congressional. Never have we been so cynical about the efficacy or integrity of our political responses to present problems. Never have politicians been so savagely attacked. Never has their intelligence, their values, and their ethical stance been so effectively diminished.

At the Victoria College Keith Davey Lecture in January 1998, Michael Ignatieff extolled the only solution to the sad state of democratic decision-making he saw about him. He spoke of the importance of the liberal imagination, the capacity of people "to enter other people's heads" and to walk in their shoes. Without this ability, democracy breaks down to a struggle of competing interest groups. The value of debate is negated by assuming that only someone with a particular experience as a woman or as a member of a minority can speak with any legitimacy on an issue involving that particular group. Discussion leading to understanding and eventual accommodation deteriorates, and ultimately the confrontation becomes violent and brutish. The arts provide the opportunity for all of us to enter the experiences of a Willy Loman, or a Shylock, and thereby learn to engage with compassion. Role-playing in the classroom, along with the study of great dramatic literature, is the very best mechanism for teaching what it feels like to be bullied, humiliated, diminished, and depreciated. There is no greater training for the reality of the give-and-take of democracy. It is training in the imagination, says Ignatieff, that "enables us each to leave our race, gender, language and ethnic origin behind and become citizens together."8

Young people are aware of the irony in being driven to acquire "marketable" skills at a time when there is little expectation that full-time jobs which will make use of these skills and accompanying knowledge will be available to them. Indeed, the obsession over government job training and retraining that has engulfed Canada and all industrial economies since the late '50s has turned decidedly sour. The Organization of Economic Cooperation and Development (OECD), in a 1994 report, states that there "is remarkably meagre support for the hypothesis that such programs are effective," and an analyst looking at the quality of the $5-billion retraining schemes in the US was brutally frank in his appraisal: "Zero is not a bad number." Nor could any real benefits be found from schemes in the UK or Sweden. A report on billions of dollars of retraining investment in Australia was so devastatingly negative that the Labour Marketing Bureau carrying out the analysis was closed down.[9] The youth who thought that badly spent years in school could be salvaged in a free government job-training program now find that this alternative gives little hope. However, there seems to be no strategy for educational reform but that of addressing the economic factors through a more literate and computer-comfortable graduate capable of discovering the secrets of business management and particularly the questions posed by the new technologies. One could describe such a program, in the long term, as little more than training students to succeed in an economic structure that the planet cannot sustain. In the short term, it is failing to excite the desperate young people who see through the ambiguity of their situation. In many cases, these are the youths who are designated as mere drop-outs. To think that more conformity and more testing will attract their attention and attendance is to engage in a grand illusion.

Young people are confused and angry about the world around them and are unimpressed by those responsible for government decision-making. In *The End of Work*, Jeremy Rifkin writes:

> Politicians everywhere have failed to grasp the fundamental nature of the changes taking place in the global business community. In corporate boardrooms, on plant floors, and in retail stores around the world, a quiet revolution has been going on. Businesses have been busy restructuring their organizations, in effect reinventing themselves, to create new management and marketing structures that can work effectively alongside the extraordinary array of new information and telecommunications technologies being hurried on

line. The result is a radical transformation in the way
the world does business that threatens to bring into
question the very role of the mass worker in the coming
century.[10]

No curriculum, even an integrated and arts-based one, can promise
a set of easy solutions to these monstrous problems, but such a learning
experience can provide self-understanding, self-confidence, flexibility
in confronting crisis, and an increased capacity for individual action.

As much as global matters attract the attention of the school, it is in
matters of personal conflict where young people sense the irony of their
predicament. In a way that no previous generation has been forced to
confront crises — that is, without the extended family, close-knit village
and neighbourhood, and supportive church intervention — the young
feel very much isolated and alone. They are bombarded with images of
the "normal" family in an endless succession of situation comedies on
television; yet so many know that the family setting may be a place of
continuing pain and frustration. In many cases it may represent deprivation rather than the warmth and relaxed good humour that exudes
from the Bill Cosby example of filial relationship. Is it any wonder that
the stories of Alice Munro or Margaret Atwood are received with deep
thanksgiving, exposing as they do that normality may wear many faces,
some of them unpleasant? In the classroom, we must replace the "bad"
art of the commercial television sitcom with revealing and meaningful
expressions that expand the understanding of young people facing the
disruption of family breakdown and the personal hell of loneliness and
spiritual deprivation.

One of the greatest lessons we receive in life is that those we love
most may hurt us the most. The years of adolescence are a valley of
darkness and terror for so many young people. The matter of close relationship is pre-eminent in the minds of teenagers. Having at least one

close friend is essential — being accepted as part of a peer group in their school is close to paradise in the minds of our young.

Down through the ages, nothing has seemed as important as gaining a close romantic relationship. Is it any wonder that the Romeo and Juliet story is so popular, whether read as Shakespeare's poetry, high drama on a temporary set in the gymnasium, or danced by Karen Kain and Rex Harrington to the glorious but heart-rending music of Sergei Prokofiev? The world of sexuality and male-female, male-male, female-female relationships is a marsh with dangers in every step.

Roseneath Theatre in Toronto is the inspiration of David Craig. It plays in school auditoriums to student audiences and produced in the mid '90s a comical but poignant play about male sexuality and intimacy. *Health Class* explores the full gamut of emotion, including the invitation to macho behaviour that is found in every corner of the world of advertising and promotion and is a threat to every woman who dates and seeks companionship with a man. The dialogue between the two teachers who make up the cast sparkles. The plot centres on the fact that these two very different instructors (one a hockey coach, the other an English teacher) have been given the task of preparing a curriculum outline on sexual intimacy for a boys' health class. The simultaneous impact of laughter and shock is palpable. Only a dramatic approach to the visceral problem would have served. Even back in 1976, Theatre Passe Muraille had the courage to put on *The Horsburgh Scandal*, a play about a celebrated controversy over whether a clergyman, in discussing with the youth in his congregation the realities of sexuality, was providing them with necessary information or was encouraging their experimentation. Canadian actors Don Harron, Eric Peterson, and David Fox gave a sympathetic interpretation of the cleric's efforts in a time less tolerant than the '90s, indicating the willingness of actors and playwright to address controversial subjects and themes around intimacy and sexuality.

The arts are characterized as fantasy and fiction. But in every way they provide the reality for young people to fend off the lies of modern advertising about the good life and how to secure it. The consumer society is fuelled by the capacity of the advertising agency to convince people in vast numbers that they should desire certain products and services. If the conserver society, preoccupied as it is with the limits of the planet and the implications of continued growth at the expense of the life chance of every future generation, is to be successfully mounted, then some response to the power of advertising must be developed. In a civil libertarian society, censorship is understandably rejected, even restraints are resented by public and the courts. The recent ruling of the Canadian Supreme Court in the matter of cigarette advertising — that even when a health hazard can be proven, censoring the spoken and written word is too extreme a solution — makes the point adequately. The arts, because they examine the multitude of issues around human behaviour and also deal with the power of communication in all its forms, may be the strongest weapon in the hands of those who see the broad issues around advertising as resolvable only in the context of intellectual freedom. Once again, however, only a connected curriculum — integrating the arts subjects to illuminate sociological, historical, and moral issues — can make such matters comprehensible to children in our classrooms.

Education must prepare young people to meet a daunting future, but it must also help them face a terrifying present. The increasing incidence of teenage suicide, the retreat by teens into the immediate comfort of drugs and alcohol, even the unintelligible attraction of tobacco, particularly among adolescent women, indicates the foolishness of treating these years as merely a period of waiting for adulthood.

There is not an artist who would not admit that music, dance, film, and video can also be paths to abuse and violence. These activities share the ambiguity of every aspect of our lives. Even religion can be both a source of profound self-knowledge or a road to self-immolation in a fiery holocaust of the faithful. An effective program of integrated arts education which examines the mountaintops of humankind's past and challenges youth to create and express in the most compelling way their own concepts and feelings, can transform the lives of these very fragile beings.

Such a program can prepare these young people to face the cruelty of blighted hopes, the disappointments that come to plague us when, in spite of our best efforts, the great plan or strategy fails. Even more, through the arts the young come to realize what a collection of weaknesses each of one of us is and learn to accommodate the personal disappointment that we must encounter every day of our lives. To do so without resorting to violence, to carry on with courage and fortitude, is a lesson that the arts portray in countless examples drawn from literature and drama. That is surely a legacy all children deserve to receive from their formal schooling. It is particularly important in a society that is bringing together people of very different races, colours, creeds, and cultures. One satisfying fact that new Canadians from other lands can hold on to is that they can bring their unique cultural insights to the land their parents have chosen for them. For this reason, arts education is the most successful and most effective way of celebrating these cultures.

For example, in areas of North York, in the north end of Toronto, it made sense to provide musical training on steel drums rather than on strings, woodwinds, and brass. The schools there, with large concentrations of students from the Caribbean, have magnificent ensembles which play the music of the islands on the instruments for which it was written. No charge of Euro-obsession can be levelled at those institutions — but these same students are introduced to the glories of other cultural traditions in music, literature, drama, visual arts, and dance as well.

A very wise friend and mentor, Rabbi Arthur Bielfeld, responded to my assessment of education as a means of coping with irony in words of caution I have never forgotten: "The problem, surely, is that young people who view the ambivalence and ambiguity contained in the concept of irony may indeed turn to cynicism as their main defence. And nothing could be more grievous and damaging to their sense of well-being." That, indeed, is the most serious attribute that teachers already see in the students the school can neither interest or excite, and it would be tragic to exacerbate the situation by emphasizing even more the ambiguities and ambivalences experienced by teenagers. However, the arts provide many shields and bucklers. At one end is the sense of the absurd which at some point every child must acquire. Theatre, film, and painting can all express the wit and humour found in the efforts of humankind to order its affairs. At the other end is the most exquisite exposition of the highest ideals humankind has explored.

The arts can also show that out of the worst depths of human degradation and dissolution can emerge qualities of courage and heroism that may overwhelm our minds and senses. Such stories have been the central themes of great literature back to the days of Greece and Rome. It is the role of the arts to help young people work their way through these realities in such a way that they come to realize that tolerance, forgiveness, and civil behaviour is the response of the transformed individual and that such transformation is one of the highest goals of a liberal education.

The arts express revelation, or the apocalyptic, in the extension of that term as identified by the Rev. Dr. William Kervin:

> Apocalyptic writers saw history as a kind of screen or curtain behind which an even greater drama was being played out. Their function was to lift the curtain, to unveil the true meaning of things. In short there is what is going on, and there is what is *really* going on. Apocalyptic is about what is *really* going on, what is *really* at stake in the events of our time.[11]

Canada has produced a prodigious number of authors who have written apocalyptically — Margaret Laurence, Robertson Davies, Margaret Atwood, Morley Callaghan, Hugh MacLennan, W.O. Mitchell, Michael Ondaatje, Barry Callaghan, Alice Munro, Timothy Findley, Carol Shields, Jane Urquhart, Carole Corbeil, and a host of others. Fortunately for Canadian theatre, a coterie of directors surfaced in Toronto in the '60s and '70s who recognized the apocalyptic — George Luscombe, Paul Thompson, Bill Glassco, Christopher Newton, Guy Sprung, Sky Gilbert, Richard Rose, Richard Greenblatt, Janet Amos, Leon Major, and Marion Andre. By that time, there were Canadian playwrights providing serious fare — Carol Bolt, George Ryga, Sharon Pollock, David Freeman, Rachel Wyatt, Anne Chislett, Charles Tidler, and many more — and the Canadian stage was graced by Robert Christie, Jane Mallet, Amelia Hall, Barbara Hamilton, William Needles, Betty Leighton, Kate Reid, David Gardner, Mavor Moore, Frances Hyland, Sandy Webster, Charmion King, Barbara Chilcott, William Hutt, Martha Henry, Gordon Pinsent, Douglas Campbell, Douglas Rain, Don Harron, Patricia Hamilton, Pat Galloway, Jennifer Phipps, R.H. Thomson, Claire Coulter, the Davis brothers, and many others skilled enough to address the issues that beckoned to be seen in the context of "what is *really* going on."

It could be said that the extraordinary development of Canadian theatre in the 1950s and '60s had as much to do with education as theatrical production. George Luscombe was the seer and the catalyst during these years, and Neil Carson makes the point that a major aspect of his contribution was in the field of learning:

> [T]here was practically no conception of drama as anything but escapist entertainment. The idea that theatre could challenge audiences, enlighten them, *change them*, had hardly occurred to his students. It was clear that a proper theatre school would have to do more than teach acting; it would need to provide an extensive cultural and political education.[12]

In short, Canada has developed a mature literary and theatre community capable of the best in book or onstage. There is a body of literature available to the curriculum writer or the classroom teacher. The advantages can be seen in Canadian theatre and must be made manifest in Canadian schools.

A recent example of insight a play can bring to a contemporary problem is provided by Urjo Kareda, artistic director of the Tarragon Theatre. Sam Shepard's *True West* was being presented as part of the 1995-96 season and Kareda had received a letter complaining about "its inconclusiveness and possible negativity." He replied:

> It seems to me that so much of the writing of the 20th century is precisely *about* a lack of resolution, about indecisiveness. As principles and standards lose their old meanings and we struggle for new values, I think that our experience, too, becomes open-ended. To my mind, the final image in *True West* — two brothers immobilized after a battle, neither willing to yield to the other — strikes me as an uncanny image, for instance, of the relationship *right now* between English Canada and Quebec. And just as in *True West*, there are two opponents who need each other to survive, who know that they need integration without being able to act upon it.

> . . . I think that the failure to resolve the conflict in the
> play is the resolution.[13]

However much things have happened on the stages and in the concert halls of our communities during the past three decades, it is in the early years of our children's lives that these connections between the arts and the world around must be established and the insights to be found in theatre and literature examined for all their meaning. It is in the classrooms of our schools that children and youth must be prepared to live in a dangerous and ironically uncertain world. To send young people into society without the confidence and understanding that the arts can provide is a travesty of all that education could and should be.

NOTES

1. John Kenneth Galbraith, *The Age of Uncertainty* (New York: Houghton Mifflin Company, 1977), p. 7.
2. Allan Bloom, *Love and Friendship* (New York: Simon and Schuster, 1993), p. 93.
3. David C. Korten, *When Corporations Rule the World* (West Hartford, Conn.: Kumarian Press, Inc. and San Francisco: Berrett-Koehler Publishers, Inc., 1995), p. 69.
4. Langdon Winner, *Autonomous Technology: Technics Out of Control as a Theme in Political Thought* (Cambridge, Mass.: The MIT Press, 1977), p. 13.
5. Ursula Franklin, *The Real World of Technology* (CBC Massey Lecture Series, Toronto: CBC Enterprises, 1990), p. 12.
6. Stephanie Pace Marshall, "Chaos, Complexity, and Flocking Behaviour: Metaphors for Learning," *Wingspread Journal of the Johnson Foundation, Inc.* Volume 18, Issue 3: p. 13. Excerpted from *The School Administrator*, January 1995.
7. Ibid., p. 13.
8. Michael Ignatieff, "The Liberal Imagination: A Defence," *The Toronto Star*, January 21, 1998, p. A16.
9. Michael Ignatieff, "The Training Wheels of Government Go Flat," *Globe and Mail*, Toronto, April 13, 1996. p. D4.
10. Jeremy Rifkin, *The End of Work* (New York: G.P. Putnam's Sons, 1995), p. 89.
11. Rev. Dr. William Kervin, "The End of the World," sermon presented on November 19, 1995.

12. Neil Carson, *Harlequin in Hogtown: George Luscombe and Toronto Workshop Productions* (Toronto: University of Toronto Press, 1995), p. 26.
13. Urjo Kareda, "Audience Feedback," in *1995-96 Tarragon Theatre Season Play-Guide*, December 1995.

Chapter 2

**The Arts in our Schools:
Their Presence and
Possibility**

If art is to be a living reality for modern man, it has to
be a pure expression of the new consciousness of the
age.

Piet Mondrian

T he arts have always had some role in the educating of our children and young people. In fact, an argument could be made
that in the past it was a more common occurrence than at
present. In the one-room schoolhouse singing was one thing that children in both the early and later grades could do together. In the elementary school, teachers were usually female and a great many were drawn
from the church manse where hymn-singing around the piano was a
Sunday-evening form of entertainment. Playing an instrument and
singing were often part of the baggage that a prospective teacher
brought with her. Thus, singing became a part of every school day, even
if few classrooms had the luxury of a resident piano.

Canada, sharing a frontier view of learning, was not unlike the United States in the manner in which the arts were treated. George Geahigan writes:

> Ever inclined toward the practical, American educators have tended to regard the arts as more enjoyable than necessary, as something to be attended to after the serious business of schooling had been finished. . . . The arts were to be regarded as ornaments, something useful to be sure, but only as a means of occupying one's leisure time.[1]

At least in those simpler days of a previous century, there was no fear that amateur performance by the classroom teacher would be judged inferior to the instrumental and vocal pyrotechnics witnessed on the television set the night before. Every young woman was expected to do things with her hands, whether it be embroidery or pencil drawing and watercolours. These skills were acquired at an early age. Soon after arriving at the front of a classroom, the newly trained teacher realized that visual arts were a good way to finish off the week. Friday afternoon was perceived as "down time" in the classroom. Both teachers and students were tired from a week of learning the important things, the three R's being central, of course. Now there was a prize: moments to be spent with pencils and crayons, perhaps even paint and clay.

In a rural community with few entertainment opportunities, the annual school concert was the event of the year. The number of great actors who first experienced the charge of energy that courses through the veins when standing before such a live audience, even one heavily laced with relatives and neighbours, is surely legion.

In time, schools found a way to involve children in a process that not only brought attention to the school, but aroused the pride of parents and colleagues. The school choir could rival the school hockey or basketball team in raising student spirit. When secondary schools became almost as obligatory to attend as elementary, the stakes were raised. Now, not only school choirs were in competition at community Kiwanis music festivals, but orchestras and bands as well. However, these were extra-curricular and not-for-credit, even though the quality of performance might reach levels of excellence rarely exhibited in the normal class-room.

As well, there were courses in music, and later in drama. Eventually dance also made its way into the secondary school curriculum after dec-ades of distressing trivialization (as an art form) in physical education classes. Visual arts were found in every school but achieved distinction in particular institutions such as Beale Collegiate in London, Ontario, and Central Tech in Toronto, as both schools produced an extraordinary number of noteworthy Canadian painters and printmakers.

Creative writing, as part of the English-language curriculum, has al-ways been in danger of a second-class rating in comparison to grammar, spelling, and business correspondence. Only in the last decade or so have film and the technological arts found their way into the class-rooms, mainly at the secondary level, though a visual artist like Aiko Su-zuki, whose fabric sculptures grace public spaces like the Toronto Reference Library, and who works in a host of visual arts media, can work wonders in video and film, even with elementary-level students.

However, it is quite clear that these arts subjects took a back seat both at the elementary and secondary school levels to languages, sci-ence, mathematics, and the humanities. Indeed they were isolated in the curriculum, lower on the pole than physical education and later ar-rivals such as family studies. In short, the arts were tolerated in most schools, used to raise morale in others, and celebrated in a few. There was recognition that some students might find a place to excel and gain confidence sufficient to become accomplished in the "important" disciplines offered by the school. Certainly, any parent who thought the school should provide an appropriate base for a professional career in the arts was quickly disabused of such notions. Indeed there have always been those who believe that all arts training should be the responsibility of the home and that it was quite normal that private lessons should be paid for by the parent. In spite of the embarrassing reality that many great composers and performers have come from poor families, the reliance on the free market to assure that only the really gifted arrived at distinction seemed entirely proper.

Certainly there was no sense that the arts could be central to our understanding both of our culture and ourselves. Nor was there any thought that learning of all kinds could be enhanced by the linking of the arts to areas of serious consideration like the sciences, mathematics, and languages. There was little reason to believe that the industrial society would need more than a handful of artists to keep the well-to-do amused. There was also a fear that artists were too often dangerous people set upon changing the society that supported them. Encouraging self-expression in non-verbal ways was a sure method of courting civil unrest. If there was evidence that the pen or well-modulated voice was stronger than the arms of those in power then even the paintbrush was a threat to civilization. The arts had to be kept in their place in the school, otherwise the discipline base would erode and children would be talking excitedly, thereby breaking the silence that was supposed to prove real learning was going on. Or even worse, these young people might be moving about rather than sitting still and passive like jars being filled with intellectual jelly — the transmission theory of learning that has dominated human history.

Geahigan writes:

> Student involvement in the arts has often been tarred
> with the suspicion that it is a matter of deviant person-
> alities engaging in compulsive behavior. Some educa-
> tors have also regarded schoolwork in the arts as a form
> of therapy appropriate for students who were not suc-
> ceeding in other areas of the curriculum.[2]

Even these limited observable phenomena of reluctant arts education development in Ontario classrooms came directly from philosophic
underpinnings emerging out of the progressive education movement
that had its beginning at the end of the 19th century in the United States
but flowered through the first half of the 20th century and very much affected the teaching of the arts. Child-centred education — a theory that
the curriculum should address the developmental needs of children and
youth with classroom activities relevant to student interests and enthusiasms — became very popular. The arts could obviously stand up well
in a curriculum based on that perception.

As well, Geahigan writes, there was a social purpose strand to the
progressive philosophy:

> Social reconstructionists sought to use the schools as a
> way of preventing or alleviating social problems in the
> society at large. . . . Social reconstructionists focused on
> preparing students to function as reflective citizens in a
> democratic society. . . .argued for instruction in solving
> problems, for new curriculum content, and for an em-
> phasis upon community life and participation in social
> activities within the school.[3]

All these theories had some effect on my own school experience. I
attended a secondary school in a large urban centre. It had been decided
that every first-year student would receive some musical education. As
a result, the single music teacher on staff was confronted with 10 or 15
identical classes for two 35-minute periods a week, meaning that he was
forced to process some 300 students each year. He used "fill in the
blank" tests to solve the problem of assessment but still had to cope with

the utterly boring and exhausting experience of facing that unconscionable number of repeat teaching assignments each day.

His survival technique to ensure continuing sanity was that of music appreciation. He played records he hoped would interest, or at least subdue, this army of students. Although I had taken piano lessons, I had never heard any classical orchestral music and was overwhelmed by the sound, the colour, the excitement of a symphony orchestra playing Tchaikovsky. The *1812 Overture* and *Marche Slav* may seem pretty meagre fare, but these recordings were my window on a new world of listening. Although my tastes have changed enormously, that experience began my frantic effort to hear more and more symphonic music. I still have the 78 RPMs of Tchaikovsky's *Pathetique Symphony* and his first piano concerto. As a teenager, I worked hard at a grocery store after school and on weekends to find the money to pay for these and many other recordings. Now Beethoven, Bach, Mozart, Brahms, Mahler, Bruckner, and Richard Strauss, and a host of contemporary Canadian composers, have replaced Tchaikovsky as favourite composers, but I have not forgotten the vista that was revealed to me in a secondary school classroom, one I might otherwise have been deprived of forever.

The ultimate irony is that the uninspiring but well-meaning efforts of that overworked and professionally abused music teacher have brought me more hours of joy and delight than those of any other instructor I was to meet in secondary school and university. Indeed, I am among those forced to agree with Friedrich Nietzsche that "without music, life would be a mistake." However, it never occurred to me that there was any relationship between what transpired in the music class and the painting and drawing in the art class down the hall, and most certainly there was no connection with the mathematics classrooms and science laboratories on the second floor. Nor did it occur to me that the arts had some linkage with the events of World War II, the event that dominated my years of secondary school education.

My learning experience of some 50 years ago would not be tolerated in a modern elementary or secondary school. The arts were indeed peripheral in the minds of administrators, teachers, and students, and it was only good luck that gave me such a life-changing breakthrough. But it would also be wrong to assume that all young people today are receiving an adequate arts education. In fact, recent budget cuts have influenced both the availability and the quality of arts programs, making more difficult the kind of integration of arts disciplines and the connection with other sectors of the curriculum that would change the learning lives of students.

In fact, the distance between what arts experience is available and what is needed for students facing a difficult and uncertain future is probably even greater in the '90s than it has been in the more certain and stable past. Like so much of what we see in education, it is not a matter of whether learning is as effective as in past generations, it is that the expectations are much higher, and so they must be — the stakes are much higher. More must be learned, and the implications of failing to learn are so much more serious. In a learning or knowledge society, the ignorant become an underclass with little access to satisfying work, to an understanding of the social context in which they find themselves, or to the experiences that bring joy to a life of accomplishment.

Throughout all these years, those who teach the arts have faced massive misunderstanding about what their roles should be. Some parents have been outraged that a student should fail visual arts or music classes. These, after all, are merely play and have nothing to do with the serious aspects of school, in particular what happens in the mathematics or science classes. It is a continuation of the perception of the arts as "play," entertainment, a kind of relaxation class at the end of the day.

Yet arts education programs in some schools are rigorous. They stretch the mind and the emotional capacity of the student. In good arts education classes there is a seriousness, an intensity that is a wonder to behold. This quality can sometimes be experienced by attending a play, a musical, or a concert in the local school gymnasium. Even during those mythical years of the '70s and '80s, when it was assumed that excellence had disappeared from the classrooms of North America entirely, the quality of music or drama at such events left the adult audiences in awe. Yet arts classes are still viewed as unimportant.

It must also be understood that arts education in our elementary schools, even in the single discipline-by-discipline expression it often receives, is not just learning to appreciate the arts or mastering a basic skill, but the releasing of the creative artist in every student. It is true there are secondary schools in which the orchestra, the brass band, and particularly the jazz band have reached near-professional standards. Nevertheless, that should not be the pre-eminent goal, and until artistic literacy is a

CHORAL MUSIC IN NORTH YORK

It's an early spring night, and hundreds of children and grown-ups descend on the Ford Centre for the Performing Arts. An evening with Show Boat, the blockbuster musical mounted to inaugurate this splendid venue? No, an evening with Professor Doreen Rao of the University of Toronto's Faculty of Music, a dozen music teachers from North York schools, and over 300 young people singing at a truly breathtaking level of quality.

The evening begins with Bach but moves quickly to a selection of more contemporary music from all around the world. It has been clearly stated that this concert is reaching out to the lands from which many of the children in the choir have come.

The drums of Africa accompany the lilting lines of the folk song. The quickening rhythm of the Hebrew dance melody features a group of Jewish students; the sounds of Macedonian choral music come from a quartet of children from that region of Europe, and so the evening goes. The vivacious, personable conductor shares the podium with the teachers with whom she has worked to prepare this ambitious repertoire.

The most memorable impression is that of the explosive joy of the voices in both unison singing and in harmony. Even the body language accompanying the rhythmic pieces is integral to the pulse of the song and the movement of the children. Here is global education and its possibilities for racial harmony being achieved through the joyful, spontaneous delight of the participants. And, perhaps, most surprising of all is the presence onstage of the regular music teachers singing with the children.

The evening is a culmination of the rethinking by coordinator Elaine Mason of the way choral music and performance is to be approached in North York. Not only have children learned to sing under the direction of a professional conductor, but teachers have been given the professional development opportunity of their lives — to work with a distinguished and experienced conductor of children and youth choirs.⌘

universal objective and until the arts are perceived as an integrated exploration connected to every other subject area in the curriculum, there is much to accomplish.

In 1960, the federal government of Canada, in an uncharacteristic display of generosity, passed the *Technical and Vocational Training and Assistance Act*, a seemingly innocuous piece of legislation that transferred substantial amounts of money for capital construction and equipment to the provincial governments, who were constitutionally responsible for education. The stated purpose was to encourage practical training at the secondary school level so that these young people would be job-ready for lower-level industrial positions at the least.

As it turned out, shop wings were added to virtually every secondary school in the province. So much money was available that music rooms fully equipped with instruments appeared and a new era in orchestral training began that influenced the curriculum of the elementary school as well.

There were fall-outs that could not have been expected. Too often secondary school students were trained to play the oboe or trumpet in the same way their colleagues down the hall were engaged in learning plumbing or woodworking. Although there were notable exceptions, most graduated with little appreciation or real knowledge of music. One might have expected an explosion of community bands and orchestras across the land as a result of the subsequent presence of tens of thousands of instrumentalists. In the southern coast of England that I visit often, there is but one symphony orchestra, in Bournemouth, but over 200 community bands, most capable of addressing a most difficult but satisfying repertoire. That was not to be in Ontario. Indeed, the most lasting effect of all these instrument purchases and the extensive construction of music rooms was the demise of choral music in many secondary schools and a de-emphasis of this important arts expression at the elementary level.

Years later, in Toronto, irony prevailed. Outside influences assured that there would be opportunities for children to sing at the highest level of quality. A choir was established by gathering students from various elementary schools under a gifted and sensitive teacher, Jean Ashworth Bartle. The Toronto Children's Chorus was founded initially as a result of the Toronto Symphony's need for a children's choir to enable the orchestra to address repertoire demanding such a component. Within four years, the choir had won first prize at the prestigious International Eisteddfod competition in Llasngollen, Wales. Now, some 20 years later, the chorus program serves some 300 choristers from age five to 16 in four choirs — Cherub, Junior, Intermediate, and the peak of choral achievement, the Chorus. This ensemble has sung on radio, recorded several discs (one with Canadian soloists Louis and Gino Quilico and another with Canadian Ben Heppner, the latest international tenor sensation), and commissioned and performed works by Canadian composers Glenn Buhr, Jean Coulthard, Malcolm Forsythe, Harry Freedman, Srul Irving Glick, Imant Raminsch, R. Murray Shafer, and Ruth Waltson Henderson, the chorus's accompanist as well as a contributor to its repertoire. Expanding that repertoire, the chorus has sung with the Toronto Symphony Orchestra under Andrew Davis, Charles Dutoit, Helmuth Rilling, Robert Shaw, Klaus Tennstedt, and Sir David Willcocks.

Every year, the TCC sings its way to Europe, Asia, or Australia and is greeted ecstatically by audiences there. The critic who perceives the arts as undemanding should experience the discipline that releases the purity of tone and clarity of text that characterizes this choir under a conductor who believes there is a musician and artist in every child.

A similar dynamic occurred when the Canadian Opera Company found it needed children's choruses for even the main repertoire, *Carmen* being the most obvious example. Lloyd Bradshaw founded the Canadian Children's Opera Chorus, an ensemble that gained such repute it soon extended its role beyond appearances with the COC, giving concerts in its own right. The lesson is obvious — with inspired leadership, Canadian children at the elementary level can excel to levels equal to their contemporaries anywhere in the world.

In the early '70s, the outstanding Canadian choral conductor Robert Cooper, who has since become conductor of the accomplished Opera in Concert Chorus and the distinguished Niagara Symphony Orchestra Chorus (now Chorus Niagara), took over the leadership of an ensemble of students from area secondary schools which had been formed through the initiative of the Toronto Mendelssohn Choir, the country's major choral organization. The Toronto Mendelssohn Youth Choir continues to reach extraordinary heights, singing a choral repertoire that would challenge the most accomplished mature choir. It presents a series of concerts every season, has toured Canada and Italy, and has been heard across the CBC network. When asked why he chose to feature the carols of obscure turn-of-the-century Canadian composers and a lesser-known work by Ralph Vaughan Williams at a recent concert, Cooper replied that his choristers needed to know the broadest repertoire as an aspect of their learning experience in the chorus. His view is that young people in his TMYC are learning more than music performance — they are engaging in a study of what Canadian cultural survival is all about.

All of this development is explainable when one realizes that the dean of Canadian choral music, the late Elmer Iseler, came to his position as conductor of his own Singers and the Toronto Mendelssohn Choir, from his post as a music teacher in a secondary school. No person has devoted his life so completely to the development of choral music in this country; no choral conductor has presented such a broad range of Canadian choral music. As a result of Iseler's work and inspiration, other centres of youth choral music have emerged across Canada. Indeed, Noel Edison, the distinguished conductor of the Elora Festival Singers and Iseler's interim successor as conductor of the Mendelssohn Choir, came from an Ontario school classroom.

With these opportunities for music-making by young musicians, it is no mystery that *Choral Concert* is one of the most popular programs on CBC radio. Hosted by conductor and music educator Howard Dyck and produced by TMYC leader Robert Cooper, it has a dedicated weekly following, which is quite astonishing for a serious music presentation. Nor is it surprising that within a single decade, Nicholas Goldschmidt, for years the artistic director of both the Guelph Spring Festival and the Algoma Festival, was inspired to organize two enormous, unique choral festivals in Toronto, bringing choirs from all over the world as well as highlighting Canadian ensembles.

However much one might want to applaud these successes — and others in Elora, Ottawa, Listowel, London, Thunder Bay, Niagara Falls, Kingston, Windsor, Kitchener, Sudbury, Hamilton, and elsewhere — in one fragment of an arts discipline, the impetus came in spite of, rather than because of, the educational system as such, even though based on the work of exemplary classroom teachers whose names are now all but forgotten. If a fully integrated arts-based curriculum had been in place, one can only imagine the achievements that might have resulted in all segments of the arts.

The strength of the arts can be attested to by the fact that even in the financially deprived '90s, miracles do happen in the most unexpected places. Parkdale Collegiate inhabits a poor Toronto neighbourhood with enormous social problems, partly resulting from the closing of a major mental-health facility that had served a large number of patients who now became dependent on the out-patient clinic and remained in the neighbourhood to receive treatment. Parkdale is also one of the most multicultural communities in Toronto. Thus, Parkdale Collegiate, a proud and historic institution, receives a continuing stream of students from every continent, most with no English-language capability. Its record of serving these newly arrived immigrant students is exemplary in spite of communication challenges that are truly monumental and a drug culture that surrounds the school like a fetid swamp.

In the midst of all these problems, a program of integrated arts emerged from the head of a devoted and compassionate English teacher and department head, Jim Craig. He is an arts lover of a magnitude rarely encountered. He enjoys every art form passionately; indeed, he pursues the arts both in his own country and in Europe and the United Kingdom every moment of his discretionary time. When a program to assist alienated youth was promulgated by his board of education, he proposed bringing in artists on a scale unprecedented in area schools, believing that the arts were the most effective force in dealing with the issues facing the young people he taught. His proposal received board funding, and artists began to arrive regularly. Storytellers, dancers, singers, and instrumentalists were involved, as virtually every art form was included in the program. The young people in that school are now comfortable with artists and, more importantly, with the creativity those artists use to challenge them.

These artists' visits are not a passive experience for students, but an opportunity for interaction. Artists are expected to enter into an animated exchange with students who, in turn, are expected to write about what has happened. In one case, Helen Porter, an outstanding storyteller, took students through the neighbourhood, helping them to see that what was familiar and perhaps ugly and worn was also filled with character and meaning. The result was a splendid publication of student writing that indicated profound thought about themselves and their neighbourhood. The arts, for these students, are a single fabric of understanding and a path to comprehending the world around them.

Certainly there have been examples of magnificent secondary school programs that have brought forth bands and orchestras of breathtaking capacity. Schools have developed reputations, largely based on winning Kiwanis Festival awards year after year. North Toronto and Barrie Collegiate spring to mind in that regard. School orchestras and choirs from Ontario have journeyed to the major centres of music in the United States, the United Kingdom, and Europe. These miracles have transpired even in the trivializing atmosphere the arts have faced in the past. Yet even the exemplary programs discovered across a vast province do not lessen the need for an effective arts program as a regular feature of an integrated curriculum that reaches every child and youth, offering a holistic learning experience that sees the arts as a window to learning in every area affecting these students' lives.

The point is simple. Teaching the arts is not merely the passing on of a skill, even if it results in performance at the international level. That is obviously some part of the expectation that comes from a student's desire to participate actively in creative activity, whether it be music, drama, or dance. But one must assume that the ultimate questions of life show through the arts even in the midst of the adolescent triumphs which in themselves are so important. Unfortunately the numbers of students touched by such programs are but a handful. There are thousands of others who could be transformed but will not even be influenced, much to their disadvantage. For some, drugs, violence, and petty crime will replace an arts experience that could have brought positive satisfaction.

Nor is teaching the arts a strategy for preparing young people for a job in the world of arts industry. This is a new phenomenon in our society. For many years, it was believed that studying the arts was a waste of time insofar as getting a real job was concerned. Indeed, that was always the major reason given for suggesting that students pursue more vocationally useful disciplines such as science, language, and math. Suddenly, as we shall see in a later chapter, it has become an accepted fact that the cultural industries have had a far greater increase in employment opportunities than can be found in the traditional industrial and commercial fields. In a period which has seen a record number of unemployed or underemployed architects, engineers, and lawyers, those associated with music, dance, and theatre have done comparably well. When one adds the arts-related areas of broadcasting, publishing, advertising, et al., it is not hard to see why some arts supporters would rank arts education with computer courses as a sure path to satisfying employment.

One way of recognizing the employment potential of young children who have a considerable talent for music, dance, or theatre has been the creation of special schools for the arts. The Claude Watson School for the Arts and Earl Haig Secondary School in Toronto are extraordinary examples, producing graduates who have received first-class arts training as well as excellent academic preparation for any post-secondary work they might wish to pursue. Recently, these schools put on a production of Carl Orff's *Carmina Burana*, normally a concert favourite for mature audiences that exposes the untraditional erotic thoughts and musings of renegade monks of the 12th and 13th centuries. Claude Watson mounted a full staged version which revealed the talents of actors, dancers, vocal, mime, and visual artists as well as the proficiency of a full symphonic orchestra which had mastered the difficult score and a well-rehearsed choir which sang without scores. However, the focus was not on the largely incomprehensible Latin text that Orff had adopted as his inspiration, but rather on the metaphor that revealed student concerns. As the director's notes in the program outlined, this performance had something to say about

> environmental concerns and dangers, the global struggle for political, economic, cultural and national development and our personal sense of health and identity. Concerning the environment, we are aware of global deforestation, species extinction at an accelerating rate, toxic pollution of the oceans, urban centres and the atmosphere. In our global struggles for development, we are constantly bombarded with images of economic exploitation and the daily horror of refugees and terrorists. As individuals, conflict about our identities on sexual, racial, ethnic, religious and cultural levels — a process heightened by an invasive and confrontational media. At the same time, this media defines "the good life" in terms of material wealth, self-interest and token tolerance.[4]

A production of such proportions, involving hundreds of young people, could not have been contemplated in a "normal" school, nor could such ambitious expectations have been successfully met. The school auditorium was filled with parents and friends as well as members of the community who saw their young people addressing matters of extreme importance and communicating their collective and individual concerns through one of the world's greatest choral triumphs.

In these and similar schools, highly qualified arts teachers have been gathered to provide a highly enriched experience for talented young people. These schools are controversial, as it is charged that they draw the best teachers and the most able students from the regular schools, thereby weakening the arts across the entire educational jurisdiction. Others would deny the charge, suggesting that only a small percentage are so attracted and that experience has shown that the regular school programs are undamaged. Indeed, these special schools can often serve as research centres for new methods and curriculum advances in the regular arts education programs. The case is not closed, but the point must be made that setting up elite arts schools for those who see their future employment in the arts and in arts-related areas of our economic system, or indeed, failing to do so, does not address the main concern — that *every* child must be brought to a level of arts literacy that will make life joyful and productive. Only by addressing the nature of the curriculum, the appropriate development of teachers, and the preparation of each child for a future in a difficult world can such an issue be resolved.

Arts education is not specifically about finding work. Yet the reality is that the new technological highway is about communication — the communication of a vast, seemingly infinite array of messages. And the arts have been about communication from the outset. The cave pictures of the earliest discovered humans were communicating important spiritual information, as were the dances about the campfire. Thus, it follows that in spite of all the emphasis on hardware and the scientific research and development that achieved the breakthroughs which have brought on the technological revolution, the arts will provide the essential element, the software, the message. This realization has led North-view Heights Collegiate and Don Mills Collegiate in Toronto to develop a curriculum around technology and the arts. Although this experiment has only recently been initiated, it signals an understanding on the part of two schools that such a linkage in curriculum emphasis provides significant opportunities for young people.

Teaching the arts as communication comes closer to the preferred aim, for it places the arts at the centre of learning, in the mainstream of the curriculum as opposed to the backwater where it is found in many schools. If the arts' essential capacity to reach out to every discipline were understood, it would provide a strong argument for recognizing the role the arts could play in the curriculum. At the same time, the arts are not simply a mechanism for sending other peoples' messages more effectively. The arts have their own set of values, and the integrity of the arts can easily be eroded if they are exploited, as indeed they are every night on commercial TV. It is in the context of the integrated arts-based curriculum that the power of the arts to express the most profound thoughts of philosophers, mathematicians, physicists, psychologists, theologians, and historians can best be utilized.

NOTES

1. George Geahigan, *The Arts, Education, and Aesthetic Knowing, Part II*, edited by Bennett Reimer and Ralph A. Smith (Chicago: The University of Chicago Press, 1992), p. 2.
2. Ibid., p. 7.
3. Ibid., p. 5.
4. Director's Notes, program for Carl Orff's *Carmina Burana* by Earl Haig Secondary School/Claude Watson School for the Arts, North York, December 1995.

Chapter 3

The Arts and the Process of Learning

Art is not a means by which we escape from life, but a stratagem by which we conquer life's disorder.

Alfred Barr

We are becoming aware of the complexities of how we come to know, realizing that the process of learning has many facets. We learn as individuals — indeed we have our own timetables and patterns of seeking understanding — yet we learn many things best in a group, especially a family unit. We learn from the moment of birth to the point of death. We learn from personal contact, but increasingly in a modern society we collect information from machines. Each of these elements of our coming to know has an enormous impact on the nature of our community and our well-being as individuals. The arts are at the very centre of all the debates on learning that have consumed our energy and purpose in the past and will most certainly engage us as the quality of our understanding becomes the basis of action before an uncertain future.

Understandings about children's learning have come through many phases in this century. However, the most pervasive and unrelenting concept has been the empty-bottle theory — that children were but empty vessels to be filled with facts, figures, and ways of doing things that society considered essential to the well-being of every productive citizen. The present organization of the traditional classroom and the dynamic of the teacher-student relationship honours this "transmission" perception of how children learn.

More sophisticated educators came to realize many years ago that school learning is a very personal activity, based on individual enthusiasms and interests as well as preparation in the home environment before schooling begins. We know that children are ready to learn a specific skill or body of knowledge at different points in their lives — learning to read at the age of two or three may be appropriate for one child and at seven or eight for another. We know that motivation plays a major role in the success of children in the classroom. We know that the informal curriculum abounds in every educational institution and that children learn much in the school's halls, gymnasiums, and playgrounds.

These rather obvious observations about schooling are but a prelude to the more sophisticated analyses of learning in school that have dominated the last half of the 20th century. In terms of the role of the arts, we have all witnessed the intense enthusiasm and concentration of young children at dance, at making music, at creating sculpture or film, and have been astounded by how much they have learned both in terms of content and skill. There is mounting evidence, most of it inconclusively anecdotal, that these young people have learned effectively and efficiently even though we might call their activity "play." However, in the past decade, more substantial evidence has emerged that makes the prevailing attitudes toward the arts in the schooling system infuriating for teachers who have observed the transformation of children learning through music, dance, theatre, and visual arts at preschool and primary levels of instruction.

Of particular interest is the impact of our new understandings about the functioning of the human brain, influenced — ironically — by comparisons with the complexities of the workings of the computer. Sharon Begley has made use of our new knowledge in mounting a case for ensuring that arts-learning opportunities for young children be pervasive and widespread. She explains:

> The child's brain is "a jumble of neurons" all waiting to be woven into the intricate tapestry of the mind. Some have been hard-wired, by the genes in the fertilized egg, into circuits that command breathing or control heartbeat, regulate body temperature or produce reflexes. But trillions upon trillions more are like the Pentium chips in a computer before the factory freeloads the software. They are pure and of almost infinite potential, unprogrammed circuits that might one day compose rap songs and do calculus, erupt in fury and melt in ecstasy. If the neurons are used, they become integrated into the circuitry of the brain by connecting to other neurons; if they are not used, they may die.[1]

She points out implications of this understanding in terms of what children should be encouraged to do with their minds and bodies both before school age and in the early years:

> It is the experiences of childhood, determining which neurons are used, that wire the circuits of the brain as surely as a programmer at a keyboard reconfigures the circuits in a computer. Which keys are typed — which experiences a child has — determines whether the child grows up to be intelligent or dull, fearful or self-assured, articulate or tongue-tied. Early experiences are

so powerful, says Harry Chugani of Wayne State University, that "they can completely change the way a person turns out."[2]

The important message in this analysis of the development of the human brain is that the natural interest that children have in the arts can become the path to that "wiring of the neurons" that means so much to their future capabilities as adults. One can select any of the art forms and discover that the play activities of children — for example, their love of drawing or their delight in playing roles in mini-dramas — are not peripheral, engaging their time until they are old enough for "serious learning," but are possibly the most important educational moments of their lives. These experiences in the very early years represent the opening of windows that close as the child matures. The irreversibility of early brain deprivation is a strong motive for arts education. The example of music is most dramatic. Lyn Nell Hancock reminds us that Plato once stated that music "is a more potent instrument than any other for education."

> Now scientists know why. Music, they believe, trains the brain for higher forms of thinking. Researchers at the University of California, Irvine, studied the power of music by observing two groups of preschoolers. One group took piano lessons and sang daily in chorus. The other did not. After eight months the musical three-year-olds were expert puzzlemasters, scoring 90% higher than their playmates did in spatial intelligence — the ability to visualize the world accurately. This skill translates into complex math and engineering skills. "Early music training can enhance a child's ability to reason," says Irvine physicist Gordon Shaw.[3]

In light of our growing knowledge about how the mind develops, the dismissing of the arts as mere "play," as unimportant and peripheral, is surely a tragedy of major proportions. We need to understand the risk a society imposes on itself when it trivializes such an instrument of learning.

Seymour Sarason, in his book *The Challenge of Art to Psychology*, points out that US culture is not one that celebrates artistic activity. He charges that, on the whole, American schools effectively extinguish whatever artistic excitement children bring to their learning during the first years of elementary education. With the emphasis on representing reality in visual arts and polished performance in dance, music, and drama, the child soon experiences negative feelings that extend into adulthood. "The result is a form of learned helplessness or inadequacy," Sarason writes.[4] He points out that artistic potential then goes underground and becomes a festering source of dissatisfaction that often is dissipated only when mature adults turn their attention to drawing, painting, photography, and drama in their retirement years. Elderhostel Canada, part of an American-based international organization providing courses for retired individuals over age 55, reports that arts courses are its most popular offering, even though these activities have featured less prominently in the lifestyle of participants throughout their working years, supporting Sarason's argument. Elliot Eisener, the eminent American arts-education advocate, tells the story of an artist shocking an audience of business tycoons by suggesting that their stress ulcers were but an "unkissed imagination . . . and undanced dance." Many of those unreached by the arts in the midst of a high-powered career are finding satisfaction and joy on the stage and at the easel in their later years. Many also feel they might have been much more interesting and productive human beings had these artistic impulses not been buried in their early years.

Thus, the arts may have become a major recreational device for adults over the past few decades simply because schools on this continent have had such a meagre commitment to teaching through the arts. In most schools, artistically engaged students are seen as very special persons whose talent sets them apart from the rest of those who make up the "normal" student body. It becomes very easy, indeed it is perceived as being financially responsible, for school boards to put few resources into the arts. That the arts have survived the perception of being both trivial and elite is an indication of their power and resilience.

If we truly believed that every child has artistic potential and that the development of mentally and spiritually healthy adults depends on the nurturing of these attributes, then skills in the arts would be considered as crucial as computer skills for the citizens of this and the next century. It is not beyond imagination — indeed everything we know points in this direction — that we are depriving our young of developing the very essence of their humanity and undermining their capacity to contribute to a decent and compassionate society. However, we have many miles to travel before we can expect that understanding to animate public policy. One school will have an excellent visual arts program, another will emphasize

SENIOR STRINGS AND THE CLAUDE WATSON SCHOOL

The downtown church is populated with older adults waiting to hear an afternoon concert by the Toronto Senior Strings. This ensemble of professional players, most of whom have recently retired from the Toronto Symphony Orchestra, is the inspired initiative of Ruth Budd, a bass string player in that orchestra for several decades.

The concert is one of a series, but today an unexpected pleasure has presented itself. The student choir from the Claude Watson School for the Arts has rehearsed an arrangement of Faure's "Pavanne" for voices and strings. It is to be the final piece on a demanding orchestral program of Corelli, Britten, and Buczynski. Victor Feldbrill, Canada's highly respected orchestral conductor, introduces the choir with the observation that in rehearsal the sound of these children overwhelmed even the most hardened pros in his orchestra and that he is sure the audience will also be thrilled. And thrilled they are, with the purity of tone, the moving dynamic, the clear unadulterated line of sound that floats out over the assembled listeners. The response of the audience is more than spirited, it is tumultuous, and deservedly so.

There is a place for young and old to find common ground in the arts, and the cooperation of professional and amateur, young and old, with the highest quality of performance as the objective, can be achieved. The arts can be an appropriate focus for intergenerational contact with the capacity to benefit all. It is a common ground for the exploration of the past through the memories of people who experienced events that young people need to know about. To lose the past is to undermine all hope for the future: young children and older citizens singing together, telling each other stories, and enjoying a visual presentation, is an opportunity for learning at the cusp.⌘

its splendid music courses and its choirs and orchestras, but few indeed have connected the individual arts in an integrated whole and fewer have seen the capacity of the arts to give meaning to the rest of the curriculum.

Even recent public examinations of the ills of the schooling system fail to give the arts any real attention. The latest Royal Commission in Ontario presented the arts educator with a splendid slogan: "Any school system that fails to open up the spirit of the arts to its students is unworthy of public support." What more could be said? The commission's report was published in the wake of excellent representations from both arts educators and artists. All the latest research findings on the value of the arts were paraded before the commission. The Ontario Arts Council, through its Arts Education Officer, Stephen Campbell, in a document entitled "Not a Frill: The Centrality of the Arts in the Education of the Future" (Appendix A), made a succinct and cogent argument for a new era in arts education, placing it at the centre of the curriculum and emphasizing its influence on learning in virtually every area of intellectual exploration. Yet, among the commission's 167 recommendations, not one mention of the arts could be found.[5] References to the arts in the commission report, "For The Love of Learning," were so sparse that the arts were diminished by such unstated and unexpressed support.

Ironically, this 1995 Royal Commission report faced with some courage the fact that the family is no longer the steadfast, ever-present element in the positive development of children that it had been considered in the past. It was this realization that parents had less time with their children at the most crucial point of their development that led to the commission's emphasis on early childhood education. But the commission failed to make the connection that learning, usually regarded as an individual activity, is also a family affair. Assigning the state even further responsibility for the learning of the very young child (though based on the early childhood education successes in other jurisdictions) may well divert people from recognizing that children learn best when surrounded by parents who are also learning. The truth of this can be observed in any children's museum, such as the Museum of Civilization in Hull, Quebec, or the Children's Museum in London, Ontario. Fathers and mothers accompany children in their exploration of Inuit igloos or the tents of native people, authentic costumes bring reality to the study of the people who wore them, and imaginative toys challenge the skill of hand and eye of every child. The Royal Ontario Museum in Toronto has a special exploration area in its basement for hands-on learning by children and their parents, emphasizing the experiential rather than simply the viewing of artifacts in cases. Thousands of parents and children experience exciting moments of learning together in these venues.

The arts have provided a perfect opportunity to engage the entire family in much more than a merely entertaining fashion. The Children's Festival at Harbourfront Centre in Toronto has enthralled both children and adults, presenting artists who have brought the joy of artistic expression but have also have been teaching profound truths about race relations, sexual stereotypes, indeed, the full spectrum of issues that bedevil our society. Parents and children learn together, ensuring that learning is seen not as yet another wall that divides the generations but rather as a binding force that brings delight and understanding to the whole family.

It should not be surprising that a Royal Commission in Ontario referred to the arts in the classroom warmly but simultaneously damned them with faint recognition. Commissions reflect the political and social environment from which they spring. We have been aware for decades that learning could be defined in left- and right-brained terms. It is now conventional wisdom that schools have served left-brain understanding — logical, linear learning that can be tested and for which objective grades can be assigned. This was the side of the brain that best addressed the needs of the old industrial system. Workers who could deal with a series of repetitive, boring tasks were as essential to the assembly line as they were to the office space crowded with filing cabinets and typewriters. It is a sad fact that many educational institutions are still labouring in the industrial mode, even with the vast array of new technological equipment now gracing their own offices and laboratories. In spite of the inevitable bow in the direction of computer literacy in a new economy, the full implications of this technological thrust in terms of reaching children's *artistic* potentials rarely move the collective minds of a Royal Commission.

To throw into the orderly process of everyday schooling a full recognition of right-brain functioning, which encourages creativity, imagination, and poetic expression, would be seen as courting disaster. The fact that we are shifting from an elemental post-industrial society into one that is global in its organization, capital-intensive in its emphasis, but comparatively incapable of providing regular jobs, appears to have escaped many administrators and educational policy makers. A number of CEOs from leading corporations (notably John Grant of Quaker Oats in Peterborough) have recognized that the employee most needed even in the present economy must have precisely the attributes emerging from an intense experience in the arts. They speak of such qualities as

creativity, imagination, initiative, and the capacity to work in teams —
all outcomes of a strong arts education program. But school boards
seem to be the last institutions to hear the message and respond to it
with alacrity and consistency.

This lack of response is even more discouraging in the wake of the
latest research about the complicated question of how children learn.
The effect of the empty-vessel theory allows the process of learning to be
seen as teachers projecting while passive students listen and react. As
well, it puts the attention on listening, reading, figuring — all the elements of the totally rational, cerebral approach to learning. The research of Professor David Perkins of Harvard University reveals that
children construct their own learning and do not passively accept what
is being done to them in the name of schooling. Not only does Perkins'
theory make sense but it corresponds to what we see when children are
learning — they create their own body of knowledge and skill in a unique
and personal manner. These observations also seem to corroborate
what we have come to know about the development of the human brain.

This theory explains why every child has his or her own learning
curve, learning enthusiasms, and learning deficiencies. And Perkins' research emphasizes that although learning is about the intellect, it is also
about the senses, the very central aspect of our humanity served by the
arts. The successful learning opportunity of every child must be con-
structed through a sensual and reasoned initiative. Eric Odelfson, chairman of the Center for Arts in the Basic Curriculum, outlines the
importance of Perkins' theory:

> I ask those who are skeptical to consider first principles
> that are driving education today. They include the idea
> that students have fixed amounts of intelligence — var-
> ious-sized "buckets," if you will. Educators will say that
> they can tell, early on, the size of students' buckets and

will put each into the appropriate track for his or her bucket's size. And educators believe that their primary job is then to fill each bucket with facts — with knowledge. But during the last 20 years, cognitive psychologists studying how people really do learn have established that children do not absorb knowledge passively — they *construct* it actively. And with that process they are able to make their buckets larger.[6]

Perkins has illuminated the role that the arts could play in his book *The Intelligent Eye: Learning To Think by Looking at Art*, in which he addresses the question of the nature of intelligence. He perceives three forms of intelligence — the neural, which he describes as "inborn and unchanging;" the experiential, an activity that "grows with learning;" and the reflective, "dependent on a rich repertoire of experience that fairly automatically and spontaneously guides us."[7] The latter intelligence allows for "the contribution of mindful self-management and strategic deployment of one's intellectual resources to intelligent behaviour" and is thus "a control system."[8] The arts, Perkins argues, play an important role in the development of reflective intelligence:

> Art is emblematic here. What is true of art holds for many other facets of life as well. Experiential intelligence working alone gets us by in familiar circumstances where the quick take and the steady habit serve. But in the face of subtlety and novelty, those four intelligence traps of narrow, hasty, fuzzy and sprawling thinking snap shut. We need the countervailing dispositions of reflective intelligence to make the most of experiential intelligence to see better, to think better, and to act more wisely.[9]

Another writer about things educational, perhaps the most influential, is Professor Howard Gardner of Harvard University. He believes there are at least seven forms of intelligence, each of them important in the development of every individual. However, we celebrate only two in the normal school setting — the linguistic and the logical/mathematical.

The others — Gardner identifies them as the musical, spatial, bodily/kinesthetic, and the personal intelligences (knowledge of self and of other people) — receive little attention, are rarely evaluated, and are seldom honoured in our traditional educational institutions.

The result is predictable. Those who achieve high marks in school are those with skills of reading, researching, and writing. Those with logical/mathematical skills excel in subjects such as the sciences and technology. Those with musical skills are consigned to having talent (not designated as intelligence at all, in most cases). Those with particular spatial and bodily/kinesthetic skills are the heroes of the football field and basketball court, but are seen as "dumb jocks" or "tomboys" by the scholarship students and mainstream staff. "Knowledge-of-others" skills turn up among those who run the student council and organize the school dances. These are also the students who provide leadership in the school's environment or multicultural day, devising a broad array of speakers and presentations. And those who have knowledge of themselves eventually discover that they have succeeded beyond their dreams in a host of careers demanding self-examination and complain bitterly about what school has failed to tell them about living a happy and satisfying life.

Gardner describes these intelligences

> as a set of "natural kinds" of building blocks, out of which productive lines of thought and action are built. . . . We might think of intelligences as elements in a chemical system, basic constituents which can enter into compounds of various sorts and into equations that yield a plethora of processes and products.[10]

He presents the working of the mind in the following way:

> [I]n normal intercourse, one typically encounters complexes of intelligences functioning together smoothly,

even seamlessly, in order to execute intricate human activities.[11]

Watching a group of children drawing and painting, singing or playing an instrument, is viewing that "construction" and the degree to which these intelligences interact directly. Complete concentration and focussed participation are the signs that the knowledge-building is under way. The arts are central to this engagement of the mind and spirit.

In an interview on the Public Broadcasting System in the United States, after a performance of his musical *Into the Woods*, Stephen Sondheim put it simply: "All art is a form of education." Sondheim's use of fairy tales to inform adults and children about very basic life values — friendship, courage, fortitude, persistence — was illustrated most charmingly, poignantly, and powerfully in the 1995 Canadian Stage production through the visual arts, movement, music, and the spoken word. Children need to confront these values and behaviours through creative literature, drama, film, and video, preferably in the context of an amalgam that preserves the integrity of each discipline, but connects to the power of their unified voice. A curriculum which fails to choreograph such a confrontation deprives these students of the most essential experience. Of all the roles we can expect an educational system to play, surely that of providing the context and opportunity for children to decide what is good and worthwhile in life is the most crucial.

The school's penchant for ignoring the wealth of ability, skill, and understanding about artistic things, leads untouched students to realize what society has already indicated — that the arts are about being entertained. One has only to review the entertainment section of the newspaper to find that what is largely created to amuse and titillate — the most mindless and pointless of offerings — is placed on the same page as the advertisement announcing the performance of a dance company, a contemporary composer's string quartet, or a play exploring the horror of the AIDS epidemic and its meaning in our lives. The daily press provides a mixed message to adults and youth that allows the weak and eroded role of arts in the schools.

Everything we know about the challenges facing today's youth tells us they must be given the chance to develop lively minds and imaginative spirits, attributes particularly enhanced through dance, music, drama, visual arts, film and video, poetry, and creative writing. The young people now in our schools know they face enormous problems. They know that they cannot depend on the wisdom of the past and that the linear, rational comprehension of the world in crisis is insufficient.

John Ralston Saul, in *Voltaire's Bastards*, his brilliant analysis of the limitations of our dependence on the rational, put the issue in all its irony, emphasizing the fragmentation which has resulted from our total preoccupation with the cerebral, thus leading to a faith in "expertise:"

> Thus, among the illusions which have invested our civilization is an absolute belief that the solution to our problems must be a more determined application of expertise. The reality is that our problems are largely the product of that application. The illusion is that we have created the most sophisticated society in the history of man. The reality is that the division of knowledge into feudal fiefdoms of expertise has made general understanding and coordinated action not simply impossible but despised and distrusted.[12]

Saul not only seizes on the limits of the narrowly rational approach, he attests to the degree to which our society has denigrated other paths to understanding, such as the intuitive, the poetic, the imaginative. Perhaps most important, this preoccupation with the rational has devalued simple common sense, an attribute that allows a woman like Jane Jacobs, with no university degrees in urban planning, to write the century's definitive book on the kind of city worth living in.

Edward de Bono has also addressed the issue of educating only a fraction of the capacities of the human mind:

> We need to move from our exclusive concern with the logic of processing, or reason, to the logic of perception. Perception is the basis of wisdom. For twenty-four centuries we have put all our intellectual effort into the logic of reason rather than the logic of perception. Yet in the conduct of human affairs perception is far more important. Why have we made this mistake?[13]

And Eric Oddleifson asks a question which is equally relevant to Canadians:

> Could it be that our schools at present allow children to play with only half a deck? In denying the arts to our children, do we deny them access to organized (as opposed to chaotic) forms of reality — since our perception of reality is a combination of the intellect and the senses? Is it possible that the failure of our schools can be attributed to a significant degree to the dismissal of the arts from the curriculum?[14]

The problems of coping with such issues as ecological disaster demand more than producing a curriculum that allows children to understand the impact of human activity on the biological balance of our planet, the climatic effects of global warming, or the thousands of interrelated factors which cumulatively lead us to realize that we live in an unsustainable ecology. These elements have been a part of our understanding for many years. What we lack is *will* based on established knowledge, emotional realization, and intuitive understanding. At present there are no images, no metaphors that move us, and these are surely the stock-in-trade of the visual arts and creative writing, of music and drama.

When the astronauts transmitted that magnificent picture of Planet Earth from space — a blue dot in the black velvet of an uninhabited universe — it gave us a clear message. We were the only living creatures in this universe that can be identified as human and we shared a small, fragile ball of energy floating in space. This image, which found its way into the minds of countless millions of the planet's inhabitants, might have had something to do with the extraordinary shift away from the inexorable tramp toward a nuclear holocaust that dominated the middle years of the 20th century. Now similar images must save us from an even more assured fate of environmental disaster. It is in the making of music and the creation of drama, the choreography of dance and the construction of poetry and prose, the invention of form on canvas or film, that these images and metaphors emerge.

Perhaps no distinguished educator has put it more effectively than Abraham Maslow, some decades ago:

> Why are the arts an essential element of a complete education? Because they are systems of communication and teach us about human interaction. . .because they demand creativity on problem solving and teach us about coping and growing. . .because they challenge our perception and teach us to sense and interpret the world around us. . .because they bring us pleasure, teach us to enjoy both learning and living. . .because they employ metaphor and teach us to discover likeness among things seemingly unlike, because they depend upon individualism and teach us to discover and appreciate our strengths and weaknesses. . . . I think the arts are so close to our psychological and biological core. . .that rather than think of these courses as a sort of whipped or luxury cream, they must become basic experiences in education.[15]

It is the perception of arts education "as a sort of whipped or luxury cream" that has held back the development of an appropriate curriculum response to the learning needs of children.

⌘ ⌘ ⌘

Fear of violence and crime has become a major preoccupation of many citizens, who no longer feel safe walking the streets. In many communities children have lost the joy of trudging home from school with companions: they must be driven by parents. The incidence of break-ins of homes, automobiles, and businesses is on a scale that police departments are incapable of adequately investigating. There is every reason to believe that the sublimation of emotional needs is connected to this worldwide phenomenon. What remains unexpressed does indeed erupt in anti-social behaviour that threatens every home, street, and shopping centre. When I began teaching some 40 years ago, the last concern that ever passed through my mind as I walked into the classroom was the possibility that this seemingly safe and unthreatening place could erupt into violence. That is no longer the case, as teachers find weapons concealed in the clothing of students, and fights erupting in the halls threaten the safety of both students and teachers. It was not an elementary school, but a post-secondary educational institution in Montreal, where the most horrific massacre of young women in Canada's history took place, all 14 of them gunned down by a psychopath resentful of their presence in a professional program he believed should have been preserved for males.

John Goodlad, in his book *A Place Called School*, makes a serious charge that the American schooling system is not at risk because insufficient mathematics and sciences are taught, or because the school days are too short, but because the nation's classrooms have become "emotional wastelands" as a result of the place that arts are given in the curriculum.[16] Could the same be said for Canadian schools? Is the image of children sitting in front of their own computers in classrooms across the nation one that suggests the school is a place to gain confidence in social relationships? Surely, an argument for the enhancement of arts programs and a more prominent place for them in the curriculum is *strengthened* by the increased emphasis on education through technology.

Educating the emotions is one of the civilizing roles that is disregarded at the highest cost. It is the inability of young people to express these emotions that results in the violence that has become so much a part of youth and adolescent culture. The implications for the quality of our society are horrendous if policing and jailing become the major interventions guaranteeing law and order in a community which has lost its ability to cope with emotional need. The society which depends on technological devices to communicate is not one that will find it easy to resolve its emotional conflicts. Machines do not train us to achieve the quality of interaction upon which every successful relationship must be based.

Ursula Franklin has commented on the effect of technologies in eliminating reciprocity from the interactions we need to experience in our daily lives:

> In school, there is no argument or negotiation with the computer. Sharing work among students takes on a different meaning. . . . The question that lingers on in my mind is this: How will our society cope with its problems when more and more people live in technologically induced human isolation?[17]

Even today, techno-stress has become a major problem in many families. We have come to expect human response to be instant and precise in the way the computer reacts to our commands. The damage such behaviour creates in the home cannot be estimated, and arts have the capacity to signal the problem and provide alternative behaviour patterns. Just as it is possible for families to expand their understanding about themselves and their society as a unit, the family can comprehend its emotional needs together and find, in the arts, an antidote to the devastated web of family relationships left unattended by our preoccupation with technological manifestations found in our homes.

As we have seen, one of the glories of the arts is that they encourage families to be involved as families. In my own family (two parents, four kids), a high point of our life together was the weekly trip to the local library, where not only could each of us stock up with an armful of books, but there was invariably someone to read stories to whet the interest of each of our children. And there were storytellers as well. Storytelling is an art which has lost some of its role in our television-obsessed society. Anyone who has watched Bob Barton, an internationally respected Canadian storyteller, narrate a tale to a circle of children knows the excitement he creates and the learning that emerges. And it is learning in every sense of the word — a rich vocabulary, imagery through words and sounds, the development of an often complex plot, the injection of humour, and almost always a thoughtful moral lesson. In short, a menu for the most sophisticated juvenile taste.

There is, in most communities, a coterie of artists who would be an asset to the work of students in the schools but as well to the activities in libraries and community centres where families congregate. There are many other opportunities. A host of children's theatre companies have sprung up in Ontario, performing at a professional level equal to those reaching out to adult audiences. Several musical organizations offer "cushion concerts," presentations of an hour or so, with splendid music and an opportunity to speak with performers and sometimes composers. A family can attend these informal affairs and experience the joy of shared learning. . .and shared delight.

For many years, there has existed in Toronto an organization called Inner City Angels, which has provided children from less prosperous neighbourhoods a place to experience the finest artists in presenting dance, music, and drama, and to join visual artists in drawing, painting, sculpting, making kites, and creating puppets. This organization also provides individuals and families on low incomes with tickets to productions where otherwise there would be empty seats.

It is a matter of some pride that a generation of children have been placed in contact with artists through the public sector in Ontario, in particular through a spectrum of programs funded by the Arts Education Office of the Ontario Arts Council. At a time when the cost of government has become an obsession and the role of government is being slashed on all sides, it is well to remember that certain good things happened as a result of positive interventions by a government agency, benefitting children, young people, and artists.

We live in a strange society where there is a cornucopia of fine artists graduating from our conservatories and faculties of fine arts, music, and drama, and yet there are limited opportunities for these young artists to perform. At the same time, many young people could benefit from the learning interaction of a live concert, play, or dance presentation. Indeed, an integrated arts-based curriculum initiative would incorporate such activity both in school and in the community. There are empty venues — not always the most luxurious to be sure, but halls, church basements, library facilities, foyers in large commercial buildings — where the magic of artistic expression could take place at a very low cost. The public performance has particular advantages in addressing children's learning across a broad spectrum, but even more important is the sense that education is taking place in the real world, along with other adults, even parents. The school is an important venue for learning, but the more that can be accomplished outside the school, in communal settings that encourage young and old to learn together, the healthier will be our civic life.

⌘ ⌘ ⌘

A revolution has taken place in our perception of learning in the past two decades. It hardly seems possible that the most internationally renowned educator Canada has ever produced, J. Roby Kidd, who died just 20 years ago, spent his entire adult life advocating on behalf of mature learners in this country and in countries on every continent. As a result of his legacy, the International Council on Adult Education, serving nations around the globe, has its headquarters in Toronto, Canada, rather than in Geneva or New York.

Today "lifelong education" has become the slogan of jurisdictions large and small. It has passed from a fringe insight of a few enthusiasts, like J. Roby Kidd, to a widely held conventional wisdom in just a few short years. It has happened as a part of the shift to the knowledge society without ever going through any process of general debate and discussion. Suddenly, adults who thought they had seen the last of the classroom realized that if they were to be employable they would have to continually take courses and complete programs. Although work-oriented education was the primary focus, many adults came to realize that learning was necessary to be a good parent or even an intelligent voter. Even more significant, adults discovered how satisfying continuing education could be when they themselves had the power to select what and how they were to learn.

During this period of transition from youth-oriented schooling to the recognition of lifelong education, the arts have blossomed as a means of learning. Although facilities, talented artists, and minimal resources could be found only in larger communities, their fortunate inhabitants were engaged in confronting the major issues of the day in

theatres, concert halls, and museums. It has not been broadly understood that wisdom could be dispensed by those who saw themselves as
performers, rather than teachers or instructors, but generations of
adults came to explore the complexity of the human condition from the
works of Shakespeare and Shaw long before festivals bearing these playwrights' names emerged in Canada.

Thousands recognized that their own understanding of beauty, its
relationship to form, colour, and texture, was being achieved in the galleries and museums available to them and that the way these institutions integrated the knowledge from history, literature, theology, and
the sciences was most satisfying. In short, the fast-developing artistic
scene which emerged in Canada after World War II was the nation's
most effective adult education process. The CBC, which in its early years
considered itself an educational, as opposed to an entertainment institution, was pre-eminent in bringing Canadians the arts in a learning
cloak — unlike the US, where broadcasting has always been a form of
business activity. (This helps explain why Canadians view cultural institutions as sources of identity rather than merely commercial entities,
much to the fury of Americans who cannot see why a free-trade agreement should not affect the world of publishing, the performing arts, or
broadcasting as it does other aspects of the economy.) Indeed, because
of Canada's size and its relatively small population, broadcasting took
on an importance unparalleled elsewhere in the world. Professional theatre had its beginnings on the small stages that Dora Mavor Moore discovered after World War II, but even more important were Andrew
Allan's weekly radio dramas, in which John Drainie, who became Canada's most celebrated actor, achieved his distinction in front of a microphone. Dora Mavor Moore's Village Players, the New Play Society, and
Robert Gill's Hart House Theatre, all in Toronto, along with radio dra-

ma at the CBC, established the basis for the Stratford Festival that now dominates Canada's theatrical life.

It is nearly a quarter of a century since Dr. Douglas Wright, who was to occupy many positions of importance, such as president of the University of Waterloo, chaired a commission which produced a report titled "The Learning Society." In this document he envisioned a society in which schools, colleges, and universities would be part of a vast network of learning opportunities available to every person through the interaction of varied institutions that would recognize their educational responsibility to the community. As we approach the millennium, such an integrated learning community seems distant in spite of the presence of the technological highway which could, in the appropriate circumstances, make all there is to know available to everyone with access to a computer and modem.

Yet in our hearts we know that data is not digestible information, nor is information necessarily a road to knowledge, and most certainly knowledge is distant from the wisdom that can empower the children of our day. The arts have the capacity to inform us of the past, and to provide us with the courage and fortitude to face the chaos of the present and the vision to see a better future. Nothing else can provide children and youth with an opportunity to connect to themselves, to be centred on their own strengths and aptitudes, and to be less diverted by peer pressures. Children should know hope, understand their own feelings, and appreciate beauty in all its forms. To experience these both as individuals and within the bonds of family must be the most effective preparation for the present and the future.

The arts can give our children the confidence to confront both the challenges that face society and the personal disappointments and frustrations that are a part of every mature life. Our modern society, with all its rush and pressure, has deprived us of much of the discretionary or leisure time we had gathered for ourselves just decades ago. It is surely the ultimate irony that we have reached what we called in the '60s the decade of the "leisure society," only to discover that those with employment are working longer hours than ever. Those with enforced leisure, or unemployment, have less motivation or opportunity to find meaning in available time, and life is less joyful for them. Those whose lives are blighted by the loss of work are in special need of artistic expression. A schooling system for the 21st century must not construct its learning programs around an assumption that lifetime full employment will be the lifestyle of every graduate.

For Canadians, access to education is one of the rights of citizenship we have cherished, along with old-age pensions, suitable unemployment benefits, effective support of the physically and mentally challenged, medicare, the education of our children and youth. These aspects of the society that we have built in the 20th century and that we wish to leave to our children are at risk in the '90s as budgetary cuts threaten the quality of learning in our elementary schools and tuition fees for college and university students soar to levels scarcely conceivable a decade ago.

⌘　⌘　⌘

We inherited from previous centuries the concept of the "commons." Most villages in the UK and Europe still have "greens," publicly owned open spaces of grass and trees that bring contentment to their citizens. The public park systems that dot our countryside and make amenable our urban spaces come from the same principle. These have become our commons. Environmentalists have declared that clean air, water, and soil is a further extension of this principle of civilizing and life-supporting services which we can only retain as a community. Today, the threatened social support systems are another form of commons that are at great risk.

Some years ago, the Ontario government brought forward what was identified as the Common Curriculum (replaced in 1998 by the Ontario Curriculum). The first stated principle underlying learning: "Learning involves values as well as knowledge and skills."[18] Other principles underlying the curriculum were that "preparation of students for the modern world requires integrated programming"[19] and that the arts are very important. Amazingly, the document stated that 25 percent of the time in the early grades should be spent in the arts:

> The arts develop the mind, nurture and reflect our spiritual aspirations, and thus enrich our experiences and enhance our capacity for self-fulfilment. From a broader perspective, the arts provide continuity with our past by stressing the universality of human experience and offer an inspiring record of human achievement that transcends barriers of race and culture. In a world of rapid and widespread change, these traditional functions of the arts take on new significance and provide the context for making education in and through the arts meaningful for students.
>
> Dance, drama, music and visual arts are expressions of the ideas, values, and concerns of individuals and societies. It is therefore important for learners to become literate in the arts — to develop an understanding and appreciation of the creative process and of the principles and techniques that serve the creative purpose in individual disciplines.[20]

Probably no directive from a provincial ministry has had less effect. It came at a time when the Ontario government was promising substantial cuts to the budgets of local school boards, thus negating the influence of its own education ministry. As well, there was no strategy for connecting these principles to the overall expectations for accountability, interpreted by most boards as an educational initiative directly related to job preparation (i.e., training on computers and familiarity with other forms of technology). The lack of preparation for teachers, and in some cases, the lack of sufficient materials and leadership from experienced coordinators, many of whom have been released or sent back to the classroom, has meant that teachers have feared more than welcomed the opportunity the Common Curriculum presented. However, the greatest hurdle was that of a general sense that the arts are peripheral and insignificant in the totality of society's judgement. The schools, faced with a wall of criticism and condemnation, had no capacity to turn that perception around.

The Common Curriculum was indeed the "commons" for the vast majority of children and youth who attend public schools. The arts as an aspect of that commons are as important as reading and computer skills as we approach the year 2000. The Ontario Curriculum has as its basis the demand for more specific objectives year by year and, although it is too early to speculate how the arts will fare in the classroom, it appears the arts have been diminished in both the elementary and secondary schools, at least in terms of time allocation. The emphasis on literacy and numeracy (in tandem with increased testing and accountability in these two areas) has triumphed. The irony is obvious: just as massive evidence is indicating that arts education is an advantage in learning across all disciplines, the opportunities are lessened. However, the strategy for turning back this seeming reduction lies in adopting a horizontal arts-based learning process that sees music, drama, dance, and technological arts expressions as part of instructional process in every discipline. That would not only ensure that the arts survive, but would improve the very skills that seem to be at the heart of the Ontario Curriculum.

The quality of life for future generations depends on how this debate about learning resolves itself in Canada. A very important aspect of this debate will be the degree to which the arts, individually as disciplines and integrated in their full power, will be recognized as essential to the well-being of every citizen, both in terms of their own legitimacy and as pathways to intellectual mastery and emotional stability in an uncertain age.

NOTES
1. Sharon Begley, "Your Child's Brain," *Newsweek*, February 1996, pp. 55-6.
2. Ibid., p. 56.
3. Lyn Nell Hancock, "Why Do Schools Flunk Biology?" *Newsweek*, February 1996, p. 58.
4. Seymour Sarason, *The Challenge of Art to Psychology* (New Haven, London: Yale University Press, 1994), pp. 4-5.
5. Ontario Royal Commission on Education, *For The Love of Learning, Volume IV* (Toronto: Queen's Printer for Ontario, 1994), p. 167.
6. Eric Oddleifson, "What Do We Want Our Schools To Do?" *Phi Delta Kappan*, Volume 75, No. 6, February 1994, p. 447.
7. David N. Perkins, *The Intelligent Eye: Learning To Think By Looking at Art* (Santa Monica, California: The Getty Centre For Education in the Arts, 1994), p. 14.
8. Ibid., p. 14.
9. Ibid., p. 85.
10. Howard Gardner, *Frames of Mind: The Theory of Multiple Intelligences* (New York: Basic Books Inc. Publishers, 1993), p. 279.
11. Ibid., p. 279.
12. John Ralston Saul, *Voltaire's Bastards: The Dictatorship of Reason in the West* (Toronto: Penguin Books, 1993), p. 8.
13. Edward de Bono, *I am Right — You Are Wrong: From Rock Logic to Water Logic* (New York: Viking/Penguin, 1972), p. 42.
14. Oddleifson, p. 448.
15. Abraham Maslow, *The Farther Reaches of Human Nature* (New York: The Viking Press, 1971), p. 179.
16. John Goodlad, *A Place Called School* (New York: McGraw-Hill, 1984), p. 62.

17. Ursula Franklin, *The Real World of Technology* (CBC Massey Lectures, Toronto: CBC Enterprises, 1990), p. 51.
18. *The Common Curriculum, Grades 1-9*, Ministry of Education, Ontario. February 1993, p. 4.
19. Ibid., p. 7.
20. Ibid., p. 12.

Chapter 4

The Arts — Living Together and Learning a Living

Art is the signature of civilization.

Beverley Sills

I t is perhaps the greatest sign of a sea change in our world that the word "job" has taken on a negative aura in this last decade of the 20th century. What was once a normal expectation has become a source of pain and disappointment. The words "downsizing," "right-sizing," and "limited contract" have invaded the field of status and satisfaction that was once inhabited by the phrase "having a job."

A horizontal or integrated arts-based curriculum may be able to prove its worth in providing a rich, varied, inclusive learning experience, appealing to a broad spectrum of students, providing a path to the mastery of other essential disciplines, bringing the students both personal growth and confidence, preparing them for an uncertain future.

However, such a curriculum must prepare them to participate in an economy unlike any that has existed in the past, one that is "job-poor," unable to heal the festering sores of enormous disparities of rich and poor, both between nations and within national boundaries. Unless integrated arts-based learning can succeed in addressing the issue of employment, there can be little hope of it attracting the attention of teachers, parents, or students. Parents must be confident that their offspring will graduate from school with skills and knowledge that will prepare them for the job market even if the time is long gone when educational institutions can honestly offer assurances of guaranteed employment to graduates.

Since the mid-1940s, two problems have concerned young people in North America and Europe — the imminent nuclear holocaust, which seemed only minutes away, and the fear that employment might not be available upon graduation from secondary school or even college and university.

With the reduction in global confrontation and the expectation that present stocks of weapons will be reduced, the state of the environment has replaced nuclear war as the second preoccupation of our young. However, full-time employment can no longer be regarded as a reward for academic accomplishment. The debilitating spectre of joblessness as an ongoing phenomenon in both "good" and "bad" times has increased its hold on the minds of students. Young people see parents who have highly responsible jobs joining the ranks of the unemployed and watch as older brothers and sisters who have graduated as engineers, architects, and lawyers find it impossible to pursue their professional paths.

When the latest recession was proclaimed to have come to an end in the early '90s, it did not mean a swath of hiring began. Indeed, the business community engaged in corporate "re-engineering," preferring to remain "downsized" or "right-sized," realizing the ebb and flow of prosperity and the pressures of global competition made it essential to be lean and flexible. At a breakfast meeting in Ottawa at which I had been invited to speak, the inevitable welcoming cup of coffee was accompanied by an announcement from a Canadian bank executive that on that very day, 1,500 of his employees would be released. In answer to my shocked comment that financial institutions had been the singular area of the business world undamaged by the recession, he replied, "What do you think those banking machines in front of our buildings are all about?" We now know from painful experience that technology has indeed destroyed millions of jobs around the world when the challenge of corporate survival depends on reducing the workforce while increasing productivity.

Jeremy Rifkin, in his widely praised book *The End of Work*, describes the consternation that workers feel about the effect of technological change:

> Today, many people are at a loss to understand how the computer and the other new technologies of the information revolution that they had so hoped would free them have instead seemed to turn into mechanical monsters, depressing wages, subsuming jobs, and threatening livelihoods. American workers have long been made to believe that by being more efficient and productive, they would eventually free themselves from endless work. Now, for the first time, it is dawning on them that productivity gains often lead not to more leisure, but to unemployment lines.[1]

There was a time when such reductions could be balanced by employment increases in other sectors of the economy. Manufacturing has picked up the results of reductions in the labour force engaged in mining, forestry, and agriculture throughout most of this century. More recently, the service sector has provided jobs as technology has decreased the need for workers on the automated assembly line. However, the fact is that the future will see an ongoing reduction of these kinds of jobs as automated processes replace people now serving hamburgers, just as they have replaced tellers in banks.

The only effective increase in employment figures in the '90s, either in government or the private sector, has been that of short-term, contract work which provides no career path and no security benefits. The rate of government defined unemployment continues to rise — the rate of real unemployment, including those who have given up looking for work and those who can be clearly designated as underemployed, is beyond accounting.

At the same time, the obsession with national deficits has led governments to reduce their civil service complement, and tens of thousands of dedicated personnel have been offered early retirement or simply let go. The unpleasant image of the future is graphically described by Ran Ide, former CEO of TVOntario, and Arthur Cordell, once secretary of the Science Council, in a paper prepared for the annual meeting of the Club of Rome in Buenos Aires in the fall of 1994:

> The problems facing society today are huge. Even when the profit and loss picture for corporations seems to be brighter, the outlook for workers remains bleak. Globalization, sparked by the ease with which money and management structures can be moved, is threatening traditional forms of government based on the sovereignty of the nation state. The planned economies of the socialist world are largely bankrupt and free market systems seem headed for a major adjustment.
>
> The underlying problem is a human one. It is unthinkable to imagine a society where 20 to 30 per cent of young people are unable to find jobs with the majority of the remainder required to accept those of the part-time and lower paying variety. . . . As one writer pointed out when discussing the nature of crises that beset par-

liamentary democracies, "the most basic concerns are about working and making a living, about security of person and property, about the stability in public and private life that allows one to plan for the day after tomorrow and not just from day to day. . . ."

The irony is that the world in general is not in a state where there are no jobs to be done but rather one of insolvent governments. The need for work related to the environment, to resolving the problem of poverty and the care of an increasing number of old and helpless people has never been greater.[2]

Schools have been placed in a particularly difficult situation. They are expected to produce job-ready graduates for the post-industrial, technologically sophisticated, knowledge-based economy that demands more highly educated workers but is unable to assure many of them a stable career in the areas they select to work in. It is no mean task for administrators and teachers to produce more highly qualified, highly motivated graduates in light of the discouraging predictions made by the most knowledgeable analysts of future trends in patterns of work.

Schools are being pressured to perform this task in the face of a seemingly inarguable charge that our educational system is failing to produce even literate and numerate graduates. It is claimed that at a time when the education of the workforce is the crucial factor in the nation's economic well-being, students are emerging from our institutions of learning unable to make any real workplace contribution. Indeed, their literacy and numeracy skills, compared on international tests to those of students of other nations, are deemed in question. Even graduates, to say nothing of dropouts, are seen to be a drag on the economy. So the story goes in letters to editors of newspapers, in the words of columnists commenting on matters educational, and in the speeches of businessmen to Rotary and Kiwanis clubs across the country.

When boom times arrive, the school is never congratulated for its success. But in a period of such economic volatility, a scapegoat must be found. Thus, teachers and schools bear the brunt of society's frustration and disappointment, resulting in an atmosphere that creates an army of depressed and battered teachers. To add to the despair, education budgets have been savaged and thousands of teachers laid off. It counts for nothing that the present teaching complement in Ontario and other provinces has never been better trained in the traditional disciplines and, unlike in parts of the United States where teaching may in some cases be the last hope for the inadequate, our teachers come from the top levels of achievement in the nation's universities. It counts for little, too, when a report from the G7 nations commends Canada's educational system as the best among the industrial countries. Teachers are faced with charges of deficiency while having to cope with the fact that rhetoric about the importance of learning is rarely supported by public investment that might fulfill the day-to-day needs of the school. Indeed, in a society that is prepared to unravel its public services and denigrate its public servants, the teacher becomes an easy victim of a rhetoric that assumes all those on a government payroll are either incompetent, lazy, or both.

The accepted wisdom has been that appropriate preparation in school should allow graduates to both fill existing jobs and create new ones. There is a further assumption that in this post-industrial, knowledge-based economy, the most appropriate preparation would be more attention to mathematics, science, and technological subjects.

It would be foolish to ignore these ways of exploring the world and the skills and knowledge which come from conquering the complexities they present, but this belief that universal acquisition of a narrow selection of skills and information in a particular discipline will solve our economic woes borders on a faith that will move mountains. Such thinking leads to an unbalanced curriculum that fails to recognize the wide variety of "intelligences" to be found in individual students. Nor does it concede the equally important contribution of other forms of knowledge and skills in a very complex economy, to say nothing of the other aspects of living in a modern world.

This trivialization of knowledge which is not included in the narrowly defined mathematical-scientific package not only fails to recognize an economy which needs a wide variety of constantly changing skills and understandings, but also fails the student who has both the capacity and enthusiasm for these trivialized disciplines but is left uninterested and frustrated by being force-fed subjects for which she or he may have little interest or aptitude. This is the student that school fails. The student becomes a dropout, for to remain in school is to be streamed into programs that lead nowhere but to a "McJob," a vocational experience that discourages further education and results in a life which never surfaces the individual's potential.

However, parents, teachers, and even some guidance officers have warned that the future is bleak for students who wish to study the arts and find a job which rewards the skills they have acquired. The image — and, in some instances, the myth — of the starving artist dies hard. Stories of superb actors who have had to wait tables in a restaurant between theatre productions are surely legion. These inadequate understandings of the world of work result in very foolish decisions about course selection and employment directions.

Part of this nervousness about job preparation for work in the arts relates to the assumption that such vocational choices are lacking in social significance. If the arts are merely entertainment, a bright graduate's life would be wasted in such activity. Except in very special cases (the millionaire rock star), such work could never be properly rewarded by a regular and adequate paycheck. Parents of artistically gifted children who have succeeded in building a career in the arts have been heard to express the hope that their offspring might soon decide to get a "real" job in a more traditional sector of the economic structure.

Another aspect of the confusion about arts education as appropriate training for work is the tendency to see jobs in the arts as synonymous with performing on the stage or in a concert hall. It must be admitted that there are areas of toil in the arts that give less hope of permanence of occupation and encourage this pessimistic view of arts employment. Recently my wife and I spent a week at a major conservatory of music in North America learning something of the works of Johannes Brahms. As a part of the experience, we attended over a dozen recitals given by young performance graduate students who were playing their instruments with obvious flair, enormous skill, and evident commitment. However, conversations with these talented musicians indicated there was little hope they would achieve their ambitions to be serious concert artists. It is an ironic reality that modern transportation has limited rather than broadened the opportunities for young potential concert and recital artists. Yo-Yo Ma can play his cello on three or four continents a week, and high-technology hype convinces audiences that he and a handful of others are the only cellists worth hearing. Thus, it is sadly true that thousands of extremely talented and thoughtful performing artists find no place to play. The number of venues increases only marginally, and thousands of people in small communities and neighbourhoods in the suburban shadows of great cities are deprived of the opportunity to hear live performance, new interpretations of classics, and the contemporary compositions that speak to our age.

This situation could be turned around if the effect of arts education in the schools was that of producing audiences for live performance. However, this will not happen until the arts are seen to be important to every child's learning and development. When students are made aware of their own creativity, they become conscious of the excitement of being in the presence of other artists producing drama, music, or dance which expresses our understanding of the world, revealing our pain and our ecstasy. In short, they become the kind of audience that inspires great art. A horizontal or integrated arts-based curriculum has the effect of developing audiences, even though it is not the central purpose.

As Ursula Franklin has observed, modern technology, whether it be the television set or the home computer, has a fragmenting, isolating influence. In spite of the window on the world, the ability to interact with individuals around the planet, this connectedness provides none of the thrill that comes from experiencing together with other people the excitement of a splendidly interpretive performance, the joy of communal understanding and appreciation. It is these events that give our lives as citizens real meaning. Canada's centennial year, 1967, will be remembered as that time when singers, dancers, and musical ensembles travelled across the country and gave us, through live performances, a sense of our history and heritage, and a feeling that Canada stood for something. As human beings, we have a need to feel part of a neighbourhood, a community, a village, a town, a city — a country. This can happen when we become part of an event that has attracted, excited, and inspired us and other fellow beings together. Thus, the function of arts education as one that encourages audiences should not be trivialized or discounted. It is this same impetus that has inspired Nicholas Goldschmidt to launch Music Canada 2000, a year of public performances of newly commissioned musical compositions to celebrate the millennium and the creativity of Canadians.

In the past, artists and arts organizations became involved in arts education to encourage this role of audience-building — and thankfully so. However, it is now conceded that the involvement of artists and arts organizations in the classroom should be devoted to the producing of creators, the encouragement of participation in these art forms, as well as the attracting of future audiences. Indeed, one could opine the fact that Canada's faculties of fine arts in our universities, the Royal Conservatory of Music, the National Ballet School, the National Theatre School, the Ontario College of Art and Design, as well as other community colleges producing artists in the performing arts, technological arts, and crafts, are producing an extraordinary number of brilliant artists who have "made it" on the world's stages and in the galleries at the centre of artistic creation. We have been significantly less successful in producing audiences and visual arts viewers.

The work of Robert Putnam, a Harvard University political scientist, gives even more significance to the public arts event. Putnam studied the regional governments created across Italy after World War II. The fact that they were initiated simultaneously allowed longitudinal studies of their effectiveness to be carried out, with rather surprising results. One would expect that economic factors would be overwhelmingly dominant in deciding the success of these jurisdictions. However, Putnam discovered that the presence of community activity — of all things, choral societies — was fundamental to the well-being of these regional governments. Human infrastructure that brought people together across a collective experience was the essential factor. A recital, a concert, a theatre or dance performance provides just this sense of community that raises the spirit and enlivens the sense of being part of a community.

Perhaps the ultimate test of the arts as a community-building activity is the First-Night experience in major cities across North America. New Year's Eve was once thought to be a night when grown-ups indulged themselves in expensive evening entertainment accompanied by rich food, flowing alcohol, and ending too often in an orgy of automobile accidents. At a lower social level, the night could be characterized by a plethora of street brawls, subway violence, and general public upheaval. Today, in a city like Toronto (Vancouver, Calgary, and several other Canadian cities would provide equally valid examples), one can take children of any age to the downtown streets for special performances of music and theatre, and feel safe and comfortable while enjoying this wide variety of artistic fare. A Camerata Choir singing folksongs in St. James Cathedral, the boisterous leaping of Morris dancers in the foyer of the market across the street, the colour and drama of the Desrosiers Dance Theatre in the John Bassett Theatre just down the road, First Nations dancers in the Metro Square, hypnotic and participatory drumming and dancing on main traffic arteries now transformed into pedestrian malls — all form an explosion of delight and laughter that makes heralding in the New Year a positive, non-alcoholic, violence-free panorama of artistic delight, strengthening both the family and the community.

Thus, community-building, audience, and local job creation become all of a piece and counteract the forces which fragment and divide to allow an atmosphere that breeds violence, crime, and civil unrest. Greg Baeker, former director of the Ontario Museum Association, has been a voice for the recognition of the economic and social implications of the arts and heritage resources of the Province of Ontario for over a

decade. He believes that urban planning programs have not been sufficiently sensitive to the cultural realities in making their decisions:

> What contributions might community cultural plan-
> ning make to this view of planning and its possibilities?
> Answers can be informed by the growing interest in
> interdisciplinary mergers of critical urban and cultural
> studies. The emphasis is on understanding cities as cul-
> tural entities — places where people meet, generate
> meaning, negotiate and renegotiate identities; these
> discourses explore how cultural dialogue can help pre-
> serve real and imaginary spaces of diversity and plural-
> ism — "construction sites" of more genuine political
> community.[3]

Certainly such understanding of the appropriate role of the arts in
the community is one way of building audiences. Another strategy is
that of reaching children at the earliest point of their lives with some realization that the arts are important to their emotional, intellectual, and
spiritual well-being, especially in the earliest grades of their schooling.

The answer is not a grand strategy of using schools and their captive
audiences to produce clients for live performances, as much as these
events encourage us to live together with civility and higher morale.
Rather, learning in the arts must be about making artistic expression so
central a preoccupation in children's lives that they will both make and
listen to music, dance and watch others dance, draw and paint but visit
museums and galleries as well, and, yes, learn to speak and act "dramatically." Then they will come to the theatre and enjoy the Martha Henrys,
the Bill Hutts, and the Fiona Reids because not to do so would be a form
of self-deprivation, would be to miss moments of intellectual excitement and spiritual renewal. They will then fill seats not only in the performance venues of our major cities but in towns and villages across the
nation. As an added advantage, the problem of finding jobs for the vast
number of gifted graduates of our conservatories and faculties of music

will have been addressed, and, even more important, the lives of smaller communities will have been enormously enhanced. Thus, living together and making a living become connected phenomena to which the school could be contributing a great deal.

Most important in bringing balance to any discussion of unemployed artists in the community is the fact that the performing arts, and particularly the solo artists within that field, represent but a fraction of the workforce involved in the arts and arts-related industry. In fact, 600,000 Canadians regard themselves as participants in the arts workforce and can be found in TV studios, publishing houses, recording studios, and darkrooms.

The arts and culture industries now contribute some $22-billion to Canada's GNP. Even during the latest recession, from the early '80s to the mid '90s, these industries expanded their sales by 40%. Thus, at a time when other basic industries were going out of business, when leading corporations were laying off many thousands of workers, the cultural industries, with few exceptions, remained strong and healthy.

If the Province of Ontario's economy is examined, the impact is even more proportionally dramatic. In 1992-93, the arts and culture sector fed $11.2-billion directly and indirectly into the gross domestic product and represented 4.6% of the entire provincial economy.[4]

As a host of commercial operations consider their futures in competing with lower-wage workers in Mexico under the North American Free Trade Agreement, people working in the arts have every confidence in being able to compete across a continent and indeed around the world. Low-wage workers in other countries cannot replace the Canadian artist who by definition must be unique and irreplaceable — irreplaceable, that is, as long as there is a Canadian culture that molds and nurtures a truly Canadian expression through film, photograph, drama, or song.

Further, arts education prepares the student for more than just a place in the burgeoning arts and arts industries. It is extraordinary how the outcomes of effective arts education can relate to the well-being of the workforce. Many of the skills that come from preparing a dramatic presentation, particularly the difficult process of learning to work with others in the dynamic relationship of a play's cast, are most necessary in the workplace of the '90s. Great industrial research and development takes place in the context of small groups working in teams to achieve a common end. Increasingly, employment is coming from the development of medium and small companies engaged in high technology that depend on just such a work style.

Rather than the pyramid structure found in large General Motors-type corporations, these companies will operate on a more horizontal, collegial basis. Indeed, Peter Drucker, the pre-eminent analyst of corporate behaviour, has suggested that the style of a symphony orchestra or a string quartet is one that modern companies should emulate. A comparable example

MIMA HOYES AND THE FAYWOOD ARTS CENTRE

It is a bleak day, but in Mima Hoyes' classroom there is the thrill of being challenged. She is exploring the basics of sculpture, puppetry, mirror-action, and robot response. Young people are learning about their bodies, giving clear, concise directions to each other as they move across the floor. In the close collaboration of group work the racial distinctions disappear as couples form and reform with no thought of cultural difference. This is a grade four class but within a few minutes it will be followed by a grade five class where "Creating a Play" is the theme.

The class is about problems and problem solving. "Plays are about conflict," Ms. Hoyes insists. The children choose "friendship" as the theme, the playground as the setting, and morning recess as the time period. Then begins the task of creating the characters and each child assumes a new identity.

From these moments of collective creative planning, the drama commences as groups of three or four develop a tableaux in a frozen stance that outlines the plot. Slowly the play develops, but much more begins to happen. Children see the nature of confrontation, their role in making it happen, their feelings when they themselves are the object of bitter words and violent action. They learn about mediation and negotiation, scarcely a topic normally imposed on children in elementary school.

The integration of word and movement, drama and poetry, is evident. Children see the wellsprings of intolerance and violence in their own hearts and minds. How easily such a lesson could be incorporated into a history class on war and revolution, a family studies program on dysfunctionality or a civics class on the Quiet Revolution. How effective could Mima Hoyes' work be in making real the textbook or today's headline. ⌘

would be a choir. The choir member must accept the leadership of the conductor, of course, but the excellence of the ensemble is determined by the commitment of every chorister to the highest quality of sound he or she is capable of, and the concentration of every mind on the interpretation being sought. What training for the marketplace!

Economic well-being no longer depends on the availability of natural resources or even access to cheap energy. In a world seeking new ways to feed, clothe, heal, and house in such a way that the planet can be sustained, worker creativity becomes a crucial factor. Creativity is a seamless cloak. The leap in thought, image, or connectivity that leads to a product based on a new technology is the same dynamic that inspires a totally new way of using sound and movement in a dazzling dance sequence to say something profound about the human spirit.

Anyone who remains in the cinema to watch the endless film credits will realize the extent to which every feature, whether a banal B-movie or a Montreal or Toronto Film Festival winner, is truly a team effort involving many players with many skills. The focus of the schooling system on individual competitiveness for grades and academic honours is not an effective training for teamwork. Ironically, we turn to the arts for preparation in what is surely one of the most important factors that leads to career success.

"Discipline" is not a popular word today as it brings forth memories of having to do things that were decided by others. Indeed, lack of discipline is the major criticism levelled at teenagers today. Their bizarre hairstyles and tattered clothing are seen as symbols of a hatred of authority and rule. Yet watching these same young people in the context of a studio, one is astounded by the single-minded concentration on the completion of a demanding sculpture, or the detail of an oil painting or the exacting procedure undertaken to produce a successful print. This generation has no reason to trust either the ethics or judgement of their elders, but their loyalty to a great idea, a special sound or image, is boundless. It has the potential to save the planet and the human species, but it will also enable them to support themselves and their families.

⌘   ⌘   ⌘

One of the greatest problems the school faces in preparing students to face the world of work is the fragmenting of knowledge into disciplines that may well have extended our understanding of the universe in the past, but now prevents our children from seeing the patterns that make life and work intelligible in the present. The requisite for a holistic approach to learning, an approach that the integrated arts-based curriculum promises, has been eloquently expressed. There are examples of teachers of mathematics who have brought new meaning to their subject by playing the fugues of Johann Sebastian Bach. Geography and history lessons have been enlivened through the exploration of the visual arts and music of an era and region, providing as profound an understanding as that which can be found in the study of maps and constitutional documents. As we proceed in the direction of global education, the arts become a legitimate and appropriate source of integration. As Canada continues to develop as a world trading nation, it will be essential that the workforce have a global understanding of that collection of markets which spell success and prosperity — effective teaching of music, drama, and visual arts in our schools is an invaluable resource.

Business has become aware of its need to comprehend the total societal context within which it is seeking to make its contribution. Nothing reveals the hidden realities and the trends of thinking within a culture more clearly than the arts. The events of the 20th century that have produced such discontinuity in our lives also influenced the non-representational painting of a Jackson Pollock, a Harold Town, or a Riopelle, the minimalism of a Mark Rothko or a Jack Bush. The dissonance which has been the problem for those seeking to understand the contemporary music of a John Weinzweig is simply the architecture of sound expression in a century that has produced two massive world wars and a holocaust of obscene heartlessness. These connections must be made through the various arts disciplines more distinctly and through the entire intellectual experience of the school curriculum. That is the overwhelming challenge to teachers and artists alike, but there needs to be a process which will bring them together, a school curriculum that will unify and integrate. Such a thrust can play a most significant role in changing Canada's understanding of the place of technology in the economy of the future.

Mysteriously, Canada has the least commitment of any developed country to the more practical, hands-on forms of educational preparation that best serves a present workplace. There is no California Institute of Technology or Massachusetts Institute of Technology as part of the spectrum of educational choice in this land. It is true that we have institutions that are producing technicians and technologists, but not at a level or in the numbers achieved by the educational systems of the industrial countries of Europe and the United States. This is quite an anomaly, as Canada has a splendid university system. Indeed, Waterloo has an international reputation in the areas of mathematics and computer science, as well as engineering, and Ryerson has become a university with a specific commitment to practical and workplace-relevant learning. However, many community college graduates (particularly in Ontario) must go south of the border to complete their work in more advanced technological studies to achieve a degree that will be recognized throughout the world.

The reason is not simple, but perhaps it is because Canada has never appreciated the skills necessary to work with both hand and head. There are those who would say this strange element in the Canadian character comes as a result of a long colonial past: working with the hands was associated with being a colonist. French Canada, after the conquest, focused on the professions associated with the Church and the law. English Canada did not break its direct links and dependencies until well into the 20th century. When that happened, it seemed to encourage an attitude of disinterest in things of a practical nature that were associated with the shop floor and the commercial establishment. Working with the hands was little respected. Even the engineering profession (hardly a "working-with-the-hands" vocation, but obviously associated with making a product) has never been respected with the same intensity one finds in Europe or Asia. It became the rule in Canadian schools that students who could not succeed in academic subjects were consigned to the shop wing. We have paid the price of such wrongheadedness down through the decades since World War I.

The present technologically based economy gives new meaning to working with "hand and head" — and employers in Canada have been highly critical of the fact that even with many thousands unemployed, there are jobs unfilled in the high-tech industries. Indeed, employers have had to find qualified employees overseas even in the '90s, when youth unemployment has reached over 20% in some areas of the country. A new emphasis on arts education is a solution. The visual artist, of all people, must translate the inspiration, the intellectual rigour of the mind, onto the canvas through hands and fingers. Anyone who thinks fashioning beautiful pots is not back-breaking in its physical demands as well as a challenge to the mind has not worked at a potter's wheel.

The 1960s and '70s saw a renewed interest in the arts and crafts. Indeed the Canadian craft movement became invigorated with an army of spinners, weavers, potters, leather and metal workers, and glass-blowers emerging and proving themselves equal to those found anywhere in the world. A few important institutions provided excellent support. Sheridan College, in Oakville, Ontario, soon joined Toronto's Ontario College of Art (now Art and Design) in graduating a plethora of fine craftspeople. The Nova Scotia Institute of Technology and Vancouver's Emily Carr Institute became national treasures as they both continued to serve the craft movement as well as the more sophisticated world of industrial design and visual communications technology.

However, the fact still remains that Canada lags behind most Western industrial states in granting the highest recognition possible to those who have imagined and thought well and then used the skills of their hands to produce a work of art that was both useful and aesthetically pleasing, thereby bringing joy to user and beholder. The arts can do nothing more crucial to this country's economic well-being than to emphasize this aspect of the successful career for many young people in the future.

There has been an overemphasis on massive conglomerates engaging in world trade as the basis for Canada's economic well-being. There is also an alternative economy that has always been present for artists and craftspeople: the small business serving the local community. Economists such as Dian Cohen and Guy Stanley have identified a major factor in the new world of work — the move to smaller production units which can be linked technologically, allowing a shift "away from national, or macro economies, to micro economies."[5] Artists are particularly adaptable to microeconomic contexts. The painter or the potter in a studio is in every way involved in a small local industry. Indeed, part of the training of visual artists and performers is now devoted to entrepreneurship — the skills of operating a small business.

Many artists have moved across the perceived isolations that make up our workforce and have made use of the training and experience they received in one area in their successful pursuit of other goals. An example is the extraordinary career of Elizabeth Strauss, who now lives in Kitchener, Ontario, but who has sung on the stages of recital halls and opera houses of Europe and North America. Having enjoyed her life as a diva, she decided to shift her career to the lecture hall or classroom, successfully completing her doctorate in arts education. Finding little opportunity in the university or school setting, she set out on a great experiment. She established a company to produce hardware products for the home — hardly an area where one would expect an opera star to excel. However, she hired a group of people to run the company, demanding the very skills she believed would assure artistic excellence, and found she had acquired a hard-working, creative, imaginative workforce that soon achieved marketplace success even in the midst of a recession that sent other companies to the wall. Having made her mark in the manufacturing industry and having made her point about the efficacy of artistic attributes, she has gone on to establish another enterprise in the area of voice and speech improvement, reaching out to executives of corporations, particularly those for whom English is a second or third language and who need better presentation skills. That business is thriving, proving her theory that work in the arts is a splendid preparation for many areas of the economy.

The saga of Elizabeth Strauss is unique, but there are many unrecorded examples of individuals who have moved from career to career and who regard their time in the studio, on the stage, and behind the scenes in the technical workshops of the opera company or theatre as the most valuable preparation for other worlds of work. Certainly, the experience of coping with uncertainty and change is essential in the volatility of the present workplace. The arts, as no other area of activity, prepares the individual to deal with these elements of the modern economy.

Indeed, in these days of youth despair over their work future, the irony and ambiguity of the arts as a preparation for the marketplace emerges with fresh impact. Those who have been prepared in the context of an effective arts education program may well have as many opportunities for a successful career in the arts and arts industries as they might find in any other sector of the economy, but more importantly, as we have seen, they will be better prepared to engage in a countless array of jobs not regarded as being connected to the arts. The advantage of ensuring that every child has a full learning experience through the development of an integrated arts-based curriculum becomes obvious.

As important for Canada's future, these graduates will have acquired minds that will examine, analyze, and critically appraise every job on the basis of the value system it represents. The arts demand a mind-set that integrates the values for living with those that emerge in making a living. In a world increasingly unable to provide for the health and shelter of its population, this issue of values will be a central preoccupation of this generation, as will the health of the natural world upon which that population must depend. Will we have created employees unwilling to look the other way when values such as protecting the environment are outraged? Will we have produced citizens who will demand a higher priority in government for the support of programs that will end world hunger and possibly world terrorism? One can only hope so.

To return to that emerging economy based on a command of information — the one that promises fewer jobs, short-term contracts in place of long-term careers, constantly changing skills and information in place of some continuity in employer expectations — Peter Drucker observes that the workforce will be divided into knowledge workers and service personnel. The former will command the highest salaries, will be in demand internationally, and will have the status and prestige of the 19th- and 20th-century captains of industry. The latter will see their jobs continue to disappear as increasingly sophisticated robots can be found to check out customers at the supermarket. The arts produce knowledge workers of a high order, individuals who create valuable and life-supporting information but also inspire others to question the inadequate values espoused by our mechanistic society. It is the new knowledge, the as yet not understood insights, that propel the arts to our attention, even when lesser matters intervene and divert us. Indeed, it will be the arts that provide the wit and will to say no to technological inventions that promise more and more devastation to our personal relationships and our sense of community. This realization has led artists to embrace and reject new technologies, incorporate them into their visual arts and theatrical happenings when appropriate, but refuse to accommodate them when their presence would undermine the thrust of the artistic integrity of the production.

The job-poor economy will be less a trauma to many artists who have never enjoyed the security of the nine-to-five job with benefits that cushion any mishap and ensure a comfortable retirement. The culture of the arts is one of forced flexibility and constant growth, one less addicted to the materialistic lifestyle that has crippled most of us in the mainstream economy. Even in their institutional reality, artists belong to organizations that rely on the whim of the public, the diminishing support of government in hard times, the restrained generosity of corporations and foundations as they shift priorities. Yet, the record indicates a continued expansion and an ongoing commitment to excellence even in these harsh winds of constrained circumstance. In a world in which technology will continue to destroy jobs at an unprecedented rate, society will be forced to find accommodations that redistribute the opportunities to contribute and the rewards for such contribution. Unfortunately the outlines of this new realignment are vague and blurred in this time of financial restraint still influenced by the perception of runaway deficits and now affected by the presence of massive public debt. The social supports which have been the pride of 20th-century compassion are still threatened. New concepts of a redesigned "well-being" state with new ethical expectations and outcomes are dampening the glow of unrestrained worship of the market economy. It is clear that new values, new forms of relationship, new behaviours, and new sharings will have to be recognized and initiated if life worth living is to be sustained in the new century.

It may well be that the voluntary sector, or the Third Sector, neither fully private nor public, possibly connected to an as yet undefined wage structure, will provide work to those unwanted by government or corporation. Viewing this sector's expectations for that foreseeable future, the Coalition of National Voluntary Organizations, in *Report Challenge 2000: Taking Voluntarism to the Year 2015*, predicts:

> In fact, it might be more appropriate to say that voluntarism will promote values that are not predominant in today's society. First the non-economic dimension will take precedence over the more materialistic values cur-

rently at the forefront of many people's interests. The concept of gross national well-being will emerge as an important development factor. The values of dignity, sanctity of the human being, meaningful participation and democracy will be more actively promoted. In addition, a range of more environmentally friendly themes will emerge. These different values represent a more holistic view of development.[6]

The arts have been at one with these values and are familiar with the form and style of the voluntary sector. There is scarcely a performing arts company or a museum or gallery that is not kept alive by the work of volunteers. Indeed, this array of fundraisers, charity event organizers, foyer merchants, and ticket-floggers have replaced the income that governments have withdrawn from cultural budgets.

In this kind of society, the role of the artist can no longer be in doubt. Indeed, the human values expressed by the arts at their best throughout the ages will be central to the sustainability of the planet and the continuing well-being of the species. The schools must produce young people who can contribute to a fast-changing, job-poor, voluntary-action-rich economy and live in a society being wrenched apart by a variety of forces. An integrated arts-based curriculum could be a unifying force which will not only serve the marketplace and the voluntary sector, but increase the chances for a decent and humane society.

NOTES
1. Jeremy Rifkin, *The End of Work*, New York: G.P. Putnam's Sons, 1995), p. 41.
2. Ran Ide, Arthur Cordell, *The New Wealth of Nations*, an unpublished paper prepared for the annual meeting of the Club of Rome, Buenos Aires, Argentina, November 30-December 2, 1994, p. 4.
3. Greg Baeker, *Comprehensive Examination, Community Cultural Planning, School of Urban and Regional Planning* (Waterloo, Ont.: University of Waterloo, August 1994, unpublished), p. 27.
4. *ArtFacts* (Ontario Arts Council Research and Policy Section),

Vol.3, No. 5, October 1995, p. 1.

5. Dian Cohen, Guy Stanley, *Class Action* (Montreal/Toronto: Robert Davies Publishing, 1993), p. 3.

6. *Challenge 2000: Taking Voluntarism to the Year 2015* (Ottawa: The Coalition of National Voluntary Organizations, May 27, 1994), p. 3.

Chapter 5

Assessment and Excellence

"Artists" of every stripe are people who share qualities such as imagination, the capacity to work hard and personal vision — qualities that will be sorely needed in the globally-oriented and fast-changing century that lies ahead.

Stephanie Perrin

W e have every reason to expect a commitment to excellence on the part of the schooling system. One value containing a universal ring of integrity is that we desire people to strive for the best they are capable of, whether in the context of a football game or a brain operation. If the adoption of an integrated arts-based curriculum means the erosion of standards of achievement, it would deserve no support even if it achieved our expectations in other areas. As our children will be confronted with problems that stagger our imaginations — problems that will only be solved by the finest workings of the best minds — any educational change that reduced the intellectual demands on our students by adjusting downward either standards of content mastery or skill acquisition would be a travesty. There is little worse our generation could inflict on our children than a sadly eroded educational system that failed to challenge their minds and spirits.

For many people, an increase in the place of the arts in the curriculum of our schools is seen as precisely the kind of undermining of standards that will doom our children to live in the squalor of a third-world economy, unable to compete with the rigorously trained students of Asian countries. To suggest that the arts, integrated and strengthened in their own roles, should be the unifying and connecting feature of a new curriculum would be tantamount to the destruction of what Canada's schools have already achieved and an end to the hope of a good life for today's students.

This belief in the lack of standards in arts instruction has a long history emerging from many decades of trivialization of the arts in North American society. Yet there is surely no fragment of our lives in which we expect such obeisance to the gods of quality as in our experience with the arts. We accept incompetence on our shopping trips, mediocrity in any number of services we request at the gas pump or the bank counter, but we demand excellence when we attend a theatre, a concert hall, a dance studio, or an art gallery. We openly express our disappointment if our favourite author has provided less insight, less excitement, less suspense than we have been led to expect from our previous encounter. Our conversation is filled with disillusionment over the couple of hours and few dollars wasted on a film that has exhibited inadequate camera technique, uninspired dialogue, or a flawed plot line.

Is it that we expect less than perfect standards in those pedestrian, day-to-day transactions that serve our basic needs, but believe we should have legitimate expectations of supreme quality when our spiritual and intellectual needs are being served? Is it because we feel artists have assumed a divine mandate to achieve the very best of which they are capable at all times? Perhaps each of us who has attempted an artistic task has been caught up by the inner demand that the outcome should be our very best, that somehow quality is perceived as an aspect of artistic outcome equal to creativity, imagination, and integrity. Thus we demand perfection, or as close to it as human frailties will allow, when we attend a concert, a play, or a dance performance.

Certainly our society constantly reveals that faith in artistic excellence. The local newspaper may provide nothing but flattery and hyperbole in its coverage of sports, business, and professional activities, but even small-town community symphony orchestras and theatres receive the critical assessment and intense evaluation normally accorded to a doctoral dissertation. There is an assumption that those so engaged are not doing it for the money, indeed, they may be subsidizing the performance from their own pockets. Therefore, there can be no other motivation but that of seeking high quality, and with no commercial objective to determine success or failure, it is presumably the task of the community's media to decide whether excellence has been achieved.

Of course, artists would agree that these standards of achievement are indeed appropriate. To them it is acceptable to have sports commentators and business analysts in those areas of public scrutiny, but we must have music and theatre *critics* gracing the arts pages of our newspapers and periodicals. The business tycoon escapes assessment and analysis until the company goes bankrupt, but the artist must risk being ground to dust at every opening-night performance.

Immediate sensationalism leading to enormous wealth is certainly an aspect of the popular arts; often it appears that individuals with a faint modicum of talent but with an enormous capacity for self-aggrandizement do win out. But only in the short-term. The number of rock stars who have faded into obscurity is surely beyond counting. Even at the more sophisticated levels of musical creation it may be that Andrew Lloyd Webber will be considerably richer and more famous, but the work of John Corigliano or Michael Tippet will last for centuries while *Cats* and *Phantom of the Opera* will have been forgotten. Indeed, Webber's own *Requiem* — rather than his mega-musicals — will be the work that takes his name into musical history. The work of the internationally acclaimed contemporary choral composers — Tavener, Pärt, Górecki, as well as Canadians Glick, Holman, Raminsh, Applebaum, Daley, Freedman, Telfer, Ruth Watson Henderson, and Schafer — may be remembered even longer.

It is this realization that leads serious artists to eschew the ephemeral and seek the eternal —those things of the mind and spirit that speak to the human condition in the present but do so in ways that reveal the elements of the age-old moral and philosophic ideals of humankind. For artists, the label "excellence" has long-term significance, in spite of the presence of the crass, the commercial, and the mediocre. One must concede that the derivative and the less-than-inspired permeates artistic output as it does every sector of our lives, and some of it, at least, is richly rewarded with enormous profits.

With all our expectations of professional artists, it is mystifying that arts subjects in the schools are perceived as "soft," lacking rigour and toughness. Why is it regarded as conventional wisdom that visual arts, drama, music, dance, technological arts are beyond assessing in schools? Why is it that universities disregard marks in secondary school arts courses even for entrance into their own fine arts programs?

There needs to be some demystification of the entire school testing and examination process that brings upon the arts the charges of lacking demanding standards. It is an important point to make, as some critics of schools truly believe that constant testing of students, with accompanying public revelation of results, is the royal road to educational reform, the "fix" that will bring to an end the ongoing discussion of what ails our schools. What a disillusionment there is in store for those newspaper columnists, editors, and politicians who have demeaned the work of schools and teachers and have put all their confidence in this simplistic solution! Indeed, they may find that the assessment process found in schools with quality arts education programs is a more reliable test of the accomplishments of the students in the skills and intelligences which will count most beyond the classroom than the objective tests for language literacy, maths and sciences.

Testing, as a diagnostic tool, is absolutely essential, and should be carried out as a continuous strategy by any excellent teacher. Judith Fine, a thoughtful and respected expert in the area of evaluation and assessment with the Peel Board of Education, believes it takes place every few minutes in a well-organized classroom, both for individual students and the class as a whole. She tells the story of the motor mechanics teacher who confided that his students were failing the test on dismantling a car engine, yet every one of them could actually do it efficiently. Her question was "What do you want them most to be able to do . . . write about it, or do it? If it is the latter, surely you should be testing their ability to carry out the task." In seeking to make her point, Fine asks four very simple questions: What do we value in our children and youths' learning? What do we wish to see as the outcomes of this learning? How do we teach them the things that are important to know or to do? How do we know we have taught them effectively? If the test or examination process answers these questions, then it is legitimate and appropriate.

All of us evaluate our actions constantly, whether we are making a meal, giving a speech, repairing a porch, or knitting a sweater. It is a part of our operating as human beings. Unless this constant evaluation gets out of hand and we become dysfunctional in our efforts to achieve perfection, it ensures that we grow and develop. There is every reason to support and encourage the kind of evaluation included in the style of any great institution or individual. On graduation, these students will be evaluated on the job, on the playing field, in the political arena, and they will want and need to know how they are performing.

It is essential that testing be connected to what we want our schools to do. Surely we no longer wish to burden our young with enormous loads of factual information which can be accessed by the most inexpensive home computer. Certainly we want our youth to emerge from our schools with basic skills, but more importantly, with the ability to think clearly, cogently, and impressively. As well, we realize that the schools' success in producing graduates who can understand themselves and others, express themselves with clarity and force, feel emotions and understand their power — the very attributes that the study of the arts encourages — deserves to be judged, and judged with some accuracy. We want young people to have some sense of what is intellectually valid. We want them to have a capacity for compassion. If these are our goals, then our testing procedures are manifestly inadequate and outdated.

Multiple-choice formats for testing assess little more than recall. If the objective is to assure that the testing procedures accurately reflect the goals of the curriculum, it is no wonder that existing tests have been found wanting, particularly in determining the acquisition of the full range of accomplishments to be expected in a quality arts education program. Howard Gardner and his colleagues make the point:

Multiple-choice items are, at least in their average and widely used forms, exercises in detection and selection rather than generation. They often enforce a view of single correct answers at the expense of recognizing culturally variegated or contrasting approaches to displaying understanding.[1]

Whether in the arts or in literature, the sciences or mathematics, or indeed, in physical education, there is a major thrust to find effective assessment tools which will reveal the success of students in accomplishing the objectives of the curriculum, treat students fairly, and inform them and their parents of their development with some accuracy and clarity. This is particularly true in the arts disciplines.

It is ironic that the most progressive leaps have been discovered in recognizing that "performance," a term identified with the arts but to be understood as more than an ephemeral moment onstage, is the word which best describes an appropriate method of assessing the mastery of an idea, a concept, or process achieved by a student. Again, Gardner and colleagues:

> Many aspects of what we need to teach beyond basic skills can be captured if we imagine thinking as performance. First, serious thinking, like any other performance, is a combination of humility and risk. It takes on noisy, ill-defined problems, alternately collecting data, observing and hazarding guesses. It involves large projects that combine invention and investigation with craft and insight and embedded accuracy. Second, like other performers, someone engaged in thought sustains a long arc of work over time and across obstacles. Thinking involves rehearsals, revisions, criticisms, and new attempts arranged in nothing like the straightforward orderings we offer in discussions of the scientific method or the directions for writing a term paper. Finally, thought, like performance involves interpretation. Like an actor or a musician, a historian or a scientist has to decide how to make sense of information and beliefs.[2]

What a clear definition of what it is to think and how impossible it is to assess such an activity with blunt, unsophisticated tools such as objective tests! This is exactly the problem for the teacher who must provide useful information to school administrators, parents, and society as a whole about the students' quality of musicianship, painting, or sculpture, and, more important, to grasp how all these expressions can reveal insights about the present and the future.

The challenge is even more demanding when test marks are placed on a curve and the assumption is made that if there are many above "average," then there are substantial numbers who must, by definition, be at the lower end of the spectrum and are thus failures. Though this is an issue that should bedevil all educators, it is particularly horrifying for the arts education teacher who believes that there is artistic potential in every student to be released and celebrated.

This raises the question of IQ tests and whether the ranking of students on such tests is, in fact, a revelation of the natural way of things, i.e., that there are a substantial number of students who must be unintelligent. Indeed if one accepts the Gardner model of multiple intelligences, the IQ test as a judgement on students becomes unsupportable. There are those who will carry the issue farther, connecting intelligence with gender, race, and culture. Such a process consigns substantial numbers of young people to the scrap heap. One can no longer comfort oneself that there will always be manual labour for the incapable male and motherhood for the incompetent female. In a knowledge society, to be marked as unintelligent will mean deprivation of the cruelest kind. There will be little manual labour, and to be a mother and not perceive oneself as an able teacher will affect the life chance of every child in the family.

Good tests or examinations tell students what they have failed to grasp and teachers what they have failed to explain — surely a prerequisite for the realignment that can then take place. Perhaps the problem was student inattention, but if we accept that students learn in many different ways, the culprit may be the inappropriate technique of instruction. An effective test reveals the problem, offering an opportunity to rectify the situation. However, most arguments for formal school examinations seem to revolve around preparing students to write them at the university level, surely a justification that begs many questions.

Even more damaging, in this era of institutional accountability, is the use of test results as justifications by governments for reducing support for education. In Ontario, setting up an Education Quality and Accountability Office was meant to assuage public pressure created by unthinking critics of the educational system who had determined that the province's schools were inadequate and that by testing at certain points in the curriculum (literacy and numeracy — broadly interpreted, to be sure), these inadequacies could be revealed and corrected. The unfortunate downside of this policy is the expectation that results will be made public and teachers and schools at the bottom of the scale will be identified and presumably punished. The ideal of accountability will be achieved.

The possibilities for disaster are unlimited unless intelligent intervention takes place. More than anything, the quality of classroom experience is dependent on the morale of teachers (already eroded in Ontario by the events surrounding the work stoppage in late 1997). It is the time, energy, and intellectual commitment that teachers give to the preparation of lessons that determines the quality of the interaction. Time in the evening, on weekends, during the Christmas, March, and summer breaks are required to master the enormous volume of infor-

THE MUKI BAUM SCHOOL OF THE ARTS

The Muki Baum School of the Arts is a very special place, where the healing power of the arts has been identified and the role of an arts program for disadvantaged children has been initiated. The school serves children and young people who have developmental and emotional disabilities. They are accepted after diagnosis for a program centred on training in a variety of arts expressions, including painting, drawing, sculpture, photography, jewellery design and fabric art under the supervision of visual artists and others with expertise. Although therapy is one of the benefits of this exposure to the arts (as it is with anyone who spends an enlivening hour with music or drama), the emphasis is on the legitimacy of the artistic product. The focus, the tension, the abandoned delight as paint finds its way to canvas, as garments emerge from a frenzy of directed activity, is extraordinary.

There is no sense that these students are being kept out of the way of "normal" learners, or out of the home so that parents can get on with their lives. It is apparent that every piece of art, whether painting, photograph, or sculpture, is an expression of the interest, the pain and distress, the joy and delight of the student artist. For some whose capacity to speak and converse is limited, it is the most important expressive moment of

mation about both the curriculum and teaching methods. The commitment of teachers to that "second mile" determines whether the classroom will be a positive, life-affirming experience or hopelessly dull, negative, and even destructive.

Any lack of teacher confidence in the testing procedures can harm the teaching and learning processes, but it can also distort the balance of discipline attention as teachers try to "beat the system" by concentrating on the areas to be tested and neglecting other needs of students. Even curriculum-building can be diverted from a broad educational purpose to that of serving test results — and a form of accountability that destroys the best schooling experience possible. Arts educators are anxious to support the very highest standards and most appropriate methods of assessing performance, but are connected to broad strategies for creating lifelong learners, excited by things of the mind and the spirit.

My reaction to testing may come from my own experience in the schooling system. I discovered that success in Grade 13 examinations was about accurate guessing of what would be on the test. I once taught history at that level when there were provincial examinations in every secondary school, graded in the shadow of the legislative buildings by an army of hired hands. It was plain that in order to assure the best marks for my students, I had to check examination papers from previous years and make an accurate prediction of the questions my students might have to face. I am ashamed to admit that I became rather good at this disgraceful enterprise. I realize that the system has now moved many miles past those very raw and inadequate testing procedures, but the impact of an uncritical faith in accountability through testing remains.

their daily lives. In front of the easel, the handicaps disappeared — all that remains is an energy and commitment that would please the finest art instructor in any college or university.

The walls of the rooms and halls are filled with art. A store provides an opportunity for the students to sell their work, the school acting as a dealer to ensure that the young artist is adequately rewarded. The Muki Baum School of the Arts is expanding into the performing arts as a further opportunity for reaching out to disabled children who need the arts as intensely as those who are free of handicaps.⌘

The matter of testing becomes even more questionable as one approaches international tests used by the media to compare entire national systems of education, particularly in mathematics, which is perceived as language- and culture-neutral. Howard Russell, a professor at the Ontario Institute for Studies in Education, has worked on both mathematics and testing throughout a career of several decades. He puts it simply: if a jurisdiction wants to achieve higher results than others, then it must teach for the tests. But while the standing of the educational jurisdiction will look very good indeed, one must be prepared for those attributes of learning that cannot be tested effectively in a written examination to be ignored — things like imagination and creativity.

Often, Canadian results have been compared with those of Japan. A cursory look at a typical Japanese classroom will reveal a singular fact — the class is made up of 100% Japanese children, all of whom will have Japanese as a first language. In the centre of Toronto, in a typical classroom, 60% of the children will have English as a second language. There will be as many as 15 different nationalities in a class of 35, with as many first languages. How much more challenging it is to develop a schooling system that accommodates, even inadequately, these differences of need, than one that wins a meaningless contest of examination results on an international test.

In examining the methods of assessment, one must suspend all awe and wonder about tests and examinations. To give the arts less priority on the basis that arts disciplines defy the provision of "objective" examination results is utterly irrational, particularly when our experience and the experience of our children tells us that there is more attention, more commitment of time and energy given to such activities than in any other sphere. One visit to a school concert often reveals quality of sound and interpretation that forces the term "amateur" to take on its real meaning — that of a *lover* of the knowledge or skill being pursued, and such love is the very best reason to expect excellence.

Even more important, in certain schools arts disciplines have developed methods of assessing the progress of students that have authenticity, rigour, and appropriateness. The portfolio, or performance folio as they are utilized in visual arts, photography, and film studies, represents a continuing assessment of the effort and understanding of the students. It is ironic that the system of assessment the world of business and industry employs is precisely the methodology the arts educator has seized upon. In place of the single-day examination, there is an evaluation of the ongoing grasp of the subject matter and an attention to hands-on production, rather than the mere theorizing that even the best examinations assess.

As well, there is the process folio, an extension of the portfolio process. These process folios may document stages in the development of any project as well as journals the students keep day-by-day, to express their own perception of the learning journey. In this way, students become familiar with the highest level of assessment — self-examination. There can be few lessons more valuable than that of learning to judge one's own strengths and weaknesses with courage and deliberation. The simple mark on a report card fades into irrelevance when placed beside an evaluation tied to learning objectives and evaluation skills that involve the student as well as the teacher.

Another argument for folios is that cooperative projects can be assessed in this longitudinal, integrated fashion. By definition, the test is a measure of an individual's response to the challenge of the examiner on a particular day. Yet much of our success in life is our capacity to work with others over a period of time, often on cooperative projects. If we are training young people as citizens and workers, family members and volunteers, then the assessment system must be connected to that objective. Portfolios and process folios can play that role effectively.

In the performing arts, the "performance" in dance, music, or drama can be an effective measure of accomplishment. It involves preparation, commitment, focus, and comparability with the capacity revealed days or weeks before. Even the ability to work in a team setting can be assessed, and worthwhile commentary and discussion with the student and her or his parents can ensue.

If these procedures are already in place, then why is there this constant perception that excellence can be assessed in the "tough" subjects like mathematics and science, but not in the "soft" subjects like music and drama? In part, it comes down once again to the trivialization of the arts throughout our society. It emerges from the industrial model of our understanding, that "real" subjects are concerned with facts that can be crammed into a brain and the grasp of these skills can be quantified exactly. How less frustrating to assess than the artistic expression that fails to specify right and wrong answers and finds that, as in our lives, there are many shades of grey.

Perhaps, most of all, the less "objective" results of an artistic expression make greater demands on the individual who must decide upon the readiness of the student to graduate or to take further education, or even more pointedly, to perform in the workplace. We search for easy answers. A simple number, 80%, has a resonance about it that exudes confidence. A collection of statements that simply express a flood of observations and expectations, no matter how relevant, measured, and qualitative, do not fit well into the file cards that dominate schools and workplace personnel offices.

Howard Gardner claims, "[t]he United States is well on the way to becoming a complete testing society." If so, Canada could be just a few years behind. He analyzes the phenomenon:

> We could encapsulate this attitude thus: If something is important, it is worth testing in this way; if it cannot be tested, then it probably ought not to be valued. Few observers have stopped to consider the domains in which such an approach might not be relevant or optimal, and most have forgotten the insights that might be gained from modes of assessment favoured in an earlier era.[3]

The assessment he selects from a bygone age is one associated with apprenticeship, that of providing day-to-day assessment on the basis of hands-on instruction by a master artisan and a perception of work well done. Ironically, that is the style that best suits the arts. It is also the rising expectation of the business world that isolated knowledge is of little use and must be woven into the fabric of real performance through practical interaction with tasks that place demands on the student similar to those found in the workplace. How better to describe the assessment of a visual artist, a dancer, a composer or an instrumentalist that is an ongoing activity? How much more relevant is such an assessment in terms of judging the artistic expressions which reveal a new world view?

Those who continue to demean the arts for their "softness" have not witnessed the latest generation of arts educators who have arrived on the scene and put effort into the outcomes of every lesson they teach. For example, the Dramatic Arts Consultants of Ontario have produced a booklet outlining the standards that should be expected from students. Although they state wisely that these performance standards are not to be seen as "stone tablets," it is clear that broad consultation across many jurisdictions took place before these standards were committed to print.

In the process of drama education, students move from being novices, to emergent understanding, to competence, to skill, and finally to mastery. The booklet identifies some 41 outcomes, and the 41st might be said to reveal the expectations of teachers most explicitly. This outcome demands that "the learner will value drama as an integral part of her/his life." At the lowest level it is assumed the student will "acknowledge drama as a separate subject area involving specific skills that are relevant to her/him when in drama class." The mastery level dictates that "the learner consciously seeks out applications in every part of her/his life for the various techniques, forms and skills originally learned in drama." Such expectations make demands on students that multiple tests scarcely touch in terms of relevance to real-life experience. This is just a beginning in the long process of helping teachers discover the answers to those basic questions: What is to be valued? What are the outcomes? How do we teach for them effectively? How do we know we have taught them?

There is every reason to have confidence in the emphasis on outcomes that now dominates the arts education community. Teachers are determining what the essential core of an integrated approach to drama, music, dance, visual arts, film, and creative writing might be. They are insisting on establishing a level of accomplishment as a starting point for assessing the progress a student has made. But in the end is a confidence that evaluation can be a positive support for all the objectives the arts can hope to achieve.

Quality of thought process and decision-making, of response to complex issues, will contribute to positive solutions; these are the elements of any "excellence" that describes the nature of the school graduate. In an effort to be accountable, schools and schooling systems have lost sight of these attributes. In some countries — the United Kingdom, for example — the state is faced with the threat of illegal actions on the part of teachers and headmasters who are determined to resist the efforts of government to use the marks in a way that will damage children and their learning futures. The government insists on a process that will set school against school in the hope that such competition will weed out the incompetent teacher or will reveal the inefficient institution. These may be worthy goals, but to use the efforts of children revealed by limited assessment procedures is a travesty of justice, threatening children, teachers, and schools.

An integrated arts-based curriculum should be constantly evaluated by teachers, artists, parents, and the concerned community. Students in such a program should know how well they are doing in every aspect of the learning process, and teachers should be aware of the shortcomings of curriculum content, skill acquisition, and the instruction model. The arts, with their emphasis on excellence and outcome, might provide the very mechanisms that will bring new confidence to the world of testing and examination throughout our school system.

NOTES
1. Dennis Wolf, Janet Bixby, John Glenn III, Howard Gardner, "To Use Their Minds Well: New Forms of Student Assessment," in *Research in Education*, Gerald Grant, editor (Washington: American Educational Research Association, 1991), p. 31.
2. Ibid., p. 34.
3. Gardner, Howard. *Multiple Intelligences: The Theory in Practice* (New York: Basic Books Inc. Publishers, 1993), p. 164.

Chapter 6

The Arts and Being Canadian

The cultural revolution of the later twentieth century can thus be understood as the triumph of the individual over society, or rather the breaking of the threads which in the past had woven human beings into social structures.

Eric Hobsbawm

There is no word in the English language so problematic as "nationalism." It conjures up images of the two great wars that have dominated the 20th century, and of the countless minor conflicts that have ended the hopes and lives of millions of people around the globe. Nationalism has become associated, at least in this century, with violence and destruction on such a monumental scale that each one of us can share the hesitations of a recent Canadian prime minister who came to believe that all of nationalism's benefits are minuscule beside the horrors that have been perpetrated in its name. Yet in spite of these hesitations, there is something pervasive and basic about the desire of people to be at one with a familiar segment of the world's population and to feel a sense of comfort and belonging not found within any other context. That is the essential attractiveness of the "nationalist claim," described by Michael Ignatieff as "that full belonging, the warm sensation that people understand not only what you say but what you mean [that] can only come when you are among your own people in your native land."[1]

R.H. Thomson, one of Canada's most celebrated actors, expressed similar thoughts some 10 years ago. He had just finished the final term at the London Academy of Music and Dramatic Art:

> Then a curious thought struck: I'm not English. What did I want to act in Britain for? Shouldn't I be acting in Canada? It seemed to my thespian heart that to act was to be an expression of your own people, people you shared a country with and perhaps understood.[2]

He was determined to share a history and pride of achievement with people who shared the language he spoke, the literature he read, the music he listened to, and to do so in a geographic area he knew and appreciated. Thus, nationalism and culture become closely entwined.

For Canadians even to believe that they have a culture to enjoy and guard is a recent phenomenon. For centuries, Canada was a colony, and a good definition of a colonist is someone who believes all the important action in the world is going on somewhere else — Paris, London, or, in the last half of this century, New York.

The triumph of these last decades has been that of maintaining a national reality in spite of the flood of programming emanating from the centre of the television universe, the United States. As Peter Herrndorf, CEO of TVOntario, stated at Toronto's Canadian Club in October 1995, "Consider that 70 to 80% of those 12,000 hours of programming our kids will tune into will be American programming full of American heroes, American values, and American commercials." To survive this cultural onslaught is no mean task, hour by hour, day by day, and year after year.

I grew up in Toronto not realizing that in that very city there were authors of books that were being read throughout the English-speaking world. Until recently, that Canada had a proud literary tradition would have been a revelation to most citizens. It is less than 30 years since T.H.B. Symons pointed out, in his landmark report, "To Know Ourselves," that there were virtually no courses in Canadian literature in our universities. He, more than any other individual, shamed the academic community into focussing on Canadian Studies, using his role as president of Trent University as a lever both to develop unique programs in his own university (thereby pressuring his colleagues in other institutions) and, through his leadership role among Commonwealth university presidents, to give the study of Canada an international status.

Of course, the question arises: What is the appropriate role of the public educational system in dealing with the reality that individuals, in order to fulfill themselves, need to feel a part of a culture or nation? The charge of propagandizing and proselytizing can be easily levelled against a public institution beholden to elected officials and dependent on the public purse. Yet much of the great music that has been composed, the great books that have been written, the great pictures painted — the very materials that make up a Canadian curriculum — have erupted from a national pride and a desire to express the strength and variety found in this country's culture and initiated in a public school classroom.

Mathematics and science are in their essence international. Languages are most assuredly tied to nation, but, unfortunately in a world whose people are largely unilingual, become somewhat limited in expressing the richness of all the varied cultures. It is the arts which not only emerge from a sense of national community, but ironically find meaning from constant association with the plays, musical compositions, and visual arts expressions of other countries. Thus, the arts, both as a central learning focus and as a path to other disciplines, emphasize the importance of the traditions from which students have come and the pride of heritage which should be the intellectual and emotional property of every child. Integrated arts-based learning becomes a strategy for Canadian cultural survival and, in Ignatieff's terms, a matter of personal well-being. It also serves as a link to the cultural well-being of children who have come from other lands.

Canada has had a unique history. Even though our independence as a nation had largely been settled by the end of World War II, our schools were still teaching a British Empire culture that emphasized English writers, playwrights, and composers. Few Canadians of the first half of the 20th century knew the music of Healey Willan and Godfrey Ridout, both writing melodic and accessible works, but many more knew of Edward Elgar and Ralph Vaughan Williams.

Schools in the last half of this century have been caught up in American culture, as one would expect when the task of sharing a continent is so dominant in the public life of the country. The acculturation of our children that has led to the acceptance of American values and American perceptions of the world has come mainly from the mass media that overwhelms every child, not only before the television set, but also in cinemas and comic-book stores. It means that Canadian children know little about major figures that have fashioned the country in which they live, but they know even less about the great artists of this century and the rich, vibrant artistic output better known and revered in other parts of the world than in Canada itself.

In spite of the limitations of cultural ignorance which hound us as a nation, it is a rare week that does not include reports of Canadian cultural triumphs from all over the world, whether it be Karen Kain dancing before an Israeli audience, an international literary award given to Michael Ondaatje, or a sold-out series of performances by the Toronto Dance Theatre in North America's centre of modern dance, New York City. A nationalist's heart is warmed when the Canadian Opera Company's Richard Bradshaw is successful in attracting Robert Lepage to direct a production of Bartók's *Bluebeard's Castle* and Schoenberg's *Erwartung*, both difficult and demanding works, and hears that the Canadian cast has received standing ovations in Edinburgh and Hong Kong. Is there a culturally aware Canadian who is not thrilled to hear that foreign orchestras, choirs, or string quartets are playing the music of R. Murray Schafer, Harry Freedman, Alexina Louie, Louis Applebaum, Srul Irving Glick, Harry Somers, John Weinzweig, Violet Archer, Victor Davies, Claude Vivier, Oscar Morawetz, Norma Beecroft, Anne Southam, Bruce Mather, Brian Cherney, or John Beckwith? Most Canadians would recognize only a handful of names in this list — but these are only a small number of the composers Canada has produced and who now have international reputations.

I can remember the pride I felt when, running along the banks of the Seine in Paris, I came across a sculpture garden and found before me a piece by Sorel Etrog, a Canadian whose work can be found on the streets and plazas of Toronto and many other North American cities. I shall not forget walking into a famous bookstore in London, England, and being confronted by two central displays of bestselling novels by Robertson Davies and Margaret Atwood. I found myself filled with conceit after visiting Stratford-on-Avon, England, to realize that the productions of Robin Phillips and John Neville at Ontario's Stratford were the equal and often surpassed those staged in the bard's homeland. I was thrilled, on a trip to Brussels, to find two Riopelles hanging on the walls of Belgium's Royal Museum of Modern Art.

Glenn Gould's career as a very Canadian artist has been the focus of every serious music magazine the world over. Maureen Forrester's renditions of Gustav Mahler's great works for voice are the delight of connoisseurs in every land. Teresa Stratas and John Vickers are household names to music-lovers in any community which receives broadcasts of the Metropolitan Opera. Now, the operatic exploits of Canadian tenors Ben Heppner, Michael Schade, and Richard Margisson are becoming a source of pride. One could go on and on, especially if one chose to include singers who spend most of their lives in other countries: Paul Frey and Jamie McLean come to mind. If the more popular fields of music are considered, the names of Anne Murray, Gordon Lightfoot, and Joni Mitchell, as well as, more recently, Bryan Adams, David Foster, Céline Dion, Jann Arden, Sarah McLachlan, Daniel Lanois, Bruce Cockburn, and Murray McLaughlan, are mentioned. These names merely begin the list of internationally recognized performers and songwriters that are on the lips of young people now in Canadian schools, colleges, and universities.

These are the outcroppings of Canada's arts achievements, but to people around the world, they and all the many others who have reached heights of excellence are the proof that more than mountains, rivers, and forests make up this nation's reality. Canada's culture is much more than what some would say are these essentially elite expressions, but an appreciation of the country's contributions to the total artistic output of the planet are certainly contained in any thinking person's definition of what it means to be a Canadian.

In short, people in other countries are very much aware that Canada produces extraordinary artists in virtually every field of artistic endeavour. Indeed it is part of the aura that surrounds Canada in the eyes of the world, completing the picture of this country as seen through United Nations surveys that identify it as the best place on earth to live. Apparently it is, as well, a wonderful place to sing, dance, paint, act, and make films.

It is not only the appreciation of the major artistic expressions of international stars that give our children some confidence in themselves. Often happening upon a performance by a lesser-known Canadian singer, dancer, or instrumentalist can reveal the depths of this country's artistic quality. Jo-Anne Bentley, a Vancouver-born mezzo-soprano now singing and teaching at the University of Toronto's Faculty of Music, is not a name familiar to many fellow citizens, but her singing is a revelation of musicality and dramatic expression. She performs a broad selection of works, tending to a repertoire that demands not only a well-trained voice, but intellectual command as well. Yet she can bring an audience to uncontrollable laughter with a sense of humour that is devastating. Mary Lou Fallis has sung across the country and overseas as a splendid oratorio soloist, but has developed a reputation as the funniest vocal performer the country has produced, using her magnificent voice in a series of solo offerings about the spouse of Johann Sebastian Bach and other equally bizarre figures. Being conscious of one's Canadianism can be the experience of visiting a music store to stumble upon a recording of Carolyn Sinclair, a soprano with international experience, but less known beyond her home in Hamilton and in Toronto, where she gives frequent recitals with her husband, harpsichordist and organist Michael Jarvis. She has chosen as a field of specialty the early music repertoire, particularly the songs of Purcell, Clarke, and Eccles, and has done so with such sweetness of sound that her performances sparkle with delight and integrity. Yet why should one be surprised at this choice of repertoire when Tafelmusik, Toronto's baroque orchestra, now plays on stages around the world and is heard frequently on radio stations in other lands; and Glyn Evans, an accomplished and consistently powerful Guelph tenor who tours Canada and beyond, is presently one of the leading interpreters of the music of Benjamin Britten?

We have become aware of this phenomenon of arts achievement at the very time when the viability of the nation state is being questioned. For Canada, this issue has particular meaning as this land is in a state of crisis regarding its identity. A significant number of people with French as their first language have indicated in a most dramatic fashion that they not longer wish to be a part of this country. Though a referendum in the Province of Quebec resulted in a majority of voters indicating their wish to remain in Canada, it was clear that most francophones had voted to leave. In a global economy, the desire for a separate state becomes entirely cultural. This, indeed, is the reason it is so difficult for English-speaking Canadians to comprehend the issue. The issue is identity and a perception that cultural survival demands separation. There is every reason to believe it will remain on the nation's agenda for years to come. Issues of identity are not solved through political or economic manipulation, but must be comprehended through cultural initiatives. Ultimately, the solution is not to be found in Ottawa or Quebec City. It will be discovered by the creative people we call artists — writers, composers, playwrights, choreographers, and filmmakers.

Thus, the school and a curriculum devoted to a cultural approach to the preparation of young people becomes a strategy for national survival. An integrated arts-based curriculum could give special attention to the work of Canadian dramatists, writers, composers, and visual artists and their understanding of this country's past. As other disciplines such as history are approached through their eyes, the capacity to give meaning and emotional content to Canadian events becomes apparent. The increasing familiarity of children with Canadian artists expressing their thoughts in both official languages and the nuances found in differing musical and choreographic traditions, along with the more recent cultural expressions of peoples from other lands, could bring not only increased unity but quality learning accurately reflecting the multicultural future for humankind on this planet. As the 21st century comes closer we realize that not only will the identity of French-Canadians be tested, but that of all who have come from every country in the world to a land which promised to provide opportunity. The challenge will be that of finding a bond of meaning that attracts all who live north of the United States. To say that the arts is central to the expression of a culture able to incorporate differentiation and celebrate minority identity is to state the obvious. It will not be the study of economics or business management which will tell the difference, but a holistic understanding of the artistic.

The possibility of such response has already emerged. In 1994, 300 young people were brought together to learn about the history and culture of their province in a project sponsored by the Citadel Theatre and inspired by the energy and commitment of its then artistic director, Robin Phillips, whose years at the helm of the Stratford Festival are remembered with warmth and appreciation. The event, called *The Alberta Quilt*, was described by Phillips at a professional development day for artists working in the classrooms sponsored by the Ontario Arts Council (Appendix B). What can be achieved by young people whose energy and spirit have been engaged is truly phenomenal. It is enough to say that these young Albertans will never look at themselves and their province in the same way again. They will talk about those weeks together for the rest of their lives. This is a program which, with appropriate content alterations, could be repeated in every province as well as the nation's capital — a model for nation-building which could transcend the barriers of language and historical enmity. It is an example of what an integrated arts-based classroom could incorporate into the process of self-discovery for every child, as well as a path to geographic and historic studies of a more traditional nature.

However, it is not only internal pressure that threatens Canada's survival as a nation. The phenomenon of globalization brings into question the viability of every nation state. We know that economic power is now in the hands of enormous business conglomerates no longer based in a particular nation state but positioned along the international information superhighways. The end of the nation state, predicted on all sides, is not a view which can be easily ignored. Indeed, "globalization" is now the fashionable word to describe the next century and the opportunities it presents.

We are realizing that globalization can be merely the ultimate form of greed — that, indeed, those nations which can co-opt the technology and expertise can be assured of a place on the global information highway while those with no capacity to acquire either will be assigned to the dustheap of our worldwide economy. We have come to realize that the values of globalization enthusiasts turn out not to be those of compassion and mutual support but of competition and the punishment of the losers. Artists have been warning us of the possible inhumanity of a world in which power is concentrated and the dignity of the individual is sacrificed in the name of economic efficiency. Margaret Atwood's novels exude that terror of the power that technology can exert if unrestrained by an ethic that perceives lack of economic success as a mark of moral turpitude. It is well that writers and playwrights have expressed these fears. Academics who question the ways things have turned out are perceived as intellectually irrelevant. Forgotten are all the warnings of those who suggested that we must make decisions about the directions that new technologies were taking us and not be the victims but the masters of our future.

John Ralston Saul, in the Massey Lectures broadcast on the CBC, dealt with this problem of loss of confidence in national governments and the transfer of power to the private sector:

> It could be argued that we are now in the midst of a coup d'etat in slow motion. Democracy is weakening; few people would disagree. Corporatism is strengthening; you only have to look around you. Yet none of us has chosen this route for our society, in spite of which our elites quite happily continue down it.[3]

Saul contends that humans are social animals who must live together in communities to fully develop their talents and capacities. In the name of fighting deficits and the big inefficient governments which have produced them, such concepts as public consultation are being pushed aside. The marketplace and the corporate structure is wrongheadedly perceived to be automatically more efficient than the process of community action and democratic determination. Democracy is, once again in this century, in question. Although few will suggest that the trappings of elected government should be abandoned, many are convinced their functions must be stripped through the mechanism of privatization to the bare necessities of law and order. Saul says that if we give over the central decision-making to the corporate world, whether local or global, we will make "A Great Leap Backward," the title of his first Massey Lecture.

The arts represent the most visible and continuing bulwark against dictatorship and the other forms of oligarchy that have enslaved people in the past, both in terms of their content and process. Books can be written, plays and operas produced, art exhibits presented, only in the context of freedom. These and all the other ways in which artists "live and move and have their being" are examples to young people of how they too can engage, with tolerance toward the views of others, in the difficult process of finding agreements and accommodations which will allow them to move to actions benefitting the common good. Thus, integrated arts-based learning, sharing this obsession of artists with freedom of expression, represents an opportunity to defend those things that are culturally central to Canada's continuity as a nation in the democratic tradition.

Amidst the complexity and ambiguity of the technological age, Canadians know they cannot achieve national survival through simple pride in the many accomplished artists we have produced for the world to watch and hear. Indeed, as culture budgets are threatened at the federal, provincial, and municipal levels, one cannot be confident that Canada's political representatives have any clear notion of the connectedness of the arts and culture to national survival and whether there will be any funds forthcoming in the years ahead either to train Canadian artists adequately or to send Canadian artists abroad to arouse the attention of the world and give us pride as a people. Indeed, of all the groups hurt in the '90s recession, none have been put at risk more than Canada's creative artists, who have shown enormous ingenuity and determination to survive. Canadian composers have found their royalty income reduced by as much as 75%, as orchestras, faced with eroding grants from government, reach for a familiar repertoire to fill seats. The commitment to play Canadian composition is all but forgotten. As well, we no longer have a Victor Feldbrill, who as a regular conductor of a Canadian symphony orchestra, always insisted on presenting a contemporary Canadian piece in his concerts. Thus, John Weinzweig's "Divertimento #5 for Trumpet, Trombone and Symphonic Wind Ensemble" would accompany a Tchaikovsky concerto; Violet Archer's "Three Sketches for Orchestra" would be programmed with a Mozart favourite; Jean Paineau-Couture's "Piece Concertante #5" would be placed beside a popular Rachmaninoff offering. Canadian composers are now more dependent for income on foreign orchestras playing their music, as artistic directors of Canadian orchestras fail to mine the rich lode of home-produced composition.

The fear that globalization will undermine the unique culture of a small country sharing a large continent with a veritable giant is exacerbated by the most recent threat — the Multilateral Agreement on Investment. Called "a constitution for the global economy" by the president of the World Trade Organization, the MAI would, if accepted by the Canadian government, require that foreign investors be treated the same as domestic, making it impossible for Canadian governments at all levels to subsidize and thereby favour its own cultural entities — its theatre companies, orchestras, book and periodical publishers — as this would mean treating them differently than foreign cultural industries operating in Canada. Furthermore, content rules for radio and television which alone defend Canadian culture from the flood of American programming would be declared illegal. In short, all the mechanisms Canadians have used to allow fellow countrymen and women to tell their own stories and sing their own songs, through both electronic and print media, would disappear.

Throughout the discussions of the Free Trade Agreement and the North American Free Trade Agreement, Canadians have sought to save the soul of the nation. The MAI would obliterate all vestiges of the strategies by which Canada has worked to protect an already eroded capacity to be a nation. It is no mean task. Audiences must be found for artists, composers, playwrights, novelists, choreographers, and filmmakers if they are to make a living in this land, rather than leave to practice their art in another country. I have a vivid memory of sitting on a staircase in a lovely home where Wayne Strongman's Tapestry Singers were taking a break from a strenuous performance. Jean Stilwell, a member of the ensemble in search of a career as a soloist, had so far been unable to find an audience. On that occasion it elicited a dispirited "one more year, and that's it." Then came the Vancouver production of *Carmen*, with Stilwell in the leading role, and a distinguished national and international career was launched. She now sings opera and offers recitals in the major houses of Europe, Asia, and North America, and sings with symphony orchestras on every continent. She is a world figure as a mezzo-soprano with a dramatic, resonant voice, a most attractive stage presence, and an intense commitment to the excellence of every performance. Good training, some luck, but most important the finding of an audience, brought about a great career. Thus, schooling an audience is very much a part of building a Canadian culture. Indeed, a knowledgeable audience capable of appreciating the very best of repertoire and performance is essential to the development of capable artists.

⌘　⌘　⌘

It has always been the litany that once educational levels have risen across the nation, the arts would be flooded with clients buying tickets for seats in every theatre and concert hall. Tom Henighan examines the assumption that increased educational credentials assures greater participation in the arts on the part of the Canadian populace:

Although some government surveys offer an optimistic view of the attachment of the Canadian public to the arts, there are sobering counter indications. For example, in 1951 there were about 189,000 Canadians with university degrees; by 1991 there were 2.4 million. While audiences for the arts also increased during the same period, the increases were far below the increase in university education.[4]

There are undoubtedly many reasons for this relative decline — the effect of television, the decrease in discretionary time available to families and the minimal increases in wages of the vast majority of workers in recent years. All can be factored into a perception that the serious art forms have not become a major factor in the lives of most people. But the fact remains that extraordinary increases in formal education have not resulted in a dramatic explosion of interest in what is transpiring in our concert halls, theatres, and galleries.

A more definitive and measured analysis has come from the nation with whom Canadians share a continent. The National Endowment for the Arts, the funding body in the United States which has a mandate not unlike that of the Canada Council, released a report in May 1996 that considered the problem of audience development. It can be assumed that the Canadian experience is close to that described in this document:

> The report suggests that people who are now middle-aged or younger do not attend orchestra concerts, musical theatre, and the other arts activities at the same rate as people who are in their 50s or older. The decline is troublesome to arts groups not only because of the drain on ticket sales and admission fees, but because many arts groups are counting on a new generation of patrons to become donors as well. For some arts organizations, the demographic time-bomb has exploded.[5]

The report goes on to state that in the age group that counts the most in terms of future support, ages 32 to 36, the attendance has gone down from 15% to 11% since 1982.

It can be argued that attendance at concerts, plays, and dance presentations is but a portion of the activities that indicate a healthy cultural life, that a better indicator would be the total creative output, or the extent of amateur performance to be found in the Canadian landscape. Unfortunately, these latter activities are unquantifiable. It is serious enough to say that in the case of the only aspect of cultural maturity where hands and feet can be counted, the results are disappointing. It does indicate that the traditional fragmented curriculum is failing the arts in the one area where there are statistics that can be analyzed.

Thus, an enthusiasm for the moments of true inspiration that follow must be tempered by the realization that all these and other exemplary programs taught, in some cases over many decades, have not produced a base of committed support for Canada's creative artists or for the professional arts organizations that bring us the results of this creativity, whether it be James Kudelka and the National Ballet, Judith Thompson and the Tarragon Theatre, Srul Irving Glick and the Iseler Singers, or Michael Snow and the Art Gallery of Ontario.

⌘ ⌘ ⌘

The desperate state of the contemporary composer and the economic pressures on Canadian publishers and authors are particularly serious. Canadian culture is at threat from within and from without, from the frightening world of cultural globalization and from the intimate relationship with the world's most aggressive cultural exporter, the United States. But an audience that has experienced an appropriate introduction to the arts, within a schooling system committed to national cultural expression, would surely demand Canadian works from its orchestras, Canadian drama from its theatre centres, Canadian art on the walls of its galleries, and Canadian singers and instrumentalists on its stages.

One of the distinctive features of this country is its enormous size. It is a huge but comparatively empty land, with most of its citizens living in a few large cities and nearly all of them just a few hundred kilometres from the American border. As a result, both in terms of its jurisdictional responsibilities and its national identity, Canada is a land obsessed by issues of transportation and communication. No other country was created and held together first by cords of steel (the Canadian Pacific Railway) and then by airwaves (the Canadian Broadcasting Corporation). Having lost beyond redemption their great railway empire, Canadians are unique in their present commitment to a national broadcasting system that can reach across these thousands of kilometres, express the realities of one region to another, and reveal to citizens from coast to coast what it means to be a Canadian. Some years ago, a thesis was written examining why Canadian young people had chosen to engage in Canadian studies programs in universities across the country. One of the common reasons given was that their parents had listened to CBC radio in their homes.

In the mid-'80s, when it seemed that the federal government had lost any understanding of the importance of transcontinental communication and was cutting the resources of the CBC below its capacity to carry out its mandate, a citizens' protest movement — at first called Friends of Public Broadcasting, then Friends of Canadian Broadcasting — arose to defend the radio and television service. To discover what was at stake, the Friends decided to commission a survey to determine whether Canadians really thought they were different and should have their own public communications network, or whether, as North Americans, they had now established a continental culture that had diluted any collective perception of uniqueness.

The results left no doubt that Canadians believed there were real contrasts between their own culture and that of the US. Canadians believed they had a better health care system, a more effective system of law and order, and a more efficient government. Even more important, they believed that they cared more about the environment, about women's rights, and about multicultural issues. In short, there was every reason to fight for a strong "peoples' broadcasting system," because there was something special to communicate. Without using the word "culture," Canadians had revealed that they believed they had one worth preserving.

Not even the North American Free Trade Agreement and the increasing pressures of economic globalization have reduced this sense in Canada that a people must have an awareness of itself. It arises even in the context of sporting events. The jubilation not just of Torontonians but of Canadians everywhere when the Blue Jays won the World Series, not once but twice, points to the presence of a national pride of

MYRNA GABBIDON'S CLASSROOM

In Myrna Gabbidon's suburban Toronto classroom, one is impressed by the quiet -- the intense silence of children who are totally focused on their own work.

The visual arts class is about "lines;" the kinds of lines that make up a drawing. Some children are finding lines in illustrations in the piles of books and magazine in the large learning resource room, others are already at a table with fellow students drawing different kinds of lines — straight, squiggly, curved, wavy, thick, and thin; the whole menu of the sketching artist.

Then there are those children on the floor who are using lines to create a mural which has at its centre a huge tree, with its many trunks and branches and leaves. But "line" turns up in other ways in this class. There is a pause for a dance that allows three children to exhibit the line of the body in their movements about the room. The music that accompanies their dance has a line of melody, and soon there is a story to be acted out with its line of plot and character development. This is no forcing of arts integration, it is just the way things are done in this class.

The seriousness about the arts is palpable. For example, these children have the opportunity to learn about dance each Saturday morning, instructed by a student from the dance program at York University. Three of the students are about to write the Royal Academy of Dance examinations. And this is a grade three class. "Challenge" and "excellence" are words that have resonance among these students.

The vocabulary expands as students speak easily of "space" and "design;" where the angry "shut up" is replaced by the measured comment: "Stay focused." It is obvious that language literacy and numeracy find their way into this class whatever the subject of the moment. The children are possessed by their learning, and teacher Myrna Gabbidon puts it simply: "For the reluctant learner, the arts are simply the way to go."

Parents are aware of the learning experience of their children. An Arts Night, to which each student must bring a parent, is held in the evening and very delighted parents return home hand in hand with their children, sharing the aura of a new understanding about what their child is becoming.❆

place, circumstance, and culture even though there was scarcely a Canadian player in the dugout. Each Olympic Games reveals its own stories of Canadian athletes proud to represent their country — sometimes, as in the case of Elvis Stojko in 1998, courageously enduring enormous pain to bring back a medal. At the other end of the scale, the debacle of the Canadian Football League in past years, opening its gates to any American city unable to acquire an NFL franchise, was the despair of the entire country. However, sports has become so obviously a business with no community loyalty and little player identification that it scarcely matters in terms of cultural identity. Indeed, it is a rare stroke of luck if any local citizens find themselves playing professional sport for their home teams. The arts, on the other hand, not only address the specific issues of our nationhood, but do so through the voices of Canadians, often citizens living on the next street. Few who happened to attend performances of the National Ballet of Canada just days after the referendum over national unity in Quebec will forget the moment when the orchestra uncharacteristically struck up the national anthem at the start of the program. People in the audience sang lustily, with tears streaming down their faces. With no country, there could be no National Ballet with Canadian dancers, an orchestra of Canadian players, and on occasions a choreographed work by a Canadian artist in its repertoire. It all came together for that audience on that evening, and since then every performance of the Canadian National Ballet opens with "O Canada."

To provide a defence for a healthy and positive nationalist culture, the arts must be understood in the most holistic terms. The ongoing quest for a Canadian identity provides a strong argument for a massive expansion in arts-based education. Every classroom is a potential place of interaction around the issues of identity within our commitment to variety and differentiation. Such an initiative must involve the creative artist, who provides the images and the sounds that assure us of our nationhood. Emerging from a unique culture, our music composition is splendidly different in significant ways from that of other lands. For example, R. Murray Schafer, a prodigious and prestigious Canadian composer, connects sound with environment to the point that some of his music must be performed on a wilderness lake or an isolated island. (He is, incidentally, a strong arts education advocate and writes music for children. Indeed, his composition "Epitaph for Moonlight" is scored for a youth chorus, with the words written by a grade seven class.) Alexina Louis's concentration on the total awareness of sound in the context of an ecological focus stirs a special response in a Shield land of forest, rock, and mountains. Srul Irving Glick's focus on peace and justice issues in his choral works reflects not only his Jewish roots but the peculiar experience of the many people who have come from many lands to build a unique culture in the north. Only a Louis Applebaum could have designed the architectural integrity of sound enhancing countless films about Canada and Canadians, often produced by the CBC or the National Film Board, frequently with Harry Rasky at the helm. These are uniquely Canadian composers whose works exude sound shapes that reflect the concerns of Canadian citizens. The music of the Canadian composer can speak to young people and encourage them to make their own music, music expressing a recognizable, legitimate nationalism for the 21st century. But the need for an intervention from the schooling system through a sensitive curriculum is crucial.

In the totality of a cultural globalism that makes the arts so important, our artists are a window on our understanding of ourselves. The Group of Seven saw that Canada's northland was not simply a rougher version of rural Europe, but that the northern forest wilderness was a dominant geographic reality and a symbol of many things that made the country different from the United States. A visit to the McMichael Collection in Kleinberg, Ontario, provides a visual expression in colour and form of Canada as a northern land, indeed as a country of the Shield. It also explains in visual terms why collective action as well as private initiative has been the rule in economics, transportation, health, education, and a host of other elements that constitute Canadian culture. Fortunately, the McMichael has a strong educational interest and connects with thousands of children. However, the McMichael and hundreds of other arts organizations could make a substantially more effective impact if schools made education through the arts a central commitment.

Canadians, so familiar with the Group of Seven, are largely unaware of the extraordinary body of works that had already been achieved by such 19th and early 20th century artists as Maurice Cullen, J.W. Morrice, Ozias Leduc, Homer Watson, G.A. Reed, Horatio Walker, Marc-Aurele De Foy Suzor-Cote, and Paul Peel. Even more unfortunately, the Group of Seven have so dominated the visual arts landscape that they have obscured a brigade of contemporary Canadian artists who, as well as depicting the vast and lonely land, have also expressed other realities, such as the melange of people and cultures that have come to share the richness of this nation, and the impact of a century of violence and chaos — Jack Bush, Harold Town, Gordon Rayner, Graham Coughtry, Paul Emile Borduas, William Ronald, Ivan Eyre, Paterson Ewan, Joyce Wieland, and Tony Urquhart, to mention only a few. Certainly, Claude Tousignant, Guido Molinari, Tony Onley, and Ron Bloore have been at the centre of nonrepresentational art while expressing a unique freshness in their colour and design. Is it a peculiar relationship of wind, water, sand, and rock in the Maritimes that brings forth such realistic images from painters Christopher Pratt, Mary Pratt, and Alex Colville? Is it the closeness to the wilderness that accounts for the extraordinary depiction of the natural world by Robert Bateman and Glen Loates? Is it possible that Canada could lead the world in developing an education system based on the strength, beauty, and integrity of its artists?

Our literature, as Margaret Atwood points out, has been about survival in a wilderness land. The magnitude and the nature of the land has fashioned this emphasis. Yet Robertson Davies expresses a modulated sophistication of expression and an incomparable command of language to remind Canadians that the nation was built on the shoulders of two ancient cultures. The country's mystery writers, like Eric Wright, express more of the gentle humour of the citizen on the street and less of the blood and gore that have characterized this genre in American literature.

The music of Harry Somers and Harry Freedman has been about the variety and richness of the regions and peoples of this country, bringing a realization that although the Western provinces and the Maritimes may not seem to fit easily into a technological economy, they nonetheless have a cultural richness that must be expressed through sounds that strike the ear, sometimes with alarm, sometimes with delight, but always with a spirit-stirring relevance. The humour of Don

Harron has a unique gentleness in its caricature of the wealthy citizens of Rosedale (an historically affluent neighbourhood in Toronto) and in his characterization of the unique dialect of the Parry Sound rural dweller. The outrageous wit of the Canadian Air Farce and more recently the Newfoundland-based humourists who make up the cast of the CBC show *This Hour Has 22 Minutes* has an influence beyond the expected because its satirical ruminations and acid pinpricks inflicted on self-important political figures is carried out without malice or mercy. Indeed, even the monarchy is lampooned in good taste! Certainly, such a capacity to see the lightness in human affairs is an attribute that should be nurtured and enhanced in this all-too-serious world and given more attention in our classrooms.

Without an experience of looking through these windows, young people can never understand themselves as Canadians. Although it is not a "hand over the heart during the national anthem" patriotism that we expect to see or would wish to encourage, an effective arts-based education program would be a strategy to achieve an understanding of the dynamic of togetherness. It could develop the collective pride and sense of involvement that encourages a people to accept the call to do great things both in support of their own and future generations' needs and those of people all over the world. Otherwise, our children become merely pawns in the global game of economic domination by the corporate giants that have been unleashed and left unrestrained either by elected governments or responsible international agencies.

Such an expectation demands an integrated, rather than fragmented, approach to both the arts and culture. Only in this way can the full spectrum of cultural reality be exposed and passed on to new generations, ensuring that there will be a flood of artists who will identify our needs and inspire our purpose. The arts thus become central to our understanding of what we are trying to achieve in the world. Canada is dealing with the results of the overconsumption which has dominated the behaviour of all industrial nations for most of the last half of the 20th century. We are now enduring a period of fiscal punishment, undeserved as it may be. However, Canada has been more egalitarian, more equity-oriented in its approach to public need, as a result of the historic influence of peoples whose role in North American society predates the arrival of Europeans. Not to understand our own culture may lead to the adoption of shortsighted fiscal fixes which have attracted the elites of other countries and may be a cure worse than the disease. It could result in the adoption of inappropriate measures that weaken the very fabric of a nation's culture, thereby courting dismemberment of the very essence of the jurisdiction it purports to be saving. A schooling system that fails to honour the memory of national achievement undermines all capacity to collectively find a sense of identity and, with it, legitimate answers to the questions posed on all sides.

Both English- and French-speaking Canada are passing through this valley of shattered hopes. The only sane course is one that recognizes the common experiences and values that have been at the heart of the French-English relationship over the centuries. To be diverted by international financial interests, whose solutions have little flexibility to accommodate the particular style that Canadians have built into their culture, is to ensure failure. Fiscal responsibility is only one of many values that must make up the Canadian response to economic distress and uncontrolled government deficit. Ensuring that a basic minimum response to health, education, and housing is central to any re-ordering of the nation's priorities, is paramount within the Canadian cultural context. Thus, Pierre Berton's examination of the 1930s depression becomes as essential to the appreciation of Canada's culture as his description of the building of the CPR. Canadian Ronnie Burkett's Theatre of Marionettes 1995 production of *Tinka's New Dress* is a reminder that any society is but a hair's breadth from totalitarianism when social problems appear to be overwhelming democratic processes. A night in the theatre watching the manipulation of wooden puppets becomes a moment of truth at a time of community crisis when decades of achievement are at risk. Burkett's performance moved young people in his audience, but also offered an introduction to the making and presenting of puppets in a context which allows them to express our individual and collective despair.

Canada must face the challenges of the '90s as a very different country than the one which survived the Depression and war of the '30s and '40s. Every decision must be made in a diverse, multicultural context, and this draws upon the strength of the arts in a particularly focussed way. It was back in the '70s that I was asked by the chairman of Metropolitan Toronto, Paul Godfrey, to explore a gathering storm of racial conflict in the City of Toronto. Much to the distress of citizens and their political representatives, newcomers from East Asia, particularly India and Pakistan, were being harassed and beaten in the city's subways. On only one or two occasions were there serious injuries, but the number of minor incidents of assault were alarmingly numerous.

The obvious and immediate problem of subway security was quickly dealt with — greater police supervision, emergency telephone lines in stations, and alarm strips in subway cars — leading to a dramatic lessening of subway violence. In other areas of society there were obvious shortcomings in our response to the immigration of visible minorities. It was clear that social workers and teachers did not understand or even recognize the extent of the tension that permeated the city, even as children of East Asian parents were beaten in the playground and chased home after school. Most serious was the lack of understanding by the police that many of these newcomers had very different expectations of support from the defenders of law and order, support that was impossible in a civil libertarian society. As well, some minority leaders had an understandable fear of the police as a result of their treatment by authorities in other cultures prior to their arrival in Canada.

In short, there was a culture gap that had to be bridged. There were a few young males who were violently acting out what they perceived to be the prejudices of the people around them. Canada, like every country, has a thread of racism that emerges when long-established residents feel some discomfort. It was now a matter of finding ways whereby the acceptance that Canadian culture had traditionally accorded to newcomers could be marshalled in support of those in the last wave, more difficult perhaps because these Canadians were visible minorities whose clothes, religious customs, and food preparations were often very different. The fact was that large numbers of people had been encouraged to come from East Asia and the Caribbean and there was little preparation for the inhabitants of neighbourhoods in which new immigrants tended to concentrate. Many citizens were baffled by and fearful of what seemed to be a major change in the makeup of the city's population.

One of the best defences against prejudice was found to be that of changing the attitudes of children and adolescents through a strong arts education program that used drama to reveal the presence and intensity of racial conflict, that warned of the results of ignoring or trivializing the impact of racial tension and, most important, that recognized the racism that exists in every one of us. Toronto discovered that differences of musical expression and dance in the many ethnic groups coming to the city could assist in overcoming the fear of losing personal identity, which is at the root of all racism. The design and colour of the contrasting clothing can be explored in a visual arts context that includes the celebration of the richness and texture of fabric that comes from other lands and cultures. Schools and boards developed essential programs which celebrated the gathering of ethnic richness and variety, and other institutions, such as Harbourfront Centre, which became Toronto's magnificent host for multicultural events on the shore.of Lake Ontario, contributed to the process of revealing the glories of the cultures from which these minorities had come. Dance, music, drama, food, and crafts all blended into an argument for revelation rather than revulsion, acceptance rather than angry rejection. And Caribana, an annual outdoor celebration of Caribbean costume, music, and food, has become a symbol of togetherness and community acceptance for the people who have come to Canada from the many islands in that part of the world.

⌘   ⌘   ⌘

Michael Ignatieff outlines the dilemma of modern nationalism in the final paragraph of his book *Blood and Belonging*:

> What's wrong with the world is not nationalism itself. Every people must have a home, every such hunger must be assuaged. What's wrong is the kind of nation, the kind of home that nationalists want to create and the means they use to seek their ends. A struggle is going on wherever I went between those who still believe that a nation should be a home to all, and that race, colour, religion and creed should be no bar to belonging, and those who want their nation to be home only to their own.[6]

It is the peculiar role of the arts to deal with the dichotomy of supporting the need of children and adults to have pride in their own past and to develop a confidence that comes from such pride, while providing bridges between that culture and the one they have come to be a part of. No small task, but one engaging the efforts of hundreds of teachers every day. In the excitement of sound, colour, form, word, and movement, these bridges have been built in our classrooms, and it is here that an integrated arts-based curriculum could create new images of national unity, new concepts of togetherness, and new understanding about tolerance of difference and mutual respect for cultural variety.

Learning for the 21st century must recognize the variety of peoples who will make up the Canadian mosaic, but, just as important, must serve the cause of international understanding if global crises — political, economic, or environmental — are to be avoided. Arts education and global education converge as the central challenge for teachers and school systems in the turbulent '90s.

James Lynch outlines the knowledge, attitudes, values, and skills that provide the basic structure for a curriculum that introduces students to the variety and complexity of a world that can be either frightening or exciting in the most positive sense. Lynch states as a primary goal the provision of "awareness of similarities and differences of human beings, their values, locations, languages, beliefs, styles of life and political institution."[7] Without a clear grasp of the ways that people express these "similarities and differences" through music, drama, visual arts, and dance, such an exploration can only result in an inadequate understanding and appreciation.

One of the most disconcerting aspects of a world of such contrasting examples of wealth and poverty is the representation of people from underdeveloped countries through pictures of the bloated bellies of the hungry and the sad faces of the diseased, without any balancing image of a people with a rich culture, a glorious literature, and a spirituality that theologian Matthew Fox believes should be the envy of the overdeveloped countries. As long as children and the young judge the worth of people on the basis of economic power, then real understanding is impossible. The injection of artistic, aesthetic values can foster an appreciation of the cultures of these lesser-developed countries, eradicating stereotypes while broadening knowledge and experience. In the fall of 1995, Harbourfront Centre brought together a program that revealed the challenges faced by contemporary Japanese artists, designers, photographers, dancers, actors, and musicians. All the 19th-century images of traditional Japanese arts were brought into question and we were able to discern the conflicting values that a modern nation on the Pacific Rim must address. It will now be easier for Canadian citizens to interpret and understand the Japanese stance on a myriad of confrontational issues which will emerge to shape that part of the globe and will affect Canada as a Pacific Rim country.

It is important to know much about the climate and geography, and thus the economy, of far-off lands whose people share the erosion of environmental health on this fragile planet. While much of this factual information can be stored and accessed on the Internet, cultural differences lead to very different responses to environmental crises and these must be comprehended if we are to share any common solutions. Cultural literacy must be the basis of any transformation that will enable us to see the connectedness of Canadian and world citizenship in any multilateral efforts to overcome planetary problems.

Global education makes the whole question of the environment central. However, environmental attitudes that lead to responsible behaviour essentially stem from the most deeply spiritual values. Those who believe as Matthew Fox that only an acceptance of creation spirituality can save our future, are harking back to aboriginal attitudes toward the earth. The oneness with nature to be found in the oral traditions and writings of native people throughout the world becomes a central strategy for nurturing the planet.

Modern technology's threat to democratic institutions is also a worldwide phenomenon. Artists were the first to sense the danger, and although many were prepared to express their ideas through technological arts, the computer's damage to the human psyche has been a theme for many years. Artists, above all others, are conscious of walking the line of public tolerance. Indeed the issue is an extension of William Morris's efforts to warn his generation, in the 19th century, that overreliance on the machine could threaten the aesthetic sensibilities of the English populace.

Engaged at every turn in spotlighting the hypocrisy and the heartlessness of modern life, the artist depends on democratic institutions as a defence against those who would silence dissent and banish dissenters. Global education recognizes the essential necessity of understanding the many forms of governance that can emerge from the variety of traditions that encompass all the nations on earth. However, the commitment to human values and the integrity of the human spirit emerges as a theme that must pervade all these forms of political activity.

Canada has not escaped the shame of racism. Our treatment of the Japanese during World War II, and our heartless refusal to respond to the plight of Jews fleeing Nazi atrocities before that war, indicate that Canadians have no monopoly on virtue and civilized behaviour. However, in comparative terms, for a country that has invited more people from more varied cultures to share its citizenship than any other, the extent of racial conflict has been demonstrably lower than one might expect. This should not be a matter of arrogant pride, but it is a place to begin the process that will make it possible for Canadians to continue the quality of performance on the world stage that has led to this nation's role as a peacekeeper and a force for international understanding.

The challenge is to enlist the enormous artistic energy that abounds in the cause of providing children with a learning experience that celebrates creativity of the past and present, thereby encouraging a pride in Canadian cultural achievement. From this knowledge, children can acquire the confidence to confront the questions of identity which erode national unity and, from a base of strengthened self-realization, can reach out to a disconcerting world.

NOTES

1. Michael Ignatieff, *Blood and Belonging* (Toronto: Viking/Penguin Books Canada, 1993), p. 7.
2. R.H. Thomson, *Toronto Free Press*, program of the Toronto Free Theatre Vol. 2, No. 2, January 1988.
3. John Ralston Saul, *The Unconscious Civilization: The 1995 Massey Lectures* (Concord, Ont.: House of Anansi Press, 1995), p. 90.
4. Tom Henighan, *The Presumption of Culture* (Vancouver: Raincoast Book Distribution Ltd., 1996), p. 19.
5. Vince Steile, "Lighthearted Strategy Draws Young People to Serious Art," *The Chronicle of Philanthropy*, May 30, 1996, p. 12.
6. Ignatieff, p. 189.
7. James Lynch, *Multicultural Education in a Global Society* (London, New York, Philadelphia: Falmer Press, 1989), p. 22.

Chapter 7

The Arts and the Abundant Life

Poetry makes reverence happen;
It comes with the coming alive;
It speaks to our condition.

Patrick Lawlor

I t has been many centuries since a Greek philosopher observed that the unexamined life is not worth living. Being human includes the capacity to reflect and judge the quality of the life one is living and the meaning of that life experience in its totality. Learning to die elegantly and confidently would be another way of describing the purpose of a life well lived.

The arts have always been perceived as a path to deeper understandings about the quality of life on earth. Countless plays, poems, paintings, musical compositions, and particularly stories have explored the complexity of knowing something beyond the obvious about why we are here and the significance of this fact as we face the unknowable future. United Church Minister Dr. Lillian Perigoe has observed, "Stories outlive systems of philosophy and armies of power. Stories of evil, stories of love: they are the way we know our God. Our tears drop into them; our terrors and our dreams flow through them." The philosopher and theologian Herbert O'Driscoll has commented that certain words are creeping back into usage in our modern world. He identifies "meaning," "values," "ethics," and particularly "spirituality" as terms which have been discounted in the recent past but are now receiving increased attention. It is reassuring to know that composers, authors, and visual artists have never been at a distance from these concepts. Donn Downey's front-page article on the death of Robertson Davies in the December 4, 1995, *Globe and Mail* calls Davies' novel *Fifth Business* a turning point in his literary career. "In *Fifth Business*, Mr. Davies had the audacity to use as his subjects nothing less than Good and Evil, guilt, atonement, and moral responsibility." These elements of a reflective nature became touchstones of his work for the rest of his life. Often the perception that artists are out of step with the modern world comes as a result of their preoccupation with these basic concerns in the process of understanding life.

Certainly the great works of philosophy and theology have provided guidance on the satisfying life that seems to elude so many people. The arts down the centuries have also been very much connected to this human desire to find the ultimate truth about life and death. The earliest cave paintings have a mystical otherworldliness about them that transcends their depiction of animal and human form. Drama, as a form of expression, came from religious rituals found in the civilization of Greece and before. Gods and goddesses abound among the magnificent sculptures from that era that fill our museums and galleries. Indeed, it is this overwhelming sense of the eternal significance of the objects in our galleries and museums which brings us back to their doors again and again. It is this desire to connect young people to those artifacts of previous generations' consideration of the divine which drives the efforts to make an arts-based learning experience central to the education of our young.

For many centuries after the fall of the Roman Empire, virtually all art in Europe was religious, as churches sought to find some way of making the stories of the Bible vivid and moving for the many who could neither read nor write. The great names of these years — Da Vinci, Raphael, Titian, and Michelangelo in Italy, and later Velázquez, El Greco, Murillo, Ribera, and Zuberan in Spain — remind us of the extraordinary skill and commitment these artists brought to their religious expression. In Canada, one cannot but be reminded of the intense and passionate manifestations of William Kurelek's less orthodox religious thought.

In the world of visual arts, it is very difficult to divide the sacred from the secular. George Santayana describes this proximity in unyielding prose:

> All invention is tentative, all art experimental, and to be sought, like salvation, with fear and trembling. There is a painful pregnancy in genius, a long incubation and waiting for the spirit, a thousand rejections and future birthpangs, before the wonderful child appears, a gift of the gods, utterly undeserved and inexplicably perfect.[1]

Of course, the musical life of a community in Europe and the British Isles took place almost entirely in the church and the cathedral. The legacy of J.S. Bach is the pinnacle of achievement of countless organists, singers, and instrumentalists who today contribute to the world of religious music. Throughout the ages, the greatest composers — Haydn, Mozart, Beethoven, Berlioz, Mendelssohn, Dvorák, Copland, and Bernstein — have used their genius to express their most profound thoughts about life and death, often making use of the Roman Catholic mass as an inspirational starting point. Indeed, it was Igor Stravinsky who opined the diminishing impact of the religious on the music of our time:

> How poorer we are without the sacred musical services, without the Masses, the Passions, the round-the-calendar cantatas of the Protestants, the motets and sacred concerts and vespers of so many others. These are not merely defunct forms but parts of the musical spirit in disuse. . . .[2]

Yet the musical calendar of any city in Canada would not be complete without a Christmas rendering of Handel's "Messiah," and Bach's St. Matthew and St. John's Passions are becoming features of the religious life at the Easter season in many communities. Could it be the effect of the vast landscape on a meagre population, or the ubiquitous tradition of the British Empire, that has led so many Canadian composers to create great choral music? Healey Willan, Godfey Ridout, Imant Raminsch, Srul Irving Glick, Derek Holman, Ruth Watson Henderson, Nancy Telfer, Eleanor Daley, Louis Applebaum, Harry Somers, Victor Davies, and Harry Freedman are but a few who have worked within the Judeo-Christian music tradition. That this explosion of creative activity should have taken place in a frontier society so recently plunged into an essentially secular industrial economy is surely a marvel.

Music may be "useless," but its presence on the Canadian landscape, transplanted to be sure from the 19th-century English landscape of passion for large-scale choral music, has been a source of inspiration, a context for serious philosophical reflection and the basis for the very earliest artistic organizational. Both the Mendelssohn Choir in Toronto and the Bach-Elgar Choir in Hamilton can look back over a century of singing the central repertoire of the Christian faith.

Dance may not have been as prominent in the Christian tradition (though it was strong and vibrant in the Jewish influence on both Catholic and Protestant church life), but Eastern religions have emphasized this form of approach to the Divine with particular effect. The experience of watching Anjali (Anne Marie Gaston), a Canadian who has been trained in East Indian dancing and has been a pioneer in presenting performances across the continent, is moving proof of the impact of body movement on the state of the soul of both performer and audience. In recent days, dance has reached the sanctuaries of more traditional churches and cathedrals. For many years, David Earle, the gifted co-founder of the Toronto Dance Theatre, has been choreographing his dance to the music of major religious choral works, providing spiritual insights that words cannot express. Both the Fauré and Mozart requiems have been presented in the context of a full communion service. Patricia Beatty, a dancer and another co-founder of the Toronto Dance Theatre, has choreographed and presented a full evening of mystical feminist contemplation which she calls "Dancing the Goddess," complete with ceremonial opening and closing. The images and movements of her choreography reflect the religious life of both Cretan and Minoan culture, as well the Jewish contribution to Christian spiritual roots.

Allan Bloom makes a point which may be unresearched but reveals a prejudice shared by a vast number of people whose personal experience points in a similar direction:

> For all of this, the novelist or poet can make claim for being very well placed. He is above all a skilled observer of human beings without any necessary prior commitment to a theory. Everything, of course, depends upon how good his eyes are, but serious artists are likely to be choice human beings. They take seriously what they see and are, in a profound sense, phenomenologists.[3]

Ultimately, there is no more personal and private question that we are forced to contemplate daily than "Am I living the most abundant and most satisfying life there can be for me?" If young people cannot face such a query, then our educational system is in deep trouble, and the development of the drug culture and a tradition of violence in North America and throughout Europe and Asia are indications of the despair in the minds of so many people. I believe that the creative artist has less trouble with this question than those of us who have not adequately explored this essential aspect of our humanity. Jean Cocteau, in his book *The Process of Inspiration*, states it well:

> These unknown forces work deep within us, with the aid of the elements of daily life. . .and when they burden us and oblige us to conquer the kind of somnolence in which we indulge ourselves like invalids who try to prolong dream and dread resuming contact with reality, in short when the work that makes itself in us and in spite of us demands to be born, we can believe that this work comes to us from beyond and is offered us by the gods.[4]

The committed life of the artist is a source of wonder in a materialist and security-obsessed world. In a way, artists are the last missionaries, visionaries who are prepared to give up creature comfort that their manifest talents could attain in order to command the dizzying heights of artistry, whether as composers, choreographers, playwrights, painters, novelists, actors, or performers.

There is a new enthusiasm for creative spirituality, a perception of the world and ourselves that its most prominent advocate, Matthew Fox, would suggest goes far back into our prehistory. Its revival has great significance for the arts and the artist:

> To encounter creation spirituality is like opening a jungle path that has been long covered with thick-rooted plants and bramble. Creation spirituality is an ancient tradition, the oldest tradition in this land for it is the

> spiritual heritage of Native Americans. It is also the basic heritage of native peoples everywhere, the Celtic peoples of Ireland, Scotland, Wales, and the Rhineland in Germany and the native peoples of Africa and Asia, of the Polynesian islands and New Zealand, or of the aboriginals of Australia. All these peoples had cosmology as the basis of their worship, prayer, economics, politics, and morality. All of them honoured the artist in all persons. All expected the divine to burst out of anyplace at anytime. To see the world this way is to be creation centred.[5]

Sculptor Henry Moore put it even more dramatically to Harry Rasky in a CBC program about the spritual roots of his work. "All art has its roots in the primitive or it becomes decadent," stated this famous British artist, whose most important collection of works can be found in Toronto's Art Gallery of Ontario.

Matthew Fox outlines his concept of the artistic force as a form of spiritual self-examination:

> Creativity is not about painting a picture or producing an object; it is about wrestling with the demons and angels in the depths of our psyches and daring to name them, to put them where they can breathe and have space and we can look at them. This process of listening to our images and birthing them allows us to embrace our "enemies" — that is, the shadow side of ourselves — as well as to embrace our biggest visions and dreams.[6]

Thus, the arts become the path to spirituality not only for artists but for those whose attention is drawn to its various manifestations. "Wonder" and "mystery" are not words that fall easily from the mouths of modern men and women. We have come to believe that a scientific age would exclude these concepts as the laws of science are discovered and less and less can be attributed to the supernatural. However, we are realizing that as humankind explores space, there is a sense that we know less rather than more when the vastness of many universes breaks through our consciousness. Awe and wonder take on new meaning. It is through the arts that young people can become familiar and comfortable with the idea that all is not revealed, that there is mystery both in nature and in human relationships that must be respected. Increasing every child's and youth's sensitivity to these not-easily-answered questions must be an objective of arts-based learning.

There was a time when the local church, synagogue, or mosque was expected to ensure that young people confronted these issues that are the foundation of building a good life experience. However, as diminishing congregations testify to the erosion in the role of the traditional religious community, as the religions of materialism, consumerism, and self-indulgence become universal, it is clear that children can become youths and adults without ever addressing the most obvious of moral questions. The school, as the single, common, institutional meeting-place, is the most likely venue for such discussion.

Yet, attention to the spiritual and moral must be accomplished without offending the sensibilities of students who come from families espousing a variety of religious traditions. The first reaction of the careful or insecure teacher is that of avoiding all reference to these matters if possible, or to bring discussion of moral and spiritual issues to a level of meaningless commonality that provides neither insight nor sustenance. The best teacher realizes that these issues must be addressed if a truly educated person is to emerge from these years of schooling. Many of these paragons discover that in the contemplation of visual arts, in the singing and playing of great music, in the engagement of making of drama, students confront these overriding issues in a context that avoids the religious and cultural trappings that lead to predictable conflicts and humiliations in the classroom. The integrated arts-based curriculum is an invitation to explore the most profound matters of the mind and spirit — not only in terms of the various arts expressions, but in the context of other disciplines as well.

Most of the students who come through our schools will make their living in business and industry, in academe, or in the social service sector. If the job-destroying impact of technology and the global preoccupation with reducing employment both in the private sector and government continue, many will likely turn to a third sector devoted to serving both people and nature — or they will join the ranks of the unemployed. In some cases, they may not have the daily excitement of creative activity and the moments of reflection and contemplation that "good" work brings with it. However, the arts, certainly for creators and participants, but even for audience members, provide those mountaintop spiritual experiences that make life a constant adventure. One night, at a Toronto Symphony concert, the Canadian actress Martha Henry was appearing as the narrator in a performance of Leonard Bernstein's *Kaddish* symphony. She kicked off her shoes, dropped the score to the floor in front of her, and proceeded to rail and scream at the patent unfairness of the divine. "Do I have your attention, majestic Father. . . . You know who I am. . .and you let this happen, Lord of Hosts? You with your manna, your pillar of fire? You ask for faith: where is your own?. . . Tin god, Your bargain is tin! It crumples in my hand!" The entire auditorium was seized with the intense confrontation of Creator and created. There seemed scarcely enough oxygen in the hall to supply an audience teetering on the edge of emotional upheaval.

In 1986, Lotfi Mansouri directed the Canadian Opera Company in a performance of Poulenc's *Dialogues of the Carmelites*, an unrelentingly powerful examination of fear, both of life and death. The paralyzing terror of death was portrayed magnificently by Maureen Forrester as the old prioress about to succumb, but the triumph of Blanche (sung by another Canadian, Irene Welhasch) — a woman brought up to dread everything about life and who overcomes all her fears, both of truly living and courageously dying, to face the reality of the guillotine — became a searing revelation of what an artistic experience can offer an audience filled with similar apprehensions.

It was from the distance of a spectator that I came to the arts. I find that so much of my delight in life revolves around music, theatre, dance and ballet, and film. It is true that part of my joy is found in making music — but only as an amateur in the full sense of that word. The thrill of being a thoughtful and reflective watcher, listener, viewer — these are the joys of artistic pleasure for me. Probably my friends and acquaintances would not be perceived as "average" (whose are in this day of wild differentiation of belief and lifestyle?), but I believe that people who are participants in the world of the arts have fuller and more meaningful lives, enhanced by the sense of well-being that infuses their conversation and increases the contribution they make to their community.

⌘ ⌘ ⌘

Individuals have found many ways of occupying their discretionary time. Bumper stickers inform me that people would rather be sailing, skiing, running — a host of physical activities that I both enjoy and encourage my best friends to indulge in. The old adage of an active mind in a healthy body still holds true. However, every study of time usage, for North Americans at least, indicates that sitting before a television set is by far the most pervasive preoccupation of our society.

I concede that the arts are in a sense at the centre of good television. In Canada, we have the Vision Network, committed to both spiritual and artistic values, and we have the CBC, which at its best can produce quality television. In Ontario, we have TVOntario, an educational television network that is the envy of most jurisdictions in North America and beyond, winning countless awards for excellence. But the statisticians reveal that most eyes are trained on the lowest common denominator of prime-time watching, the sitcom, which is — with its repetitiveness, its stereotyping, its predictable plots — the antithesis of what we regard as the core of arts integrity. Those who watch television indiscriminately do not, in my experience, light up with delight at the mention of their predilection. It is considered mere entertainment, an often time-filling, passive, and mind-numbing activity that may provide a momentary escape from the pressures of real life, but fails to excite, inform, or inspire.

As Tom Henighan observes in his recent examination of the state of Canadian culture:

> Let us be brutally accurate and reflect the real (if mostly unacknowledged) experience of most viewers. Television viewing is never a creative act; it is a lethargy-inducing habit, which removes us from actual learning and from the body. . . . Television creates a kind of median consciousness; it slightly raises the awareness level of the deprived, while lowering that of the more fortunately endowed. . . . It conveys no important human experience accurately and well, offering no sense of the world in which we live and on which we are dependent; it is hopelessly superficial at conveying ideas and even information.[7]

When television does seek to be intellectually challenging, the number of viewers declines. The reason is that the medium was monopolized by the marketplace in North America and has never recovered from that initial transaction, in spite of the efforts of public and educational networks to raise the expectation of viewers. It may be the nature of the medium itself, with its small screen that trivializes every activity, its constant search for dramatic mini-bites, its frantic changes of direction and image to cater to short attention spans, but the last object one would want on a desert island would be a connected television set in working order.

My own life experience has not been unusual for an individual brought up in the Christian faith (though involved with at least three separate denominations of mainline church activity) and influenced by an essentially British tradition (both parents being recent immigrants from the "old country"). Throughout my youth I lived in a very Anglo-Saxon neighbourhood in a largely Protestant Anglo-Saxon city, governed by adherents of the Loyal Orange Order. Most of my childhood was spent in Canada, and as one might expect I grew up with a colonial mind and spirit. A series of events — World War II, and, later, a growing family and intense educational pursuits — deprived both my wife and I of "going home," that is, back to our parents' birthplaces, until well into mid-life. Yet, once in England we felt right at home. Our Canadian educational system had ensured that we were properly inoculated against any erosion of our "Britishness." On one occasion we were taken to a "Last Night at the Proms" concert in southwest England, by a group of friends who were surprised to find that we knew all the words to Parry's "Jerusalem" and Elgar's "Land of Hope and Glory." The Ontario education system of the '30s and '40s had done its job.

My parents rarely attended plays or concerts but had an interest in the arts and were determined that their only son should be made aware of the arts' existence. Thus, piano lessons came early in life and continued into the teenage years. My mother and father both sang in a church choir and encouraged me to join while still an adolescent. That turned out to be an important influence, not because of any great interest in choral music manifesting itself in a very modest, working-class congregation, but because, at the end of World War II, there was an extraordinary availability of fine musicians, who, now that the conflict was ended, were studying at the Faculty of Music in the University of Toronto and at the Royal Conservatory in the same city and were available for hire by small churches. As a result, I received an introduction to the traditional choral repertoire that has served me well through the years.

As a child I had enjoyed some experience of ensemble singing in elementary school. I can remember with delight singing in a boys' choir which won a first prize at the Kiwanis Festival. The test piece, Handel's "Where'er You Walk," has been a favourite ever since. My nostalgia also includes a grade eight mixed choir which did not fare as well. Just days before the event, the teacher-leader withdrew the choir because she did not think it was up to her standards. I cannot bear to listen to "The Bells of Aberdovey," the test piece in that mixed-voice choir competition, without a grimace and mild curse.

At the secondary level, my interest turned to instrumental music, perhaps because my wife-to-be had a musician father who gave us tickets to the Toronto Symphony concerts. As well, we both enjoyed the "Pops" concerts in Toronto's Varsity Arena in the summer. In any case, I purchased a clarinet and joined the school orchestra, a modest ensemble that played while students seated themselves at the weekly assembly. The music was taken from a book of pieces for such orchestras, noteworthy only because every selection sounded exactly the same. Only for the annual concert was more interesting repertoire found. The conductor was a truly fine musician and science teacher, Herman Couke, who conducted the orchestra with extraordinary skill as his extracurricular contribution to school life. Through him and his successor, Karl Davidson, I discovered something of the discipline that must be endured to achieve anything in the field of orchestral presentation.

I also discovered other advantages to playing an instrument. Every spring there was an inspection of the cadet corps and a band was regard-

THE FIRST ANNUAL VISUAL ARTS AWARDS IN NORTH YORK

It is a spring evening and twilight is late. In the modern, angular secondary school, lights blaze and the sound of steel drums greets the visitor to this new initiative of the visual arts coordinator, the warm and congenial Jon Mergler. He would, of course, deny his own central role in this extravaganza, and, indeed, he is supported by a host of arts teachers, without whose commitment and capacity the event would have been impossible.

Mr. Mergler, formerly Coordinator of Visual Arts and Dance for the North York Board of Education, has been the ultimate arts education advocate, both within his own board and across the province. Some years ago, he arranged a showing of school art at the board of education offices. The trustees no doubt expected a glorious display of colourful flowers to decorate the dull and pedestrian walkways of their recently built, utilitarian Education Centre. Instead they were shocked to find bleak and stark images on canvas, dramatic slashes of brush and knife that disturbed rather than delighted. Sculptures of metal, wood, and plastic rose to the ceiling, screaming out adolescent frustration and despair. Several of the trustees were angry. Their response to the display was simplistic and predictable: "Art was

ed as essential. As this band could play or march but not do both simultaneously, it was sequestered in one corner of the athletic field, to be heard but not seen. Thus, its members were able to avoid the endless tramping about that characterized cadet training. I must confess that I never mastered the clarinet — I listen to James Campbell, a splendid Canadian virtuoso on the instrument, in abject awe. When a penniless Christmas season forced me to sell my instrument, it was no loss to the making of music in this country. It is painfully obvious that I had an inadequate arts education in elementary and secondary school, certainly not one that gave me any insight into the advantages of integrating the presentation of arts disciplines. Nor did I receive any understanding of the world through the connection of these studies and the broader selection of studies making up the public school curriculum.

My contact with the arts during my university years was lessened by the pressures of academic life and the need to find income to pay tuition fees and living costs. Thus, at a time when the golden age of Hart House Theatre was providing homegrown acting at . a level never before witnessed in Canada, I was largely unaware of the outstanding productions which featured those very people who were to launch radio drama over the CBC, initiate the theatre seasons of the Crest Theatre in North Toronto, enliven the city's world with laughter at Spring Thaw in the Museum Theatre, and make the Stratford and Shaw Festivals a reality only a decade or so later.

A year at the Ontario College of Education, a teacher-training institution for those planning to work in the secondary schools of the province, revealed that only those who were specializing in the arts could expect any training in the esoteric world of music, visual arts, or drama. As a potential history teacher, it was all politics and constitutional matters, with arts scarcely mentioned in the last few pages of textbook chapters dealing in some cases with an entire century or two of humankind's story. As a result, I deprived my students in their formative years of the knowledge that political and economic history was but a fraction of the culture they should know something of. I now realize to what extent both their and my understanding and appreciation of history and geography were the poorer for that inadequate preparation.

meant to bring delight to the eyes of the viewer. What will parents think about this exposure to the ugliness and violence that is obviously the subject of these pieces?" The argument for the integrity of the art show was made, but the trustees were not mollified. Nor were the teachers and administrators prepared to tear down this "monstrous" exhibition to satisfy their political masters. The matter of censorship rose its ugly head and tested the courage of all those responsible, especially Mr. Mergler.

But on this night, all that is forgotten. Tonight, awards for the victorious submissions of visual arts students in a range of differing media and grade levels are to be presented. The evening has the support of local businesses, who have generously endorsed both the event itself and the awards to individual students.

It is not just visual artists who are present — the entire community has been invited. After marching past the steel band playing the exotic melodies and rhythms of the Caribbean, one is confronted with a bevy of clowns gesturing toward a sumptuous feast, a table heaped with sweets unequaled in any educational gathering of my experience, revealing both a respect for the culinary arts and the generosity of the North York corporate community.

After guests view the pieces -- which fill the walls of special rooms, hallways and foyers -- they are ushered to a gymnasium, now transformed with fabric and lighting into a most attractive theatre. The following hour is filled with the music of orchestra and choir and the piano solos of an accomplished group of young performers.

The time for recognizing the artists arrives, but not before Director of Education Veronica Lacey (now Deputy Minister of the Ministry of Education and Training), a totally committed advocate of arts education, eloquently explains to the audience of parents, student artists, and businesspeople, that the arts education program is not an add-on but an integral part of her strategy for excellence and achievement on all fronts in North York schools.

However, more important for the arts educator than the artworks themselves is the element of personal revelation found in the comments accompanying each selection. The statements indicate the depth of concern over virtually every major social issue facing civilization.

The search for identity, the obsession of the teenage mentality, is exposed by a painting of a lonely figure clothed in a red jump suit and blue boots. The painter explains his image: "A portrait in pastel of a superhero. The superhero who thinks, wonders, and worries. The one who is considered an outcast yet also a saviour. The one who is mystic, powerful,

Soon after I began teaching, I moved to a smaller community in the eastern Ontario city of Peterborough. I soon found both the disadvantages and the delights of leaving the big city. A splendid little theatre (enlivened by the active participation of Robertson Davies and his wife, Brenda) made one forget the now developing theatre world of the great metropolis, though I can remember that the stories brought back by a prominent local clergyman, Barry Day, of his magnificent evenings at strangely named venues such as "Tarragon" and "TWP," aroused feelings of envy for those inhabiting such a land of cultural feasting. Though there was a community orchestra in Peterborough, one did pine for an ensemble which could scale the heights of Mahler, Bruckner, and Shostakovich, a fact that ensured that my wife and I kept our subscription to the Toronto Symphony Orchestra and braved the snow-driven hills of the highways leading to that musical experience.

It was this comparative isolation which may have led me to value the record player more than any of the many other appliances which have flooded our homes in this century. Buying records became the ultimate consumer experience for our family, and I now realize how much I imposed my classical tastes and voracious desire for full sound on a too-tolerant family who had other enthusiasms. Thus, the arts and the "good life" became synonymous in my mind, and the word "abundance" took on a cultural interpretation in my life experience.

This diversion into my own past is in the nature of a "mea culpa" as I seek to explore this most personal of issues around the good life. Connecting my perception of life's richness and joy to an indulgence in the arts may seem entirely unique and tied inexorably to my own experience. Indeed, it does say something about the relative absence of real poverty in the life of the individual who can express such an insight about those things which have satisfied him most.

At a time when food banks are increasing in number and clientele, abundance must first be related to the securing of basic needs, such as food, shelter, and, in the Western democratic model, educational and health services. But the 20th century has revealed how much wider we must extend the opportunities for a good life to all if there is to be a decent civil society in which to live and work. There is no greater wastage

and different. The one who is contemplating his life and its status."

Another artist addresses the controversy over the response of the school to homosexuality, with a photograph of two men holding hands. It is a back view, but the setting reveals a strong, supportive relationship. The observation of the artist is disturbing: "This image is very powerful to me. It is hardly ever seen where two men or two women are holding hands. What I found amusing was that these men can only feel safe holding hands in a small community where they are accepted. That is where I took the picture. If they were somewhere else they would probably be risking their lives."

The role of gender is examined by a male artist who produced a large sculpture of a female figure hung on wood. The artistry that created such an icon, entitled simply "She," is obviously mature. The sculptor reflects with sardonic humour: "Although men and women are becoming equal these days, there are still a lot of women still under men's control. Some of them even think they are born to be weaker than men. Set them free!"

A female artist addresses the same problem and, using the inspiration of Modigliani, has produced "The Carytid," in which a ceiling descends on a stereotypical female figure. The artist's intention is to "raise the viewer's consciousness. I did not paint out of hatred but rather to inform…to educate our young to ensure a better future."

A splendid life-drawing of a nude figure depicts the loneliness experienced by every young person. Although the grace and line of the body are both strongly outlined, the artist was obviously more concerned with the soul of the model and how it mirrored her own feelings. She states, "To me, it [the particular pose] represents those times when you are alone and surrounded by your own silence.... One tends to think about the worries and anxieties that disturb us...represented by the dark ink on the negative space...and tends to mix the colours on her body." Surely, this is a young woman whose brush is connected to both her emotions and her intellect.

This same young artist painted a still life which included a doll clothed in the costume of an Andean native surrounded by other cultural clues. She expresses an ancient truth, that through the arts we come to know cultures different from our own, but more important, we come to understand. "This piece represents my culture. I was born in Argentina and even though we lived in the city, my family became interested in the native culture, music, and costumes. We began to appreciate all this to the point that it became a part of us."

"Joyce" is a traditional depiction of a life-drawing model. But to the artist, it reveals a spectrum of attributes that infuse the work. The

than empty seats in theatres and concert halls. It is scandalous when actors and musicians, able and willing to express their genius before multitudes of people who would find joy and inspiration, find that opportunities are restricted because those very people are unaware that such satisfaction awaits them and have not the financial resources to attend.

This is particularly true as we reach the end of this century of materialism which has deemed the job and its income and possible security as the most significant element in achieving the good life. It can certainly be proven that the industrial system has prospered a greater number than the agricultural industry economy. Indeed, the justification for capitalism has been that creating more rich would ultimately benefit those less well-off. The trickle-down theory has many devotees to this day, indeed it could be called the basic rationale for the neo-conservatism inspired by Ronald Reagan and Margaret Thatcher. Certainly, there are more very rich, measured by the number of millionaires in North America. As well, the prosperity of the '50s and '60s encouraged an effective trade union movement which raised the wages of those working on the line to the level of the lower echelons of the professions. If one adds the surge of income increase within the professions (doctors, lawyers, and teachers) to the unionized worker and the small retail and service business community, one is impressed by the pervasiveness of the "middle class." Any poll indicates that most people think of themselves as members of the middle class, though the income of those at the upper levels of that "middle" might be many times that of those at the lower levels.

However, the '90s have called into question some of the assumptions generally held by most people. The degree to which all nations have been living above their means is now measurable in terms of the debt load carried by each. Some would pinpoint the cause as the cost of the defence industry during the protracted Cold War, while others (wrongheadedly, on the basis of all the available statistics) would single out the system of social services which have eroded the old values, both for government and the individual, of saving for the future, buying when one had the money and borrowing only in crisis. Lately, more attention has been given to the role of the main financial institutions fashioned after World War II —

artist speculates, "In the life-drawing classroom, models come and go, rarely leaving more than a fleeting impression of their three dimensionality. 'Joyce' is a faceless figure because of her quiet presence and timidness. The delicate and rich colours are used to describe her graceful and soft-spoken demeanour."

A face in torment sculpted in wood is the offering of a woman from a family recently arrived from the Middle East. Called "My Family," it reveals the enormous difficulty that family units experience as they move into a totally alien culture. The effect? One brother is depicted "lonely and cold [as] he recoils from direct communication." The other brother the artist describes as "confused with a constantly changing identity." The work expresses all the pain that words cannot begin to expose.

In another piece, seemingly overwhelming societal problems are represented in paint, photograph, and sculpture in such a way that their meaning is palpable. A weathered board acquired from a larger structure gives the piece its name: "The Bridge". On this piece of wood are placed fragmented photographs of the glories of untainted nature. The artist says, "I tried to express man's struggle in understanding nature as it is seen in the world. I entitled it 'The Bridge' to show the gap between man and understanding nature."

Another artist addresses the threat of environmental disaster more directly. In "Death of Man," a vibrant, muscular figure steps into a polluted landscape and emerges in skeletal form. The piece seeks to shock the viewer to contemplate the "horrors of living in a polluted world" and asks the poignant question: "What will be left for the next generation?"

The question of mercy-killing led one artist to use the image of the syringe and bodies falling into oblivion to state his total opposition to this solution for an unacceptable life experience. Rather than dwell on the issues of suicide or assisted death, the painter speaks of his artistry: "I have painted in the style of Francis Bacon. His work appealed to me because of the unbearable tension between the shocking violence of his vision and the luminous beauty of his brushwork."

It matters little who wins an award this evening. What happened in the months preceding is stunningly revealed. A significant number of young people have been inspired to express through their own creativity their awareness of humanity's battered lives and a planet at risk.36

the World Bank and the International Monetary Fund. Many feel the policies of these institutions, coordinated through the central banks of every nation in arrangement with the actions of transnational corporations, have created a world in which every country is burdened with debt and in which the gap between rich and poor countries, and the rich and poor people within them, has widened. Whatever the interpretation of the causes of the crisis that has dominated the '90s, this preoccupation with fiscal responsibility has undermined one of the major responses, that of using government to create jobs directly, thereby incurring further national debt if necessary in order to heat up the economy.

Full-time employment is much less an expected style of career development than ever before. Part-time, contract jobs appear to be the order of the day. Indeed, wages have decreased for many jobs, particularly those protected by the trade union movement, itself under siege as its membership plummets. The upsurge in the number of two-income families dramatically shrouded the degree to which individual incomes had eroded in the '70s and '80s. As well, the rough measurement of progress as simply the yearly addition to the GNP or GDP is now seen as a most inadequate accounting of the reality of these decades. If one were to factor in the environmental devastation, the human misery of broken families, the increase in crime rates, it would quickly become apparent that quality of life even for the richest industrial nations has declined for the majority since 1970. For this reason, many observers would like to move to such an accounting, perhaps referring to the new measure as the GPI (genuine progress indicator), as outlined in a recent highly publicized article in the American mass-circulation periodical *Atlantic Monthly*.[8]

The disparities of income and well-being between the rich northern hemisphere and the poorer countries largely found in the southern hemisphere is now reaching critical levels. If nothing else can secure the attention of the well-to-do countries, there is the fact that less-developed nations can despoil the environment sufficiently to make the planet uninhabitable. That fact, plus the capacity for any despairing group of people to turn to violence and terrorism on a global scale, with weapons unparalleled in human history in their potential destructiveness, has made us realize how small the global village is. In this context, the arts as a survival mechanism have crucial relevance, and without adequate attention to the arts in the school, they can play only a very limited role in influencing social and economic policy.

During the 19th century, the industrial system had the effect of segregating the fine arts from the popular arts, but failed to liberate the former from the power of the church and aristocracy that had dominated the development of the arts in previous centuries. Today, the poor are still not expected to be seen at the opera or the ballet, or in the art gallery. In 1992, Statistics Canada's General Social Survey included a special supplement which enabled it to collect data on the participation of Canadians in a variety of arts and culture leisure activities for the first time. The Ontario Arts Council isolated the behaviour of Ontarians in its publication "Time for the Arts: The Participation of Ontario in Arts Activities." This document dispels any false perceptions that broad access to the arts has been achieved in our society.

There is most certainly a segment of the community that enjoys all the forms of artistic expression. For example, museum and art gallery visitors are two to three times as likely than the general population to attend a performing arts event, and much more likely (69% compared to 44%) to visit a cinema. People who have attended a college or a university, a clear indicator of relative affluence, are twice as likely to visit a museum or art gallery at least once in a year, or attend a performing arts event. Annual household income is most certainly a major factor, as those whose income is greater than $60,000 per year are almost three times as likely to attend a professional performing arts event as those earning less than $30,000.

Within the 32% of the total population who, in a given year, attend any professional performing arts event and the 31% who visit a museum or art gallery, educational and income factors are most telling. Compulsory attendance at elementary and secondary school (now the common experience for virtually the entire youth population) has obviously failed to create anything close to universal interest. It is painfully clear that the fragmented experience of children in our schools has been insufficient to bring them as adults to serious music, drama, theatre, or film. If the abundant life, as expressed by contact with the arts, is closely related to both income and educational opportunity at the post-secondary level, then conclusions can be drawn about the quality of arts learning in the early years of schooling. It is a well-established fact that young people who have effective arts experiences in those early years are more likely to become both artists and arts lovers. For many of those who attend our schools this does not happen, and their lives are that much poorer in terms of their enjoyment of the arts.

Arts organizations themselves may be partly at fault. Their brochures are filled with pictures of patrons in black ties and sumptuous gowns, attending expensive banquets and dances — all in the name of fund-raising. In short, the educational and inspirational qualities of "high art" are seen, at least in these publications, to be confined to those with comparatively high incomes. Some arts organizations are counteracting this perception; for example, the Toronto Symphony Orchestra offers "casual concerts," with an invitation to "come as you are" for both performers and audience, and most fringe theatres in warehouse venues also encourage such sartorial behaviour.

In spite of these positive efforts, there is no strategy for bringing people of varied income levels and educational backgrounds joyfully together through the arts, even though it was the tax resources of all citizens that has brought about the enormous expansion in arts activity in post-World War II Canada. The expansion of support from the Canada Council and provincial arts councils, from cultural ministries at both levels over the '60s, '70s, and early '80s, and the increase of support from the private sector and municipal level in the '80s, failed to overcome this problem, at least in part because the elementary and secondary education of young people did not create a thirst for the arts which only a participatory experience could quench.

There had been the hope that if the infrastructure of performance venues and arts organizations continued to expand, the next phase of development would be that of striving for universal access. Strategies for drawing people of all cultural backgrounds, income levels, and educational experience should have been the crusade of the '90s, but bad times and the ever-present deficit and debt problems became the preoccupations of the public sector. Even the advances made in the '70s and '80s now seem in jeopardy. Indeed, it appears that even the basic needs of people are to be put at risk both within nations and between nations around the globe.

If trends continue, the good life, and the presence of the arts as its expression, will become the preserve of an even smaller percentage of the world's peoples than at present. Yet, ironically, it has been in bad times in the past that the role of the arts has increased and has been extended to reach a far wider spectrum of citizens. The Roosevelt New Deal included programs which encouraged the creation of symphony orchestras, theatre companies, even dance ensembles. It was as a result of the World War II years that the United Kingdom set up the British Arts Council. During the worst of the bombing of major cities in Britain, artists like Myra Hess had performed concerts organized in churches, galleries, and museums to raise morale. The role the arts played in the war effort led to a belief that in peacetime, particularly in the difficult rebuilding period, the arts could have a positive effect on the national psyche. The British example led to the establishment of the Canada Council and, ultimately, to provincial agencies like the Saskatchewan, Manitoba, and Ontario arts councils. The resulting surge of public support, meagre though it was in the beginning, gave the energy and resources that led to the enormous expansion of cultural activities during the '60s, '70s, and '80s in Canada.

The tragedy for the arts and artists has been that the public response has failed to keep pace with the expansion of traditional artistic activity and the variety of new arts expressions. The arts have never been able to convince the electorate of the centrality of culture to the well-being of the state and its citizens. Audiences for serious music, theatre, and dance actually went down in the early '90s — not a happy trend, whether as a result of less disposable income, the impact of home-centred electronic entertainment, or the exploding commercial arts industry as expressed, for example, in imported mega-musicals saturating the market in large urban centres to the detriment of theatres offering more modest fare. After all these years of attempting to broaden the outreach for the arts, Canadians have been unable to leap beyond the perception that the arts are about entertainment and belong in the commerical marketplace. One purpose of the "Arts Council" idea was that prices for productions or visits to museums, galleries, or films could be reduced to open the arts to a much broader spectrum of society. However, the public resources were never enough to make the arts universally accessible to the public, as we have come to expect, for example, of elementary and secondary education, health and hospital care. No one perceived such access to the arts as essential, and to that extent the teaching of the arts in schools has patently failed to place the arts high on the personal development agendas of Canadian citizens.

It may well be that the troubles predicted for the next century may bring the arts and the culture they expose into the centre of our collective consciousness. If "buying happiness" in the shopping centre and travel to exotic climes dominated the North American definition of the abundant life in the past, then the perceptions of life in the 21st century may bring a new realism to the discussion of what the good life is all about. We may see a dramatic turnaround of the worst aspects of marketplace domination of our values and a recognition that continuous economic growth is impossible on a finite planet. Jeremy Seabrook expresses the dilemma succinctly:

> In the West, the buying of things (and indeed services, experiences and sensations) has become inextricably bound up with the roots of human identity. We seek to express who we are through our purchases; and at this point, the process of buying and selling ceases to be mere mechanisms, but comes to give purpose and even meaning to our lives. What was an important aspect of

all cultures has become the universalized focus of world culture. The market economy in the West, being the dominant force in the lives of people, becomes a source, not only of well-being, but of morality; and in the absence of any other force that can match its power, it is looked to as a bringer of truth. In other words, the market economy has been not merely moralized in our time, but sanctified as it has never been before.[9]

Though the term "culture" has been little used in this commentary on arts education, one must recognize that the arts represent the way we come to know ourselves in the profoundest sense and, through that knowledge, to influence our behaviour. As the market economy in developed countries becomes increasingly less capable of providing employment and satisfaction, and as the limit of available resources to feed, clothe, and house burgeoning populations in lesser-developed lands become increasingly apparent, the transformation of society we have seen in the '90s will continue. That transformation can be negative — people may well turn to crime, violence, drugs, and alcohol abuse to assuage their personal desperation. On the other hand, the arts may become the most compelling path to personal and collective meaning, indeed may become the inspiration for forces which will reverse the last decade's globalization in the name of profits. The impact of the arts could be a significant factor in turning around a world moving toward a destructive future, but only if the arts are seen as central to our well-being as humans and as a relevant factor in the changing of public attitudes and actions. This is the ultimate challenge to those who help our children learn, to those who must learn to teach the arts in all their unifying power and their capacity to reach into every way we have of understanding the world about us. The integrated arts-based curriculum can be the tool for a society which desires a different kind of future than that predicted for the new century.

In that society, leading the good life will not simply mean having a good job and indulging in consumerism, but will involve using our time and energy in a way that best serves both our fellow humans and our mental and spiritual well-being. If limited employment and a better sharing of the results of national enterprise are the directions of the future, then the arts become a concomitant adjunct of a new cultural paradigm stretching toward greater equality and justice, toward national environmental goals that sustain the economy, toward a style of technological sharing that ends the domination of the north and the submissive stance of the southern hemisphere.

In such a culture, arts education contributes to the actual, rather than the theoretical, access to the best quality our artists are capable of producing. US educators have discovered that it is not enough to say that the very best concerts presented by the New York Philharmonic in Avery Fisher Hall are available on television if only 3% of the American population take any notice, or that the Metropolitan Opera is coming live from Lincoln Centre into American living rooms if only a fraction of the population has a level of music literacy that will allow them to enjoy it. Only when culture becomes recognized as superceding the obsessions of economics, when spiritual and mental health are considered as essential to the good of the individual and the state as physical health, will the place of the arts be assured.

It may be the special role of the arts to reveal that a more restrained lifestyle in terms of material rewards can be an opening up to both new opportunities and valued experiences that are very old in our folklore. More time for family and friends, more conversation and debate, more true intimacy and understanding — these are surely valuable assets in most people's definition of the good life. Indeed, the concept of knowing oneself and relating to the wider community is close to the reality of creativity. Carolyn Jongeward, a weaver and design artist, has expressed it clearly:

> Activities of daily living often make us lose sight of the mystery and wonder of being in the world. Yet creativity exists in everything we do, in every moment of our lives, if only we can see it this way. Essentially, creating is a way of being in the world. . .using our gifts well and acknowledging that we have something to give in return.
>
> Creating involves attending to relationships of all kinds including connecting to self and others who are close. By attending to relationships within art making, we bring something into being that reflects the extent of our openness, intimacy and responsiveness.[10]

More time for reading and writing, for drama as both creator and viewer, more opportunity to explore the treasure trove of great music, both early and contemporary, as participant and audience member are all among thinking people's resolutions for the new century. To have the time to ponder the questions which only the theologian and the philosopher have ever approached in the past is yet another aspect of the future lifestyle. These and many other manifestations of the restrained lifestyle beckon us toward a society which will be healthier — physically, mentally, and spiritually — with less conflict and violence, less litigious and more cooperative behaviour. In short, an emanation of abundance could reach out to all on earth as environmentally responsible and universally just and equitable.

Men and women in the 21st century will need access to the ways by which transformation is possible. Throughout the ages, great songs, poems, novels, and music have moved minds and hearts toward greater understanding and self-realization. They have provided the images which have impelled us to act in the best interests of ourselves and the collective. The power of the arts to arouse compassion and generosity of spirit is well recognized. There is a lesson in the fact that the "charity performance" is the most effective way of reaching the sympathy and pocketbook of the potential donor. As government resources dwindle, the term "donor" may take on a much broader meaning, as both rich, middle income, and, by Western standards, poor will have to learn how to share time, energy, and resources to an unprecedented degree. The arts will be the essential path to our understanding of ourselves and the world we live in as the cultural supercedes the economic and political definitions of our humanity. These years of transition will be fraught with wars, revolutions, and terrorism unless we can find what one philosopher described as a "moral equivalent" which will divert the energies, ambitions, and aggressiveness of humankind in more positive directions.

Individually, as well as collectively, we are engaged in a search for quality of life. Technology cannot provide us with private pleasures that have meaning, joy, ecstasy, contemplative quiet, and the creative satisfaction that signal the presence of a good life. There is reason to believe that a connection with the creative spirit that leads to the writing of poetry, music, or prose, the depiction of reality in line, colour, texture, or movement, can give special delight. The performance of the work of those who have plumbed the depths of human despair or climbed the heights of spiritual transformation provide a unique moment of personal delight. For most of us, being a reader of fine literature, a part of an audience, is how we must seek to connect with the ecstatic excitement that indicates a contact with greatness of idea or concept. This sense of involvement in the profundity that has come down through the ages provides the inspiration to make a contribution to the life of the neighbourhood, the community, and the nation, making the good life spiritually productive as well as personally satisfying.

The present arts education experience of children has not created people who have savoured life with all the intensity that we could have hoped for. The history of this century indicates that collectively we have indulged in violence and self-destructive behaviour that has characterized our age as one of enormous inhumanity, cruelty, and deprivation inflicted on a considerable proportion of the planet's inhabitants. One must believe that saturating humanity's minds with the highest thoughts and filling its eyes with the most beautiful expressions of nature and art would change that story of torment and despair.

Integrated arts-based learning must focus children's minds on those things that give life meaning and make life qualitative. Certainly, an education that provides the skill and knowledge to allow the individual to make a living and that ensures a feeling of belonging through an appreciation of a cultural heritage is valuable. However, each of us is essentially alone in what seems an indifferent, if not hostile, world. To find philosophic and spiritual comfort is a step toward a life of personal joy and collective contribution. An integrated arts-based learning experience would encourage and enhance such a journey.

NOTES
1. George Santayana, *Reason in Art*, Volume Four of *The Life of Reason* (originally published by New York: Scribner, 1905), p. 8.
2. Quoted by Kenneth Winters, *TSO Program*, January-February 1983, 38:3.
3. Allan Bloom, *Love and Friendship* (New York: Simon and Schuster, 1993), p. 263.
4. Quoted in Hugh Lytton, *Creativity and Education* (London: Routledge and Kegan Paul, 1971), p. 19.
5. Matthew Fox, *Creation Spirituality: Liberating Gifts for the Peoples of the Earth* (San Francisco: Harper, 1991), pp. 13 -14.
6. Ibid., p. 21.
7. Tom Henighan, *The Presumption of Culture* (Vancouver: Raincoast Book Distribution Limited, 1996), p. 45.
8. Clifford Cobb, Ted Halstead and Jonathon Rowe, "If The GDP Is

Up, Why Is America Down?" in *The Atlantic Monthly*, October 1995, pp. 59-78.

9. Jeremy Seabrook, *The Myth of the Market* (Montreal: Black Rose Books, 1991), p. 11.

10. Carolyn Jongeward, "Connecting With Creativity: Adult Learning Through Art Making Within a Supportive Group," unpublished Ed.D. Thesis, University of Toronto, 1995, p. 180.

Chapter 8 **Integrating The Arts —
Integrating the Curriculum**

If you want to know what is going on in the world you
have to ask the artist as well as the technician and the
scientist.

Marshall McLuhan

One of the films nominated for an Academy Award in 1995 was *Mr. Holland's Opus*, the story of a composer of classical music who could not support himself in his chosen vocation and in desperation became a high school music teacher. The film did not win the Academy Award as best picture, nor should it have. It was a typical, Hollywood-style, manipulative tear-jerker. Only Richard Dreyfuss's performance merited attention. However, it did portray the power of the arts — music in particular — to engage young people, capture their commitment, give them confidence and pride of achievement, and prepare them for challenges beyond the classroom.

Ironically, *Mr. Holland's Opus* did have an immediate impact.

Dreyfuss became a cult hero, appearing on television talk shows where he made highly emotional appeals to school officials to encourage the expansion of arts education programs. For all its faults, *Mr. Holland's Opus* placed arts education on the agenda of school boards across that nation, at least for a few months.

However, there were already signs that pockets of quality arts programs were being developed in American schools. In the first few years of the '90s, some 20 collaborative ventures could be identified, Cleveland's Initiative for Cultural Arts in Education, Chicago's Arts Partnership in Education, North Carolina's A+ Schools Program, and San Francisco's Arts Education Funders' Collaborative being the most prominent. All had a component of arts instruction with an emphasis on effective learning across the whole curriculum.

In December 1993, American philanthropist Walter Annenberg announced a $500-million Challenge to the Nation to be funded through the Annenberg Foundation. Proposals were invited that supported "the unique role of the arts, culture and technology in accelerating and expanding school reform efforts and helping children succeed in school." In December 1995, it was announced that the Galef Institute had been granted a $10-million challenge grant to administer a new program, The Arts, Culture and Technology Initiative, promising to show, based on its research, "that one of the most powerful ways to keep children motivated to learn and raise their levels of academic achievements is to use the arts and technology as tools for learning. Children are fully engaged when music, drama, visual arts, literature, and the full range of media and communications technology are integrated into all aspects of teaching and learning."[1] More specifically, the classrooms engaged by this program would:

- use their knowledge as a foundation for new learning;

- work together to research compelling issues, finding multiple answers to perplexing questions;

- move around the classroom with easy access to multiple resources such as computers, reference books, drawing supplies and each other;

- work in small groups learning to collaborate on projects, helping one another to understand and express new concepts;

- use all their talents — logical and mathematical, intuitive, artistic, social, and verbal intelligences — in pursuit of deep understanding and to show and shape what they know and are able to do;

- explore and honor their home culture and that of their peers;

- analyze and reflect on what they learn as a natural part of the learning process.[2]

A national working group in the United States will plan and coordinate the initiative as it moves into school boards across the nation.

On December 24, 1995, the *New York Times* Sunday edition carried a major article revealing that the Annenberg Foundation, with some $30-million as an initial investment over a five-year period, and with the cooperation of the Metropolitan Museum of Art, the Museum of Modern Art, the New York Philharmonic — indeed, the full panoply of professional arts organizations in that great city — would be establishing a program to take over from the Board of Education all responsibility for arts education in New York City. It is too early to assess how this initiative will be integrated with the day-to-day arts activities in every classroom, or whether other subjects in the curriculum will be affected by the injection of such major proportions, but it is enough to say at this point that a new era of artistic awareness will be launched in that city, focussed entirely on children and youth.

There are reasons for the intervention of forward-looking foundations in the United States. They have been influenced by a number of research studies showing that student involvement in the arts has important ramifications across a student's total learning experience. For example, according to the US College Entrance Examination Board, 1995 Scholastic Assessment Test (SAT) "scores for students who had studied the arts for more than four years were 59 points higher on the verbal and 49 points higher on the math portion than students with no course work or experience in the arts."[3] Not surprisingly, the same board reported in 1996 that

> students with experience in musical performance scored 51 points higher on the verbal part of the SAT and 39 points higher on the math section than the national average. "Study in music and other arts generally seems to have a cumulative effect and is undeniably correlated with improvement over time in students' standardized test scores," concluded Edward J. Kelt, director of the School of Music at Central Michigan University in Mount Vernon.[4]

In a more general analysis of the effect of the arts experience on learning:

> In a comprehensive review of hundreds of empirically based studies between 1972 and 1992, three educators associated with the Future of Music Project found that music instruction aids reading, languages (including foreign languages), mathematics, and overall academic achievement. The investigators also found that music enhances creativity, improves student self-esteem, develops social skills and increases perceptual motor skill development and psycho motor development.[5]

There is a tendency for Canada to be a decade or so behind in adopting new trends that capture the American imagination, but in the area of education, this timeline may have been shortened. The Learning

Partnership is a recently formed organization of Canadian school boards, colleges, universities, major corporations, and financial institutions dedicated to cooperative approaches by public and private sectors in achieving educational improvements. Gordon Cressy, a man with a lifetime of experience in both educational and fund-raising activities, took the helm of this organization.

In late 1996, Cressy decided to include the arts as a focus, along with already developed programs in mathematics, science, and technology. A more propitious moment could not have been chosen. The federal Ministry of Education and Training had announced its willingness to accept for partial funding programs designed to encourage children in grades one to three to improve literacy and numeracy skills as well as improve their capacity to deal with new learning technologies. Two million dollars was forthcoming, which allowed the Learning Partnership to approach Silicon Graphics, a substantial corporation engaged in learning technology, who generously provided some $16-million worth of equipment. A further fund-raising initiative among the partners could raise another $4- or $5-million.

Kidsmuse, the name assigned to the program, will prepare some 500 elementary teachers to instruct children in both the new technology and the arts in 92 schools in the Greater Toronto area. All arts organizations in the area will be asked to cooperate, with the Art Gallery of Ontario taking a leadership role, in a program that could rival those found elsewhere on the continent. Although Kidsmuse has been established as a three-year experiment, it can be hoped that, if successful, it will spread across the province. It is surely time.

Des Dixon, a former teacher, principal, and administrator, in his book *Future Schools: And How To Get There From Here*, makes the point that minor adjustments to the schooling process will be inadequate if we are to prepare young people for the world of the future:

> I have stated that this is not a book about reforming
> schools — it is about transforming the learning process
> to take into account the inherent artistry of every child,
> the connection of that artistry and the needs of society.[6]

The integrating of the arts in the curriculum is a matter of transforming the concepts that we have about young people and the way they
learn. Dixon put his finger on the need to end the preoccupation with
facts and figures for their own sake and to realize that literacy — scientific, mathematical, social, economic, and artistic — is about the basic
structures of knowledge. These must be the proper concern of the educational process. Such an emphasis would be inherent in the creation of
an integrated arts-based curriculum in our schools.

However, there are a number of steps to be taken to achieve the goal
of creating school systems which will draw out the creative artist in every child, will bring the joy of the arts to every student, will enlarge the
insight of every youth who must face the enormous challenges ahead.
There must be opportunity for teachers to prepare themselves to instruct not only in their own arts discipline, but in the integrated arts
style that perceives the connections that give meaning to the process of
understanding. What will give special meaning is a response to learning
that addresses the problems to be faced in our society — whether they
be political or economic, social or environmental — and that involves
music, drama, dance, visual arts, creative writing, and media arts as
paths to their solution. To shift teachers' focus to that extent demands a
lifetime commitment that will require massive amounts of personal
time and energy on the part of those participating teachers. However,
such a commitment will enliven and transform the professional life of
all who inhabit every sector of the educational enterprise.

Even though the integrated arts-based curriculum would logically begin as an elementary school phenomenon, the students who enjoy this way of knowing will inevitably arrive at the secondary school. They will have experienced a more horizontal approach to knowledge. It need not mean that they will have forsaken the skills and procedures which have brought such advances in our century and previous centuries — the scientific method and the historical approach will not be abandoned — but ultimately arts-based interdisciplinary studies will be as relevant to their secondary and post-secondary experience as it will have been to their elementary learning years. Thus, it becomes paramount to reach out and convince teachers in the other fields and disciplines that an arts-based curriculum would be a blessing to both students and teachers engaged in the serious task of preparing themselves as scholars in languages, history, geography, physical education, mathematics, science — indeed all the disciplines in the elementary and secondary school curriculum. This emphasis would in no way diminish these areas of exploration, rather it would enrich and enliven each one while connecting every learning activity to the central need to tap the creativity, imagination, insight, and intellectual power of the student.

With these changes we would have achieved the integrated arts-based curriculum, an institutional expression of surely the most effective way of learning that has come out of the educational reform movements in the 20th century. R. Craig Sautter writes:

> The arts have proved to be a powerful tool for complex and diversified learning for children and teenagers. But what we need is a new "arts education" model of school reform: the arts-integrated school. The arts-integrated school seeks to inspire and instruct students through the many art forms that appeal so strongly to young people; it encourages students to learn in as many artistic and creative ways as they can imagine. Instead of putting them through an endless and often mindless text-book driven repetition of isolated drills-to-build-

skills and other traditional methods of rote instruction, the arts-integrated school seeks to stimulate young people to investigate many ways of knowing and many kinds of human experience.7

These are not uncharted waters. Such schools have been in place for over a decade in the United States and Europe, and the idea has been the basis of independent schools like Montessori for decades. In Toronto the Avenue Road Arts School, an independent institution established several years ago by Lola Rasminsky, provides courses in all the arts disciplines and explores the connections of music and drama, sculpture and storytelling in classes both for pre-school and in-school children, and adults as well. To visit that school is to be overwhelmed by the joy of children's creativity. Every room (even the washroom) is an explosion of colour, texture, and imaginative design.

The integrated arts-based curriculum will not emerge full-blown in classrooms as a complete overturning of everything now being accomplished. Rather, it will be an evolutionary process occuring in many different guises and forms. Some teachers may sense the transformation possible when the arts are combined to release the potential of students in their classrooms; others may decide to address whether the cognitive skills of their students can be improved by using music and drama in the study of Greek mythology, for example, as occurred in one Toronto school. The introduction of the curriculum may be an effort to see how students' creative writing might improve through the use of drama with the assistance of an artist coming into the classroom. Or it may come as a decision of an entire school that the future needs of their students would be accommodated by an infusion of arts study into every subject area at all levels.

In some cases, innovation toward the goal of an arts-based curriculum may come as an intervention from outside the educational system.

The Royal Conservatory of Music is surely one of Canada's most respected arts education institutions. When it secured its independence from the University of Toronto, its new principal, Peter Simon, decided that providing individual instruction with the old "one-on-one" teacher-student method must be revised as the seemingly single recognized role for the Royal Conservatory. Simon and his colleagues determined that the conservatory was to be perceived as a force in the schools of the country, and with a generous contribution from Canadian philanthropist Garfield Weston, a project, Learning Through the Arts, was launched. It began with an assessment by Mitchell Korn, president of Artvision, a New York State educational consultancy firm. Although the entire area of Greater Toronto was seen as the appropriate venue, it was realized that a small start, in one or two schools, under a supportive school board, was the best strategy for success.

The proposed program is not simply an extension of the familiar process of teaching an instrument, it is a program based on the recognition that the arts are the connecting tissue linking the major learning needs of young people. The first school to engage in the process, Gateway Public School in North York, has a student body in which 70% of the children speak English as a second language. The principal of Gateway, David McGee, sees literacy as the main challenge of that school: "We want to be able to say at the end of this these children are better readers and writers because of their involvement in the arts."[8] Teachers across the province are watching this project, still in its infancy but with extraordinary possibilities, given the reputation of the Royal Conservatory of Music.

In spite of these examples of advanced thinking and action, the greatest assault on arts education in many boards in Ontario is coming from the fact that those working with the arts in schools — consultants, curriculum planners, and coordinators — are being released or sent back to the classroom. Nor is there time or resources for teacher development or the extra funds necessary to bring artists and arts groups into the school and funds to transport young people to the rich community resources of art galleries, museums, and theatres. In Ontario there is an expectation that the secondary school program will be shortened in order to save public funds, thereby influencing young people to select only the mainstream courses in languages, mathematics, and science, making more difficult the process of providing an integrated arts experience, particularly at the secondary level.

But these are short-term, immediate concerns and pale in significance to the major task, that of achieving an acceptance of the major intellectual and emotional shift that a move toward an integrated arts-based curriculum would demand. It is on the basis of such a curriculum that we can be sure that students will be empowered to make use of the arts to learn about themselves and the very dangerous world they live in and have the confidence to take the action necessary to make that world both livable and sustainable. That, surely, is the responsible

STEELESVIEW PUBLIC SCHOOL

To visit this school is to experience learning at the edge. One is met first by a smiling, comfortable principal, Helen Dewling, whose confidence in her teaching staff and her students bubbles up in every comment. My introduction to Ms. Dewling came in the form of an opportunity to view her school's "Barnes Collection" (the name of a major show of Impressionist painters that was a sellout at the Art Gallery of Ontario). These pieces of splendid student art are properly mounted, framed, and hung in the professional manner that one would expect in a well-run gallery.

This is a school in which team teaching takes on new meaning. Each morning students meet a triumvirate of thoughtful, well-prepared professionals, who cooperate to choreograph an entire day's proceedings with learning every minute as the objective.

As one wanders the hall, the sweet strains of a recorder orchestra waft by. A glance in the room reveals a circle of children totally focused on the task of playing a delightful dance tune with the grace and skill of a senior class. But, surprisingly, in light of the quality of sound, this school only has classes from junior kindergarten to grade six. This level of accomplishment is the result of a greater commitment to the arts and more focused instruction.

Classrooms in the traditional sense do not exist; one strolls past groups of children gathered in circles around teachers, working in small groups and individually on projects that consume their energy and their interest. As I wander by one gathering, the teachers are taking them through a lesson on sculpture, and examining examples from the caves of prehistory to the modern day, using a picture book as a teaching aid. The steps from the raw materials of stone or metal, to the translation of sketches to the creation of more recognizable form are dealt with in clear, concise terms that would have delighted a Henry Moore, a Barbara Hepworth, or a Sorel Etrog.

I come upon a group who are being taught by a young teacher, Alison Edwards, who makes up for any inexperience with a commitment to personal goals and a clear idea of what her class is to achieve. With flexibility to cope with every child's need, her organizational techniques are extraordinary, excelled only by her warmth and approachability. For this teacher, knowledge and understanding comprise a tightly woven fabric. The very walls are filled with the brightly coloured interactions of multiplication tables and problem-solving techniques, the reality of the environmental deterioration beside the particular qualities of nature stressed by the artist the children are studying, the student-researched stories of local

and global perspective, the only legitimate one in these days of crisis.

The next phase in developing an arts-based curriculum is that of ensuring that the arts disciplines themselves are seen to have an internal unity that demands an integrated approach. Although many individuals have lived out their lives with a single-minded concentration on a particular arts discipline in the past, such a narrow band of focus will not see young people through their lives in the decades ahead. As long as each arts discipline is isolated, neither arts educators nor the students they teach can scale the heights of holistic understanding that will allow students to make the changes in themselves and in our society that must come if a decent life is to be lived individually and survival is to be assured collectively.

When we speak of the integration of the arts, we do not mean some interdisciplinary mush that degrades and trivializes music, visual arts, dance, drama, film, and creative writing. Each of these activities has a legitimate body of knowledge that it is essential to grasp. Each involves certain skills that must be recognized and appreciated even if never personally achieved. It is likely that individuals will still concentrate on one discipline, using the insights of the others to lead to new understanding of both process and outcome. There is also an artistic literacy that must be transmitted through the exploration, not only of the individual arts disciplines, but, as well, through the ways that these disciplines together enrich and give meaning to each other.

Teachers mainly interested in the visual arts will learn to appreciate what it means to be a musician, a dancer, a creative writer, and an actor by learning the skills of these disciplines and be willing to pass on the power of their combined insight to their students. This is the only strategy that has any validity in the 21st century, an age which will stress the integration of all knowledge in its efforts to address the needs of the planet. This world will present problems that make increasing demands on all the various literacies we have developed in previous centuries, whether they be linguistic, socio-economic, scientific, or artistic ways of exploring reality and seeking solutions.

Fragmented and single-discipline-driven, the arts have been driven to the periphery of our educational system. Indeed, in many secondary schools, dance, drama, music, and visual arts compete with each

people (later published in the form of a student newspaper), and pictures of the days to remember in the life of the class.

This particular lesson is on colour, but it is about so much more. Ms. Edwards has chosen Ted Harrison, a Canadian artist of the north, whose pictures exude the vitality and excitement of the Inuit culture, as a way to make colour important to every child. From the illustrated books about Canadian folklore, the students select the pictures they find most appealing. Then comes the study of the colour wheel, the gradations of colour achieved through mixing paints, the importance of the sketch, and finally a painting of the "Harrison" that brought together all these skills. Students describe their own artistic journey in letters to the artist, inviting him to their own art show, and visit the local art gallery which is featuring his work. The group explores the environmental impetus behind Harrison's work and the gentle humour in his depiction of children.

For these students in this extraordinary school, the arts are a constant source of inspiration and information. A professional artist, in this case, Ted Harrison, has something to say to them about their future on a fragile planet. As adults, these young people will find their way to art galleries and museums, not merely for an afternoon's entertainment, but to further their learning and experience-gathering.✖

other for students, time, and resources. As school boards seek to save even more money, one by one the study of each arts discipline will be increasingly difficult to justify, and if, as suggested in some jurisdictions, there should be fewer years of secondary schooling, one can see the arts subjects in still greater jeopardy. Only the integration of the arts with an enlarged and globally conceived mandate, that involves every other discipline, can save the arts from gradual abandonment in our schools.

We think of the arts as those activities through which we express our humanity — music, drama, dance, and visual expression in paint and sculpture, as well as creative writing, crafts, and a host of media and electronic extensions. We know that to separate these apparent expressions of our reality and our imagination from the limitless activities, ideas, and behaviours which comprise our culture is to make them less meaningful and more isolated. It is this perception that allows these artistic expressions to be seen as mere self-indulgence.

If the arts are to have significance in a holistic conception of human endeavour, then these disciplines must themselves be seen as an integrating effort to express our human understandings and hopes. As long as artists and teachers of the arts are caught in the same web of fragmentation and specialization that obliterates the connectedness of the universe for the scientist, the engineer, the doctor, and the economist, then arts education is still part of the problem, not a contribution to any solutions. In the arts, the first step must be that of returning to those earliest childhood behaviours that are the basis of any integrity in teaching the various arts disciplines. Children do not see the world as one divided into separate boxes of discipline exploration, each demanding our attention, each convinced of the singular truth of its perception. The world is "whole" as seen in its entirety by the mind of the child. When children draw, they are working out their own stories, often accompanied by hummed tunes and body movements that are part of that visual arts expression. When children put on their own play, the production includes mother's hat and perhaps father's bathrobe because the visual is important along with the creative literary expression (often including song and dance) of depicting some event that has caught their attention.

Picasso, surely the greatest visual artist of this century, once stated, "I used to draw like Raphael, but it has taken me a lifetime to learn to draw like a child." Anyone who has visited the Picasso Museum in Barcelona will have seen "First Communion," a large painting depicting that important religious event in the life of the faithful. It is one of his earliest works, exhibiting superb technique and exciting composition, but it is indeed Raphaelesque and, when compared to his later work, one can only agree with the artist's observation.

Louis Applebaum, the eminent Canadian composer, has opined the fact that he sees children who are bubbling over with creative impulse in their early years but have "the arts beaten out of them by the time they are teenagers." The interest of children in the arts appears to wane just as they are confronted with music, theatre, dance, and drawing as disciplines rather than as a single, exciting process of expressing their feelings and thoughts about the world around them.

To suggest an integrated approach to the arts is not to denigrate that desire of children and youth to reach higher levels of skill in whatever discipline particularly excites them. Nor does it trivialize the efforts of music teachers, drama coaches, and dance instructors who have raised the capacities of their students to astounding levels of excellence. It is not a matter of one approach or another — both can and must be accommodated. But all within the philosophical dome of an integrated arts expression that allows a horizontal understanding of the world and its problems.

Integration is not just a matter of weaving music, drama, film, dance, and visual arts into a single garment, it includes the challenge of finding connections with the rest of those windows that open to help us understand our lives and environment. Indeed, the integration of the arts is but one step. The integration of the total curriculum, while recognizing the special literacies involved in every discipline, is the direction of education for the future. Northrop Frye has pointed out that children realize that the time spent learning is as close to real life as they are ever likely to get. In light of this observation, integration becomes even more critical as students seek, so often in vain, to find reasons why they should remain in school when their learning seems to say so little that is relevant to the personal and societal problems they see about them.

To integrate the arts and other disciplines is to follow the natural behaviour of children in learning about what is new in their environment. Children learn the alphabet and numbers by singing songs ("One, Two, Buckle Your Shoe"); they comprehend biology first through rhymes ("Old Macdonald Had a Farm"); and come to a simple philosophy with a song ("Twinkle, Twinkle, Little Star"). We refer to this predilection to see the world in its totality as childlike. One great religious leader has observed that it is this capacity to see things whole that adults must achieve if they are to know heaven. In secular terms, "heaven" becomes the capacity to understand life in the full spectrum of all that our senses and rational analysis perceive to be valid.

An extension of this childlike behaviour would inform us that the arts must reach out through one of its discipline forms. It is not a matter of "using" music to learn numbers, rather of recognizing the special quality of creativity in every phase of knowledge. Bach was surely one of the greatest mathematicians who ever lived, and one must not miss that aspect of his music to experience its full impact. Yet one cannot allow the structure of Bach's music to obliterate the inspiration it exudes. Dancers explore the mysteries of movements that go beyond bodily activity, revealing patterns of emotional and intellectual power that transform the actions of exercise to those of spiritual expression. The painter addresses the scientific questions of colour and form, but the painting has psychic, dramatic, and psychological effects that go far beyond the form, texture, and vibrant hues that grace the canvas. History could be taught entirely as a cultural feast emphasizing an era's music, art and sculpture, drama and literature as a path to the political and economic story, rather than a dreary recitation of dates and events. In short, a seamless curriculum based on rich cultural extravaganza should drive the efforts of teachers and students.

This is certainly the trend in the arts outside the school. More and more, performance art, involving the visual, sound, movement, and drama, is becoming the way by which artists seek to express the truth they feel has been revealed to them. Even in the more traditional venues, this integration can be seen at work. The Tarragon Theatre in Toronto has consistently featured plays about visual artists. In the 1994-95 season, the life of Georgia O'Keeffe was examined in the context of her environment and relationships. Indeed the set was derived from her paintings and could have been the result of her own brush.

In the early '90s, both the National Ballet Company and the Canadian Opera Company presented *Eugene Onegin*. Both productions revealed, in tragic detail, the power of human emotions to devastate and kill, at the same time revealing the capacity of humankind to overcome the horror of lost love and achieve a positive equilibrium. In this example, it was an opportunity for integration in the minds of the audiences who could capture the nuances in the story line that were revealed differently in dance and vocal expression.

⌘   ⌘   ⌘

The integrated arts within the integrated curriculum is a rational response to the world which now exists, an incorporation of all we know about learning and the human condition in the task of addressing the problems we know children will have to face and overcome. To achieve competence and eventual excellence in the teaching of such a curriculum will be as difficult for arts teachers as for the teachers of every other discipline. Arts-oriented teachers are often as caught up in their own discipline as are teachers of history, science, mathematics, or languages.

Yet teachers who fear new disciplines can be inspired by artists who have made these leaps from one art form to another. Harry Freedman was a fine visual artist before shifting his attention to music. Murray Adaskin showed his interest in Canadian painting through a musical composition for string orchestra and harp which he called "In Praise of Canadian Painting in the Thirties: Paraseva Clark, Louis Muhlotock, Charles Comfort," and Harry Somers has written a "Picasso Suite" for full orchestra. Louis Applebaum has for decades written at least one score per season at the Stratford Festival, thereby enhancing the understanding and enjoyment of Shakespeare's classics through the medium of expressive sound.

It is Patricia Beatty, dancer and choreographer, who brought together visual artists Gordon Rayner, Graham Coughtry, and Aiko Suzuki for a performance she called "Painters and the Dance," with the music of Ann Southam, Michael Baker, and Robert Daigneault. She describes her desire to create "a dance to celebrate painterly qualities." The difficulties were apparent:

> Change seems to be the essence of life, or at least one of
> its greatest demands. So it is with collaboration. Work-

ing with these painters has been very different than with composers. I think it is because they are used to working alone. This has forced us all to be more dependent on each other, and in a very big way. But, painters with empty canvases are used to risks, certainly those within the tradition of abstract expressionism — their very gestures are born of risk.[9]

The key word in speaking of integrated arts is "risk." Arts educators' experience has been with mining the meaning of individual disciplines, as their reputations are so often tied to qualifications related to music or drama or visual arts. Once we seek to find the horizontal linkages and the insights they reveal, we have every reason to feel nervous — that is, until the rich payoffs are visible and obvious. Teaching has always been seen as a "safe" profession, one with considerable assurance of continued employment and, within the classroom with its door shut, a role which allows wide individualistic behaviour. Integrating the arts demands opening the classroom door and inviting the participation of colleagues, artists, and perhaps even parents. We have to learn more about the other ways of knowing that scientists, mathematicians, and historians have discovered. We must venture into unfamiliar intellectual territory.

It will not be the diffident, going-through-the-paces teacher who will have the greatest difficulty with the transition. Rather, it will be the superb professional, well-trained, perhaps still a practicing artist, who knows all the best techniques, who is flexible and accountable, who cares deeply about every student but believes above all else that the specific single-discipline arts experience in her classroom is the most important moment in her students' day. The irony is that these teachers, once convinced of and committed to an integrated curriculum, will reach heights of accomplishment beyond their dreams. There is little doubt that such a curriculum, particularly when it addresses subject areas beyond the arts, will create major dissonance. Many still believe in a hierarchy of knowledge that places those concerned with the measurable and objective at the top and those concerned with the experiential and subjective at the bottom.

The scholarship of the past few decades has blurred this simplistic distinction. What seemed objective now appears to have its own subjectivity, and every advance in space exploration, for example, seems to raise more questions rather than provide answers. We have become overwhelmed by the fact that all knowledge seems highly tentative, that the most well-informed and sophisticated scholars, who recognize that easy, assured answers, even in the most mathematically valid areas of scientific research, are but a point in our understanding that must ultimately be revised. Thus, the integration of the arts and the rest of the curriculum is not the contrast of apples and oranges that it once seemed to be.

John Polanyi, Canada's recent Nobel Prize winner from the University of Toronto, has continually stressed not only the role of the scientist as an interventionist in public affairs, but also the intimate relationship of the sciences and the arts. In addressing an Artswork Conference at the Ontario Institute for Studies in Education in Toronto in 1991, he stated:

> There have been two events in this century that marked the dawn of a new age. They reinforced one another in such a way as to change the course of history, as it is changed only once in the course of several millennia. The first of these events was attitudinal and the second technological. I have in mind first of all the concept of total war. This many of us have come to associate with the Spanish town of Guernica. The second pivotal event which came a few years later, was the invention of nuclear weapons, which made total war a threat to the

very existence of our species. Neither of these events is, in my view, reversible.

What is required of us is that we educate ourselves to a new view of the world in which we put our humanity and our obligation to the future of humankind ahead of sectarian interests. It is a vast challenge to education.

The challenge, though presented in part by science, can only be met through marshaling the enormous power of the arts: speech, literature, theater, poetry, painting, sculpture, music and dance.

To recapitulate, I have said two things. First, that scientific discovery, since it depends upon giving shape to observations, draws strength from the arts. And second that our ability to adjust to a world transformed by science will depend once again on the power of the arts, to stimulate and guide our thinking.[10]

Polanyi went on to examine the process by which science and the arts can give meaning to each other:

The scientist and the artist communicate with the world they inhabit, as a blind person does with a cane. If he holds the cane tightly he is a scientist receiving impressions that nature makes on the probe, with minimal involvement of the instrument of measurement. If he holds the cane loosely he is more of an artist, since he seeks to be conscious not only of the world but also of the instrument through which he perceives it, be it a chisel, a brush or a baton.

The difference between the artist and the scientist as an explorer is a subtle one, and I have surely failed to do it justice. But it is the similarity that is more important. Both categories of explorer, when they succeed, become discoverers. Since the world they explore is the same, the means by which they explore it must be complementary. They have an unlimited amount of power to teach one another.[11]

We are overwhelmed by the technology that permeates our every waking moment. In the knowledge that scientific research and discovery have created all these instruments which define our lives, we believe that our very survival depends on a strong and viable science and technology knowledge industry.

There is indeed truth in this analysis. Without the capacity to compete in the new global economy, we will soon be a Third World country trying desperately to maintain our standard of living, our social programs, and the enormous investment we have in our artistic and intellectual well-being — our symphony orchestras, our libraries, our universities, as well as our basic transportation and communication infrastructure. Most important, we will lose our capacity to assist less-developed countries, even to the minimal levels we have achieved in this century.

Yet we sometimes lose sight of the fact that the hardware of technology — the computer, the television, the VCR, the fax machine — are but the carriers of messages. Without a valid story to tell — stories that make it possible to be uniquely inventive and creative — we have no message to transmit. It is from the arts that many of these stories will come, and without them, all these machines are but ashes in the mouth.

Indeed, that reality hits home when we are told that 500 television networks will be available through a pizza-sized disk even though it is apparent that there is not enough quality programming to fill the program hours of networks now available to cable television subscribers. We are buried in our own access-to-information capacity. We hear stories of people who are leaving the Internet because sifting through the mountain of information to find the important material is so time-wasting and frustrating that personal mental health demands restraint. We are discovering what we already knew in our bones — that science and technology can solve only a fraction of the complex spectrum that makes up every societal problem, and that only a new recognition of the importance of the arts can reveal solutions.

E.F. Schumacher, author of the seminal volume *Small Is Beautiful*, regrets that science in the 20th century has dispensed with the exploration of great questions in order to prove mere fragments of reality. Whereas scientists such as Kepler and Newton constantly asked the question: "What is Man?," the modern scientist has, for the most part, refused to tackle such contemplative enquiries. In the context of an arts-technology-science-humanities curriculum relationship, these questions can, once again, be best framed. All we know about being human brings us inexorably to such issues as social justice, gender relationships, and compassionate behaviour toward one another. The artist confronts such questions whenever she puts pen to paper, brush to canvas, or picks up an instrument.

The answers influence how we will think and act when faced with a deteriorating environment, a massive deficit and debt that can be used to threaten our social programs, a society of enormous disparity of rich and poor, and a belief that violence solves every human problem. We know so much more than we are able to use effectively. It is not a matter of not having enough facts or statistical information; our failure revolves around our inability to see broadly enough and across sufficient dimension, which results in hesitancy, lack of will, and lack of decision.

It has been a role of the arts to signal the dangers which threaten every generation. The playwright who forces us to face the impact of sexism and racism tells us that another holocaust may well be around the corner. The arts sketch the vision of what can be, if we bring to the problems the full weight of our creativity within a value system that celebrates life for all creatures and a societal pattern which provides sustainability and justice. Rodin, the giant of the world of sculpture, put it well: "Great works of art say all that can be said about man and the world and then convey that there is something more that cannot be said." Never in the annals of time have we needed more the words and images of the artist. . .and a community able and willing to listen.

In this spirit of dire necessity, a curriculum based on human values and the capacity to communicate characterizes the best of the arts so essential to every child. Such a curriculum must incorporate the skills and understandings which a society determines essential to every child who will eventually earn a living, play the role of citizen and, hopefully, live a good life, productive and personally satisfying. A curriculum which thematically ranges across the various literacies, which makes use of all disciplines but refuses to be captured by their limitations — that is the learning which will prepare young people for a disconcerting present and an uncertain future.

The English philospher John Locke said that "hell is truth seen too late." It is time to address the essential task of learning the arts before any number of hells come upon our children.

NOTES
1. The Brown University News Bureau, "National Initiative to expand role of arts and technology in education receives $10-million challenge grant from Annenberg Foundation," Providence RI, December 7, 1995, p. 1.
2. Ibid., p. 2.
3. The College Board Profile of SAT and Achievement Test Takers, 1995. Cited in Murfee, E., *Eloquent Evidence: Arts at the Core of Learning* (Washington: President's Committee on the Arts and the Humanities, and the National Assembly of State Arts Agencies, 1995).
4. Don Campbell, *The Mozart Effect* (New York: Avon Books, 1997), p. 177.
5. Ibid., p. 179.
6. Des Dixon, *Future Schools: And How To Get There From Here* (Toronto: ECW Press, 1992), p. 434.
7. R. Craig Sautter, "An Arts Education School Reform Strategy," *Phi Delta Kappan*, February 1994, p. 434.
8. Stuart Hoffman, "Royal Conservatory Sings a New Tune," *Globe*

and Mail, January 29, 1996, p. D2.

9. Patricia Beatty, program notes for "Painters and the Dance," pp. 4-5. Unpublished.

10. John Polanyi, Address to the Artswork Conference, Ontario Institute for Studies in Education, 1991, pp. 5-6. Unpublished.

11. Ibid., pp. 5-6.

Chapter 9   # Artists and Teachers, Parents and Community

Arts is not a means by which we escape from life, but a strategem by which we conquer life's disorders.

Alfred Barr

lthough the message expressing the possibilities of integrated arts-based learning has not been heard by many teachers, there are, as we have seen, pockets of excitement and excellence to be found in particular schools and classrooms. If a strong grounding in the arts and an appreciation of the fact that their interrelationship prepares young people to live in an unsure world and participate in a volatile marketplace, then surely it is only a matter of time before the arts move to the centre of the curriculum in North American schools. However, in spite of all the successful examples of learning achievement through the arts, in spite of the personal, transcendent arts experiences that have transformed countless individuals, nothing will happen in these days of restraint and in-the-trenches mentality unless there is an alliance of artist, educator, parent, and the community of caring individuals who seek a better future for all children.

In the winter of 1998, one of the most important studies on arts education was released by the US Department of Education. A full decade before, Dr. James Catterall at UCLA had initiated this longitudinal study involving 25,000 secondary school students. There have been studies of smaller groups of students and studies involving one or another art form (usually music), but never had there been a study of this magnitude taking place over so many years.

The released results were not limited to the examination of the scholarly success of students but rather included the broader learning experience that determines other significant facets of the good life. The study found that "involvement in the arts is linked to higher academic performance, increased standardized test scores, more community service, and lower drop-out rates."[1] And, significantly, these results were valid whatever the socioeconomic status of the students' parents might be.

It must be understood that the schooling system reflects the society that supports it, and that society is far from understanding the directions that must be pursued in the world of the late '90s and early 2000s and the role of the arts in that strategy. Even if that comprehension came about tomorrow, it would take years to turn the juggernaut of the educational system in an appropriate direction. At present our whole society is enmeshed in value systems and collective behaviours that deny the viability and validity of such a thrust in arts education. The definition of arts as mere entertainment to fill in the hours, as most people characterize their function, does not lead to a belief in their essentiality to the learning function in our classrooms. Without a perception of a world in desperate need to be rescued and realigned through the mechanisms that the arts provide, there is little hope for humankind in this age of ironic uncertainty, with all its political dichotomy and violence.

The first step must be that of finding the bridges that will link artist and teacher. In the United States, an Ad Hoc National Arts Education Group, made up of representatives of the American Council for the Arts and the Music Educators National Conference, organized the Interlochen Symposium, which met in November 1987. The purpose of the gathering was simple — to strengthen arts education in the schools. An underlying assumption of the committee, identified in a paper presented by Richard Sinatra and Paul Lehman, states:

> [T]he arts are an essential part of the curriculum and. . .they should play a major role in the educational program of every young American. This has been the position of every writer and thinker who has made a major contribution to Western educational thought. It is no less true of major contributors to the current debate on educational reform.[2]

That statement of purpose was a starting point for any effective development in schools after the symposium, involving both artists and teachers.

One thing was very clear to the organizers of Interlochen — no change was possible without the interaction of those associated with teaching and those who are professional artists. In some cases, there is considerable overlap in the kinds of people who become teachers and artists. Often they share the same motivations, the same missionary zeal, the same idealism that leads them to vocations that may provide a life that has meaning in the satisfaction it brings, but has little hope of material reward commensurate with ability or hours of work. Often members of both groups have comparable skills in communication.

Strangely, there has been little contact between artist and teacher and even less indication of mutual support.

At the Interlochen Symposium, even after many months of planning and the assembling of a highly compatible list of invitees, the problems of the interface of artist and educator were painfully evident:

> The arts community had developed a vocabulary of its own, one little understood by educators; on the other hand, educators used terminology standard to that field. Each world viewed the other as suspect due to a lack of basic understanding of how the other functioned. At this point in the symposium, eight hours had not been enough to heal wounds that had developed over the years or to bridge the wide gulf of understanding that permeated the teaching of the arts.[3]

Yet, in the end, teachers and artists were able to agree on a strategy, the Philadelphia Resolution, which would see the arts as a major component of the curriculum in every classroom in the United States (Appendix C). At that time, there had been no such meeting of the minds in Canada. Understandably, in a country which places education squarely in the hands of the provincial authorities, it is difficult to achieve an effective national voice except through the Council of Ministers of Education, a body not noted for making dramatic interventions in the affairs of individual provinces. However, in the summer of 1997, the Canadian Music Educators Association convened a National Symposium on Arts Education in Cape Breton. The excitement initiated by this gathering of educators from various discipline areas has spread to every province and a second meeting was held in 1998.

The symposium passed the following resolution, a hurriedly promulgated first salvo which signals many more resolutions to come:

> Given the values of the art for learning;

Given the ability of education in the arts to nurture qualities necessary in the workplace of the 21st century;

Given the ability of the arts to generate partnerships and strategic alliances with other sectors, including business, tourism, health and education;

Given the rapidly growing work opportunities in the cultural sector;

Given the need for creative uses of and content for new technologies, which artists provide;

Given the central role of the arts in the development of the whole human being;

Given the central role of the arts in the well-being of communities;

Given the ability of the arts to respond to and embrace the movement of globalization, both affirming distinct culture and understanding others;

The participants in the National Symposium on Arts Education '97, including artists, educators, arts administrators and education administrators from across Canada, urge the Minister of Education, through the Council of Ministers of Education, to take steps to ensure that the arts are a fundamental and sustained part of the Canadian educational system for all students in all schools, by developing a vision and common outcomes for arts education in Canada.[4]

At this time, the Council of Ministers of Education can hide behind the constitution and do little or nothing. But a groundswell of concern can secure even this body's attention and lead to important changes.

However, even if there were a federal presence in the education field, it would be of little help without a shift of philosophy and priority. When the Canada Council, the leading government arts-funding organization, announced in the early '90s that it would no longer be able to provide resources even for national training institutions engaged in professional development of artists, it was the abandonment of an area the Council had recognized as its responsibility for many years, thereby putting at risk a number of institutions serving dancers, actors, and musicians. The Council explained that continuing cutbacks in federal government support had forced a change in priorities. However, the fact that such training could be perceived as expendable by the nation's major arts-funding body is an indication of the distance that must be travelled. The internationally recognized National Ballet School was one of these institutions abandoned by the Canada Council and was given a two-year guarantee of funds by a federal government department only to discover that its provincial grant in Ontario was being withdrawn. The National Theatre School in Montreal, which has provided outstanding actors and technical personnel to the Stratford and Shaw festivals and regional theatres across Canada, was placed in the same situation by a similar decision of the Canada Council. In a world of decreasing revenues, the message is clear: provincial or federal governments will not be kind to arts-training institutions, whether they serve dance, drama, music, or visual arts.

As the '90s conclude, Canada's landscape is bleak. Stephen Campbell, the energetic and thoughtful Arts Education Officer at the Ontario Arts Council, has had considerable success over several years in presenting a program of professional development for artists engaged in arts education. A full day of activities was organized, drawing hundreds of artists who wanted to know more about schools and the way the arts are taught in them. In small groups, outstanding artists and arts educators addressed the major problems likely to be encountered in the context of a teacher-artist collaboration in a classroom. The stress experienced by the participants was palpable even in this non-threatening forum, but in the process artists did come to a more profound understanding of the context in which their work in the schools takes

place. As well, they learned something of the frustrations of the classroom teacher. Unfortunately, the recent cuts in support of the Ontario
Arts Council has put this initiative on hold. Indeed, a scaled-down version of this event did transpire in 1997, but it is unlikely that even such
a successful program can be remounted in its totality if the cuts to the
Council's budget continue.

As it was discovered at Interlochen, the recognition of this gulf between artist and educator is a first step to their cooperation in the learning enterprise. Artists envy the relatively high salaries and assured
employment future of the full-time teacher; teachers salivate to think of
the freedom of artists — from administrivia, from the pressure of being
in the presence of 30 or more active, boisterous students every moment
of the day, and from the drudgery of marking and grading. The artist
dreams of the security and collegial support that the schooling system
provides; the teacher fantasizes about the joys of a more flexible and
self-indulgent lifestyle. Neither truly knows the world the other inhabits.

It is essential to reach across this abyss to achieve any success in
bringing arts education to the centre of the classroom curriculum.
School programs in the arts need the energy, commitment and integrity
that artists bring to their work, whether it be in the studio, on the stage,
in the darkroom, or in the school and the classroom. It is equally important to know that without the understanding of how learning takes place
and how the whole system works to achieve common goals, the very
strengths teachers bring to such a program can soon drift into right-
minded intentions but wrongheaded chaos.

Sometimes there is a happy combination of teacher and artist in a
single person. In Scarborough, in eastern Toronto, just such a teacher
has achieved a remarkable reputation. A few years ago, Myles Crawford

was selected as Teacher of the Year, an award sponsored by a major newspaper, the *Toronto Sun*. He won over hundreds of other nominees from the region. Crawford teaches music and believes there is no better learning experience for a student than watching a professional in the workplace where they must perform with energy and commitment night after night for hours at a time. He takes his students to concerts, but also to jazz clubs and bars when appropriate — and parents who might have been outraged by having their children frequent the latter venues were responsible for nominating him for the Teacher of the Year Award. Myles Crawford is himself a professional musician, and his career points up the advantage when the person associated with the transmission of knowledge is also the creator of such knowledge.

One cannot expect every teacher of the arts, particularly those engaged at the elementary level, to become a practicing artist, but there are ways in which the demands of artistic integrity can be experienced in effective ways. Very often, it is in the challenge of a little theatre, an amateur playhouse that puts on good drama where teachers can release the artist within, that the mutual understanding can be fostered. Scarborough music consultant Lee Willingham, with a few colleagues, launched a choir made up of teachers and graduates of school music programs, insisting on a challenging repertoire and demanding an extraordinary quality of public performance. The production of CD recordings of the choir's wide range of choral competence, and a European tour with concerts in major cities like Vienna, Prague, Budapest, and Salzburg, soon gave the Bell'Arte Singers, now an ensemble of 60, a niche in the musical life of Toronto. It has become one of the finest choirs in the country. Most important, a substantial coterie of teachers discovered what it was like to be a performing artist, and their students benefitted from that knowledge and experience. There are countless visual arts teachers who maintain a studio in their homes and draw and paint, not just to relieve the pressures of their professional life, but because they have a personal need to feel that surge of creativity which enlivens their art. Indeed, in these days of severe teacher stress there is reason to believe that those who survive stress best are those who have an active artistic life outside the classroom, as creators, performers, or members of audiences at concerts, plays, and dance presentations.

One artist in Ontario, Elke Scholz, has made an effort to reach out to teachers in Bracebridge, Muskoka, and beyond. As a result of her work, teachers found that they had gained strength and health. Some benefits that were identified:

- being more relaxed in their classroom and in their lives

- a few teachers reported their relief from insomnia

- their own increased confidence in themselves and their art skills

- noticing their own language change and the positive impact on their students

- feeling re-energized and motivated

- felt inspired by the variety and zest they could add to their current programmes and lesson plans[5]

Teachers in every school board deserve a resident professional developer like Scholz.

Finding ways in which artists and teachers can unite is crucial. The stakes are high, and in this decade of deficits and cutbacks they will be even higher. The very survival of arts disciplines depends on a greater degree of unity among those who have chosen an arts role as their contribution to the educational life of their communities and those who have chosen teaching the arts as their profession. It will require political action on the part of both and, as communicators, both can be most effective. In the City of Toronto, a unified effort on the part of artists at a recent civic election resulted, a few years ago, in a successful mayoralty campaign for Barbara Hall, an outspoken arts advocate. For many years, music teachers have been encouraged to become political. Laurie Rowbotham, a splendid music teacher and choir leader in Listowel, Ontario, and for some years the editor of *The Recorder*, the journal of the Ontario Music Educators' Association, used the editorial page to encourage his colleagues:

> [H]ave you ever written your "director of education" outlining your concerns and registering your ideas in matters as such as poor facilities, inadequate budgets, lack of a music consultant available to you or unsuitable lengths of instruction time for your students? Have you ever phoned a trustee to invite [him/her] to a class, a concert or a trip as a chaperone?[6]

When the Royal Commission on Learning in Ontario was considering reforms to the schooling system, all the major arts organizations in the province with an educational outreach program joined to present the Ontario Arts Education Accord, an inspiring statement of agreement on the goals of a rational educational system (Appendix D). Teachers had enlisted their support at a crucial moment of decision, and it was Reid Anderson, then artistic director of the National Ballet, who was the spokesperson at the meeting with commission members.

To achieve any kind of political effectiveness, this linkage of arts teachers and artists must have a continuing institutional presence. In an effort to extend the concept of integrated arts, an Arts Education Council of Ontario was formed by a number of teachers and consultants anxious to enrich the experience of students. Jon Mergler, the council's first chair, gave effective and tireless leadership, and teachers of all art forms, consultants in every area of the arts curriculum — essentially those associated with the presentation of the arts in the classroom —

joined to create a strong organization. The mandate of the council was very straightforward — to act as an advocate for arts education in all its forms and to provide information and assistance for effective teaching, including the publication and distribution of a triannual periodical, *The Artspaper*, with articles of broad interest. Jane Cutler and Wayne Fairhead, both arts consultants with Toronto area boards, Bob Phillips, a classroom arts teacher, and Paterson Fardell of Young People's Theatre, have followed Mergler, bringing energy and purpose to this effort to strengthen the arts presence in the province's schools.

At the same time, a Coalition for the Arts was formed by artists who were working in the schools both on a continuing basis at the college level, or intermittently in elementary and secondary classroom arts projects funded by schools (often with financial assistance from the Ontario Arts Council). Many of the participants were involved in musical and theatrical presentations on makeshift stages in gymnasiums and cafetoriums across the province and were aware of the fragility of their role as artists in the classroom and community when budget cuts singled out that function for obliteration.

The final organizational piece was put in place when the educational officers of the major performing arts organizations (Stratford, Toronto Symphony, Shaw, Young Peoples' Theatre, et al.) created a third entity, the Performing Arts Organizations Network for Education, to increase the role of their enterprises in the public education system.

Most importantly, these organizations have maintained a close relationship and have cooperated in various projects, bringing both teachers and artists together for common goals. They realize that as long as teachers and artists are divided by the disciplines — music, dance, drama, visual and technological arts, and creative writing — there will be no hope of advocating on behalf of the arts effectively at the school, board, or provincial levels. Nor will there be any hope of influencing the total curriculum and thereby achieving the goals that the arts have, through the ages, set for themselves.

Perhaps the greatest block to effective arts education, at least at the elementary school, has been the lack of commitment to the arts exhibited by most faculties of education devoted to pre-service teacher education. In many cases, elementary school teachers arrive in their first classroom with but an hour or two of preparatory attention to arts education. These inexperienced teachers lack both skill and confidence and tend to avoid the arts, where there is no textbook to lean on. The initial year of teaching becomes the pattern for a career. The need for immediate intervention by both experienced teachers and artists is obvious. Such programs have been initiated at both the Lincoln and Kennedy Centers in the US with different organization and purpose, but both bring teachers and artists together for lectures, workshops, and performances during the summer. Arrangements are made for professional artists and musical and dramatic groups to visit the schools of teachers represented at these programs, thus linking the entire school with some artistic involve-

TORONTO "YOUNG AT ART" EXHIBITION

The Harbourfront Gallery overlooks the lake on a dull day — but the pictures, prints, sculptures, and happenings fill the eyes with color and exciting contrast. These are works that students in Toronto schools, both secondary and senior elementary, have worked on with pride and commitment.

These are not decorative pieces to liven up the recreation room wall. These are statements about their lives, emotions, and relationships. Pictures that reveal the pain of confused identity, environmental crises, the conflict between nature and urbanity, the confrontation between technology and human values, are here.

The quality of the work, the obvious technique that has been grasped, is impressive. But far more important is the intellectual activity that has preceded these extraordinary expressions of teenage concern.

It is an occasion of celebration, but to watch the students as they view the works of their peers from other schools is to know how seriously they regard their own creations. Not only have teachers accompanied them to the opening, but artists, colleagues and collaborators, who have worked with these students in visual arts classrooms throughout the city, are here to provide both encouragement and criticism. The arts have become a matter of seeking excellence, of challenging students to produce the best they are capable of. The sculptor's knife and the painter's brush have become means of making a statement of joy, of anger — a comment more articulate than the rock through a store window or the ugly graffiti on the wall of the railway overpass.⊯

ment for months after the summer course has been completed.

In Ontario, in the late '80s, there was a window of opportunity with the launching of the Common Curriculum for the early grades of elementary school. This document, a guide for every school in the province, expressed the expectation that a quarter of the time during these crucial grades would be spent in the arts, with mathematics and science, languages and verbal expression, and the social sciences making up the other quarters of the curriculum pie. Unfortunately, many teachers felt uncomfortable with their work in any or all of the various disciplines that make up the arts in the classroom and as a result the full impact of the Common Curriculum was hardly felt by students. It scarcely needs stating that the development of an integrated arts-based learning strategy would make even greater demands on teachers in the primary and intermediate grade classrooms across the province.

It was this situation that led the Arts Education Council of Ontario and the Coalition for the Arts to cooperate in devising a new program that would concentrate on the elementary level, adopting a new pattern of in-service learning for teachers, focussing on the involvement of both artists and arts educators. Under the auspices of a combined initiative, now called the Arts Education Institute of Ontario, the first offering was made possible in the summer of 1995 through cooperative arrangements between the Faculty of Education of York University and the school boards of Greater Toronto. Dr. Barbara Soren, a professor of dance with a doctorate in museum studies, became the coordinator of the program, and her commitment and experience, along with an outstanding team of instructors, made the summer a great success.

Perhaps the most important element in the successful launching of the program was the enthusiastic support of the major arts organizations in the provincial jurisdiction, including the Canadian Opera Company, the National Ballet of Canada, the Shaw and Stratford Festivals, the Toronto Symphony Orchestra, Young Peoples' Theatre, the Art Gallery of Ontario, the Royal Ontario Museum, and a spectrum of smaller theatre, music, dance, and visual arts organizations. It would be hard to determine whether the motivation was the need for the performing and visual arts to be involved in the educational system in order to sell seats to their organizations' presentations (all had active educational departments with effective staff) or whether there was the profound belief that without a new clientele reached through a committed teaching force, the future of the art form was in question. Nevertheless, the involvement of the arts organizations was crucial, as much of the program was planned to extend beyond a two-week summer course and would be presented by these organizations on weekends throughout the fall and winter.

Equally important was the decision that the venue for the course should not be a classroom, but a setting which honoured and celebrated the arts, showing the relationship that each discipline had with every other. The offer of the Royal Ontario Museum to provide facilities ensured that the venue would express this philosophy of integrated arts expression as the core of an effective educational system.

Little could have been accomplished without the financial support of the Laidlaw Foundation and the interest of its executive director, Nathan Gilbert. This foundation saw the program as a contributor to its funding theme, Children at Risk, and provided a home as well as money. The Ontario Arts Council made a major commitment, as did the Samuel and Saidye Bronfman Foundation and SOCAN, the composers' organization responsible for the administration and distribution to artists of royalties from public performance.

The final crucial element was the concept that a team of artists and educators could work together to plan and offer the program, given the tension between artists and teachers, and the jealousies between the proponents of the various art forms. The staff of artists and arts educators met for weeks and became a closely knit team that banished all the ghosts of past conflict. When some 60 teachers, along with a sprinkling of artists who were working in the schools, arrived in mid-August, they were confronted with a dynamic, animated group of professionals eager to ensure the success of the project.

Heather Miller, former arts coordinator for the York Region Board of Education, reflected on her experience as one of the instructors on the course, and in doing so focussed on the questions she now had to confront as a result of this experience:

> The Institute provided an opportunity for all participants to see and feel the power of the arts. As a teacher, I stretched and grew through my interaction with each person there. It was a privilege to be part of that dynamic community of learners. Because of them the questions that settled in my mind call out for answers. What if teachers really had time during the course of their busy days to discuss their work as we did during the planning and implementation of the Institute? What if we had artists-in-residence in all our schools empowering teachers and students to learn through the arts? What if our students had easy and frequent access to our art galleries and museums?[7]

Visitors to the museum that summer were confronted with dance and music, drama and visual arts in the Chinese Gallery, in the shadow of the dinosaur exhibit, amidst the galaxies of the astrocentre. Child visitors to the ROM made masks and crowns while adults watched with intense interest as drama emerged from the Greek statues and the extraordinary reality of a simulated bat cave and a northern hardwood forest. Students were divided into groups and worked with the leadership team members of each individual discipline in the morning, while the afternoon was given over to the integrating of each of these disciplines with another. The final project was a presentation that included all the disciplines. The emphasis was on activity, not instruction — these teacher-students made masks and collages, composed music with instruments and percussion, danced and acted out their own creative impulses.

The two weeks of intense interaction became a transformational experience. Teachers who had never seen modern dance found themselves moving with ease and excitement, others who "could not draw a straight line" found that this capacity was not essential once one was digging deep into one's soul to find images that demanded expression. In short, fears about teacher-artist tension were essentially banished. Every participant discovered artistic creativity awaiting release and found tools to encourage their students to experience a similar joy.

The words of the participants best express the impact of the experience. One teacher stated, "The summer institute opened my eyes, enhanced my hearing, put me in touch with my body as an instrument of communication and gave me great joy." Another put it quite simply: "I have reconnected with the starved artist within me and can now unleash it in my classroom." An elementary school teacher expressed her delight as seen through eyes of her family: "From the first day my family could sense a difference in me (having lived with me through other courses, they were prepared for less than a happy time). They commented on my enthusiasm and energy, even when I was tired, trying to take in all the ideas." Another teacher identified the unique aspect of this professional development opportunity: "A rare and wonderful opportunity to work with artists and innovators in education. I am inspired by the creativity I have experienced and witnessed in this program." And finally, an expression of hope: "The arts experiences have empowered me as a classroom teacher to bring all the arts into my classroom in a meaningful and energetic manner."

A major part of the program for those pursuing advanced qualification was the practical research project that every student must undertake. Teachers were expected to find resources which would allow them to engage guest artists and measure the impact of such an intervention on the learning experiences of their students. They were expected to address a learning problem and assess how the integrated arts response enabled their students to overcome a particular difficulty. It was not a matter of searching the literature, but a process of devising a procedure that would enable teachers to evaluate their own approaches and strategies. This forced every participant to think through the effect that arts teaching in his or her classroom was truly having on the students. The results were astonishing as teachers who had never before engaged in hands-on classroom research discovered the power such reflective activity brings to the instructor.

As well, money was found to evaluate the program in its entirety, particularly the change in professional behaviour that comes from such an intense experience. Too often experimentation in educational matters is not assessed with any rigour and, in the end, the program cannot justify itself. As well as an ongoing evaluation and observation, there has been formal reporting that documents the real effects of the experience on the professional behaviours of all the participants.

An aspect of the program that worked amazingly well was the opportunity it gave teachers to meet artists outside the classroom. For many years, the Stratford Festival's education officer, Pat Quigley, has been offering teachers a program under the auspices of the University of Toronto's Faculty of Education that would bring teachers into contact with actors, designers, directors — indeed the entire spectrum of artists who produce an enormous explosion of drama in that small Ontario town. The Shaw Festival, though much smaller, has, for decades, opened up its operation to the educational system. Both Stratford and Shaw have special matinee performances on the shoulder season before July and after August for student audiences, and the Canadian Opera has rehearsals as well as live performances open for students and their teachers. The National Ballet has initiated a program of "making dance" not only in its home base in Toronto, but in Ottawa and the Niagara Peninsula. This project, initiated by Assis Arreiro, brings together dancers, musicians, and designers, who assist students to create their own dance presentation.

The Toronto Symphony can trace its work with students back to 1925 when its precursor, the New Symphony Orchestra, gave an "orchestral concert for children." For some eight decades, student concerts in Massey Hall and later Roy Thomson Hall have been a part of the regular season, and smaller groups of musicians have gone into area schools to such an extent that well over a hundred thousand students have been reached each year. Perhaps the most innovative is the Adopt-a-Player program in which an elementary school class "adopts" a TSO musician and spends one afternoon a week over a five-week period composing a new piece of music. Often the composition is given a public performance before a TSO audience. All of this activity on the part of major arts organizations kept the flame alive, but now it is essential that a new alliance — a much more potent and intimate relationship between arts organizations and the artists they represent and the schools and their teachers — be initiated.

The format for artistic involvement in the school has been worked upon by a major supporter of the Ontario Arts Education Institute, the Young Peoples' Theatre in Toronto. For over a decade, this theatre, founded by Susan Rubes and her colleagues, has mounted a season of plays appropriate for young audiences in a beautifully refurbished warehouse in the centre of the city. As well, workshops and special performances have been available for teachers. The theatre is regarded as a treasure, and its caring for teachers and students has reached legendary proportions while the quality of its productions has thrilled its young clientele. Recent presentations of *Macbeth* and *The Diary of Anne Frank* have been of a calibre envied by theatres reaching for adult audiences. It is in the spirit and focus of YPT that the future lies for organizations who have realized that without young audiences their future is uncertain at best.

During the planning of the Arts Education Institute summer program for teachers, the arts organizations not only took a major role in providing venues at which teachers and artists could work together, but contributed maturity and wisdom that led to increasing commitment to an integrated approach. Surprisingly, it was the single-discipline arts organizations that spoke most strongly in favour of integration. Indeed, Julie Stone, then Department Head, Gallery Tours and School Programs, at the Art Gallery of Ontario, spoke with missionary fervour, connecting her enthusiasm for integration to her concern for global education. This commitment heralds a new age in the role of the arts in education — a new clientele in the community's galleries and a new audience in the seats of its theatres and concert halls.

However, it will take more than the combination of artists and arts organizations, teachers and administrators to realize the dramatic change that is essential. One of the significant realizations of every commission looking at the reform of schools and education is that learning can no longer be left to the professionals. In spite of all the evidence that parents' discretionary time has been reduced to a minimum, every expert in educational practice is now demanding that the community have a voice, particularly the mothers and fathers who have the primary responsibility for the development of their children. The opportunities for reaching out to that community are legion. In the best of all situations, a commitment to arts-based learning should spring from the excitement of every family which has come to see learning through the arts as a central feature of its life together.

In one sense, a new era has arrived. The isolation of the school is to end. In Ontario, this means that parents are to be welcomed into the classrooms, the halls, and the playgrounds of the province and, most important, school advisory councils involving parents and the community are to be mandatory. The concept of parents taking on the role of voluntary assistants to teachers is being revived. In the context of a society providing fewer hours of paid employment, the future seems pregnant with possibility. Engaging in the process of schooling may become one of the most useful roles that the temporarily unemployed and underemployed can play, bringing them together with their own children and those of their neighbours.

As the concept of school advisory councils participating in educational policy-making emerges as a reality in Ontario, it is essential that they not be seen at worst as troublesome critics of the professionals, or at best, effective fundraisers for the projects the principal has devised. It is a paradox that whenever parents are asked whether they think an arts experience is important to the development of their children, they invariably answer yes, even if the society they are a part of seems determined to diminish and trivialize what the arts are doing in the schools.

Now these parents will have the opportunity of expressing their enthusiasm through a decision-making process that could enhance the learning of every child in every classroom. There are artists in every community awaiting an opportunity to contribute their skill and insight. Marshalling the artistic resources of the school district should be an immediate initiative of every school council.

In these cost-conscious days, the question will be asked, "Won't the involvement of professional artists put financial demands on the system?" Artists must make a decent living and they deserve to be compensated for the efforts and deprivations they have suffered on behalf of their art — but this would represent a miniscule charge to a school budget. The incorporation of fees for artists would represent scarcely a percentage point of the total cost of instruction. The development of schools with an integrated arts-based learning commitment is not a matter of sharply increased expenses, but of enhancing the professional development of teachers, both pre-service and in-service, at a fraction of the total public response to the learning needs of children. It means a shift in the way both the arts and all other subjects are approached, how the content is organized and expressed in a variety of instructional methods, how all disciplines are connected by artistic expression.

In every way, the integration of the arts in the classroom is a question of philosophy and priorities rather than dollars. In the midst of the havoc created by an overall cutting of school budgets, the provision of technological hardware and software seems to be beyond restraint. In an article, "Surfing Back to School, High-tech Glory or Glorified Play," *Maclean's Magazine* makes the point with staggering impact:

> Alberta, which has cut $224-million from public education since 1993, announced in February that it will invest $45-million in technology over the next three years. After slashing $400 million from schools last

March, Ontario doubled its commitment — to $40-million — to a program that matches private sector investments in public school technology. Only six months after piloting a unique CD-ROM-based Grade 9 math curriculum in 16 schools last spring, the four western provinces are taking it to almost every high school in the region this fall. And as classes ended in June, New Brunswick completed a three-year $23-million drive to connect every public school to the World Wide Web.[8]

The contrast, in terms of cost, with an integrated arts-based program could not be greater. Schools which now stress the arts and give students an enriched program do not cost any more than traditional schools. Faywood School in North York provides a good example. It is a regular elementary school serving a normal neighbourhood "clientele" with no special budget or provisions of extra help that might advantage the teachers. There is, however, a commitment on the part of teachers and students to the arts, and the normal budget allocation is directed in such a way that artists, theatre groups, and musical ensembles perform in the gymnasium of that school more often than in other schools under the same board. However, the success of the program revolves around the commitment and energy of a group of teachers who are convinced that a balanced program of arts expression is essential to the well-being of their students.

The willingness of parents to support the trips of choirs and orchestras to exotic places all over the globe is some indication that excellence, commitment, and effort can be rewarded. School advisory councils, with appropriate representation from parents concerned about a balanced curriculum, could ensure that a minimal budget for artists and artistic activities is provided. What parents do not accept is costly schooling that bores and under-challenges, and that situation should never arise in an integrated arts-based learning program.

There may be circumstances that make impossible any shift of resources within the school budget and any extra funds from either parents or the community. Where inner-city conditions make the acquisition of sufficient funds for a truly arts-based educational experience difficult to take place, the theory of the "commons" that has infused the environmental debate for decades and suggests a basic right to public services, must prevail as a provincial policy. No child's life should be damaged, no community's well-being should be threatened by an absence of an opportunity to know oneself and one's environment. The arts are basic to every child's mental and spiritual well-being and must be provided in a public schooling system in a modern society.

The strategies for change are not complicated, but they are difficult to achieve. Artists and teachers must be brought together as allies in a struggle to transform a curriculum and a schooling system. Both must be engaged in a learning process that enables them to reach across to unfamiliar areas of knowing, in a way that recognizes and celebrates the past achievements of both but recognizes the new directions that integration will impose on their activities. The strategy must be one that reaches out to administrators, principals, board of education trustees, and, most importantly, parents, who must come to understand the significance of what an integrated arts-based curriculum in an arts-integrated school can really mean to the learning life of their children.

The weaving of a new tapestry of learning demands that strands of interest and involvement be inserted from the broader community. Arts education cannot come through some isolated eruption within a particular school. It must emerge as an iterative and interactive transformation that consumes both the school and the classroom, the parent, the teacher, and the artist.

Over many years, Mavor Moore, a consummate actor, writer, speaker, and arts administrator who once was chair of the Canada Council, has pointed out that, in the end, all that remains of a civilization is its artistic expression. The politics, the trade, the wars and battles leave little to inspire and exalt future generations. The architecture, the pottery and glass, the painting, the literature and drama — and the ideas that initiated them — all remain with us for study, enlightenment, and enjoyment. Does it not make sense to base our learning on those things which are enduring, on those activities on which our civilization will be evaluated and judged? If the social and economic concerns of the future do not move us to engage the artistic spirit, if the obvious needs of children and youth do not compel us to action, surely the lessons of human life on this planet should inspire us to create a learning experience that has lasting significance.

NOTES

1. Paul Lehman and Richard Sinatra, "Assessing Arts Curricula in the Schools," in *Towards a New Era in Arts Education: The Report of the Interlochen Symposium*, American Council for the Arts, 1988, p. 55.
2. Ibid., p. 25.
3. Ibid., p. 25.
4. Nash Symposium on Arts Education, Cape Breton, August 1996, unpublished.
5. Unpublished letter, Elke Scholz to author. November 24, 1995.
6. Laurie Rowbotham, "The Power of One," Editor's Notebook, *The Recorder: The Journal of the Ontario Music Educators' Association*, February 1990, 32:2, p. 49.
7. Miller, Heather. "The Ontario Arts Education Institute — A Remarkable Thing!" in *The Artspaper*, Autumn 1995, 6:1, p. 3.
8. Victor Dwyer, "Surfing Back to School, High-tech Glory or Glorified Play?" *Maclean's*, August 26, 1996, p. 41.

Chapter 10   **Strategies for Change**

It is not incumbent upon you to complete the task: but
neither are you free to exempt yourself from it.

Rabbi Tarfon (2nd century)

s we have seen, the early '90s' optimistic anticipation of the
new century has dissipated. John Vidal, writing in the *Guard-*
ian, has expressed the gloom and cynicism that now characterizes so much talk of the millennium:

> In recent years a powerful new orthodoxy has gained
> ground. The world that has emerged after the fall of
> communism is seen as far more disorderly. New levels
> of violence and crime are widely forecast and new
> forms of civil and grassroots dissent are being predict-
> ed.
>
> Authorities, institutions and international companies
> once seen as the hope of developing states are being re-
> evaluated as, at best, self-serving and unable to change

things for the better, or as new economic colonists. The global model of development — based on state intervention, big agriculture, big dams, roads, factories, media and markets — is accused of failing.

The poor and homeless are finding new ways to oppose the rich, and there is talk of the real limits of the free market. Meanwhile, the United Nations says the conflicts of the future may be over ever-scarcer resources such as water, and that cities will be unable to cope with the new environmental and social pressures. . . .

This analysis ignores hundreds of thousands of small community initiatives going on everywhere. But the hard evidence from development groups and charities is that new levels of social disease are leading straight to dissent and conflict.

These reasons are given for the protests erupting in every continent: rapidly growing inequalities of wealth, both among and within countries; the approach of ecological limits that force the poor to compete for declining resources; and emergence of a new dispossessed class in all countries.[1]

This was not the way things were expected to be. Several decades ago Marshall McLuhan spoke confidently of the global village, a now over utilized image of a planet joined by threads of new technology in such a way that humankind would be one in confronting the scourges of poverty, hunger, disease, and homelessness. However, it was assumed that the values of the village would prevail — intimacy with one's neighbours, a caring for all those disadvantaged who were part of the extended community, a sense of common ownership of those things which create community from ballparks, city squares, theatres, and concert halls to social programs. Instead, we have the value system of a global casino — individual wealth is all that really matters, accompanied by little concern for the losers, a terrible feeling of alienation and powerless-

YOUNG PEOPLES' THEATRE: THE DRAGON'S PEARL

Ontario's most committed theatre company devoted to drama for children is playing to a tough audience: 200 young people, ranging in age from junior kindergarten to grade five. As well, there is an older group of mentally challenged students who have been invited to join the regular students in attendance in the school gymnasium.

The children have been effectively briefed on the role of the audience, not just "no talking" but the more demanding issues of appropriate interaction with live performers. To some extent, this preparation is required as a result of the pervasive behavioural influence of television viewing, where response, whether positive or negative, has little communal importance.

This production of the Young Peoples' Theatre, a play set in the Far East called The Dragon's Pearl, has intriguing features. Three of the four actors are Asian. Percussive music (tambourines, drums) is played by the children themselves and there is a simple, energetic dance at one point in the drama. The costuming, though obviously from a foreign culture, has recognizable features for the children in the audience. Indeed the actors wear costumes that resemble the "costumes" of their older brothers and sisters in their daily lives.

ness on the part of a great mass of players, and a lack of any common ideals or behaviours that seem appropriate.

The most disconcerting aspect of this vision of the future is that most of the increased population that will inhabit the earth in the first decades of the new century will be found in the developing world. Needless to say, the countries least able to clothe and feed these new citizens will bear the brunt of that increase. If that population were capable of feeding itself on the land, the pressure would be lessened, but alas, by the first quarter of the next century, there will be eight billion people on the planet, and five billion of them in cities and villages in those poorer countries. It is estimated that by the year 2015 there will be 33 megacities (metropolitan areas with populations of over eight million) and 27 of them will be in the developing world.

One has only to consider the enormous problems that the Western world has confronted in dealing with housing, transportation, waste, water, and law and order in high-population areas to realize what an enormous challenge lies ahead. For we can be sure of one thing: unlike the comparative passivity and relative silence of the dispossessed in rural communities, the discontent of the masses of people in those cities will be most visible. It will be expressed in ways that will disrupt the lives of children now sitting in Canadian classrooms. The technology of destruction that has largely been the legacy of rich nations will be in the hands of unstable and despairing countries, making it a threat to every citizen on the planet.

If the 20th century has taught us anything, it is that the simple, logical theories of town planning that were popular in the post-World War II era have been inadequate. Only the creation of neighbourhoods with strategies for developing local employment, for moving people about, for providing the motivation and processes for reusing and recycling our waste, for providing intellectual, artistic, and emotional sustenance, can make cities work. It is the holistic, cultural perception of dealing with people that can prevail in either a city or on an overcrowded planet. In the wake of challenges such as overpopulation and urbanization, educational systems can no longer avoid the cultural role they must play.

In a way that no one could have predicted, the solution to collective problems has

The story is simple, but not patronizing. The dialogue stretches the vocabulary without baffling even the youngest in attendance, and the plot holds their attention with suspense that is gentle but ever-present.

The themes are clearly defined: the importance of demonstrating respect for the environment as revealed by the dependence of these peasants on rain, the reality of poverty in this region, and the degree to which sharing is the strategy for survival. The play also examines the effect of sudden riches as one family, favoured with the magic Dragon's Pearl, sees its relationship with another disrupted by greed and selfishness.

After the performance, the members of the cast call for questions, and though the children are obviously overwhelmed by the props and the visual effects they have witnessed, it is clear the messages have been heard. One issue in particular, the question of sharing, will undoubtedly be the pre-eminent issue of the 21st century. The needs of the lesser-developed regions of Africa, Central and South America, and Asia will be massive, especially if the more advantaged nations in North America and Europe are reluctant to act with generosity and compassion. The future for these young people will be at risk as violence becomes the defence of those who are hungry, diseased, and without shelter. This drama in a school gymnasium strikes at the very centre of the human dilemma and thus serves a curriculum devoted to the understanding children require if they, as adults, are to eventually influence the public agenda and enhance the quality of their lives.⌘ an increasing connection to individual intellectual and moral awareness. The idea that slick theories or a capacity to assemble statistical data would improve the daily life of the urban dweller, without confronting value systems which lead to chaos, is now proven ludicrous. Any curriculum change in our schools that deserves consideration must address the individual needs of students, even those perceived as bored and withdrawn, at sea morally and spiritually, anxious to drop out, seemingly enthusiastic about nothing but bizarre dress and hairstyle, drugs, beer, and rock music. The integrated arts-based curriculum must perforce satisfy the essential need for identity, but also confront the students' sense of impending disaster. That curriculum must address the themes which incorporate universal concerns around political, economic, and environmental challenges as well as answering questions that children have about who they are in a way that goes beyond the answers found on television and in the marketplace.

At a time when schools around the world have adopted the view that their primary responsibility is to train young people to compete in this planetary gaming house, where the cultural, the intellectual, and the artistic are dismissed as irrelevant, where the right thing is interpreted as merely staying within the limits of the law — or at least not getting caught — there is the quest for a new direction. George Grant describes the point of view that once gave schools and teachers such an honourable place down the centuries and made the creation and maintenance of a fine public school system so important to civilized nations on all continents:

> In the old theory of education, when a man began to see what was the ultimate purpose of human life, he was

said to be wise — to have the virtue of wisdom. Wisdom
was then the purpose of education. It was the condition
that men reached through reason, as they came to
know what were the purposes in human life truly worthy of a rational soul.[2]

Seeking "the ultimate purpose of human life" and acquiring "the
virtue of wisdom" must surely be restored as the central role of the
school. Wisdom, however, cannot be reached through a narrowly defined concept of the rational. The emotions are valid, as well as the enhancement of all the various intelligences by which we come to know
ourselves, reach out to others in understanding, and seek to do those
things that are valid and appropriate.

This will not happen simply through teaching children to conquer
the various technologies that surround them, nor through a total preoccupation with skill training for vocational purposes. Rather, it will be
the result of integrating all forms of knowledge in a cultural thrust that
stresses the centrality of dealing with the basic problems facing our civilization, that emphasizes the interaction of all forms of wisdom identified over the centuries of human activity, and that perceives the artistic
as the connecting tissue which can give coherence and intelligibility
while emphasizing the human values that will sustain the planet.

A few basic strategies that could change our schools must be identified:

1. A COMMITMENT TO CREATIVITY

It scarcely needs saying that schools which trivialize what emerges
from the thoughts and imagination of the child should be abolished, and
teachers who fail to encourage the creativity of children should be encouraged to seek alternative employment. It is time for every school advisory council, every teachers' and parents' organization, every board of

education and provincial education ministry, to state unequivocally its belief in children's creative potential and, as well, the importance of making it possible for this creativity to emerge. Without this commitment, it is possible to lose sight of the extraordinary need to ensure that the process of surfacing, exposing, and enhancing the creative impulse of each child not be lost in the host of other expectations the school faces from parents, community, politicians, business leaders, and media commentators. Only such a statement can free the teacher to risk, to experiment, both alone and in association with artists — a linkage essential to the success of any integrated arts-based program. The first step in the political sphere for artists and teachers together might well be the extraction of such a commitment from every level of administration in the schooling system.

A commitment to the creativity of children is, by implication, a vote of confidence in the creativity of the professionals engaged in teaching them. One of the most effective changes that could happen immediately would be that of raising the morale of the teaching community. In Ontario, teachers at all levels staged a protest in the fall of 1997. Some 116,000 teachers demonstrated in front of schools all across the province, the largest assembly of its kind in North American history.

It could be said that this event was the culmination of many years of continuous criticism of teachers in the media and in the halls of government, as well as severe cutbacks in resources available to the schools. The effect has been to undermine the sense of dedication and willingness of teachers to walk the extra mile that has always characterized the best teachers and has created the best classrooms. A new vision that brings together all who care about learning is a strategy for achieving a new unity of purpose.

2. A COMMITMENT TO THE CONCEPT OF LIFELONG LEARNING FOR CREATIVITY

There must be an end to the idea that narrowly cast adult learning for the workplace is an appropriate role for the school board, the college, the university, or indeed any publicly funded educational institution. Arts courses and arts units within courses must balance the offerings that have an obvious vocational purpose.

Such a principle recognizes that learning is a lifelong process and thereby rejects the child-centred concept by which we concentrate the formal schooling of people in the first years of their lives. Lifelong learning must be perceived not simply as a means of training and re-training people for the numerous jobs or voluntary sector roles they might assume over a lifetime. Learning must be perceived as the basis for enabling individuals to survive on a very precious but threatened planet on which there now exists the means of wreaking havoc and destruction to the point of eliminating the species.

Every program teaching a technological skill should have a cultural component, and workers, teachers, and artists should be campaigning to see that such richness is provided. As well, the web of artistic activity in the public sector — the performance of music, drama, dance, and serious film and the presentation of visual arts — must be seen as a valid continuing education opportunity for every adult after the school has disappeared as the focus of learning. It is on the basis of this essential learning role, rather than on the providing of entertainment for the masses, that public funding philosophies should be based. Every arts organization, artist, and teacher must share that mission.

3.   RECOGNIZING THE UNIVERSALITY OF THE CULTURAL APPROACH

There must come a realization that the cultural approach to all human problems is the only sane course in the days ahead. This strategy in no way denigrates the knowledge and understanding of the engineer, the scientist, the lawyer, the doctor, the philosopher, the linguist; it simply recognizes the futility of narrowly based strategies to confront the problems facing humankind. Thus, learning the arts becomes the mastering of the pre-eminent force which can lead young minds to the wonders of science and mathematics, which can link what we know of the past to what we perceive of the present, can make intelligible what we know of our minds, bodies, and spirits. Through the arts, the vast majority will find the philosophic capacity to reach a value system that is the basis for sustainable living. This path will replace the consumerism and personal greed that has dominated human society as we approach the millennium.

Arts organizations must consider how they might broaden their patrons' understanding of the cultural approach as part of the fabric of lifelong learning. The programs of every theatre, concert hall, dance studio, and art gallery must be devoted to some aspect of the supremacy of the creative. This does not suggest a humourless and deadly serious arts scene in every venue or performance space. Indeed, laughter and fun are very much the ways by which the cupidity and greed of our present context can best be revealed. It does mean a more focussed search for a coherent role for each arts organization devoted to arts disciplines interconnecting to explore the human condition. It most certainly impels the educational community to reconsider its role, its practices, its priorities, and its commitment.

4. DEVELOPING AN INTEGRATED ARTS-BASED CURRICULUM

As we have seen, there are steps to take before an integrated arts-based curriculum can be put in place, even at the earliest primary levels of the school. Teachers must be given the opportunity to explore the necessity of a holistic approach to learning both for themselves and their students. Introducing such a curriculum will be an evolutionary process. In some classrooms it will begin with an invitation to an artist or a group of artists to enhance an existing theme that unites the arts subjects and reaches out as well to science and mathematics, history and geography, and linguistics. Or it might be a theme built around visits to the museum or art gallery that provides an introduction to myriad alternatives in understanding a particular aspect of life that has attracted the attention of students and can be revealed by various artifacts.

In another school, it might be the preparation of a particular segment based on the theme of exploring the universe. Holst's "The Planets" might be an entrance, along with Haydn's "The Creation," moving to visual expressions of planetary reality, from photographs taken from space to painters like Van Gogh, who revealed space as conceived in his own mind, to the reading of books which express the wonder and awe that attend the enormous extension of our scientific knowledge. Such exploration would lead logically to an examination of the value system that must permeate the thinking of those who live on a single planet on which life as we define it has developed. Concepts of time, both in music and in the measuring of a universe, become further opportunities for the discussion and contemplation of the purpose and goal of human experience. The skills of reading and writing, effectively working in groups to explore particular planetary systems — all these represent entry points in a curriculum which seeks to expose children to all the facets of their intelligences. A part of every school day must be given over to the planning of this interrelated approach. Teachers must constantly work together to discover their own collective wisdom in creating an arts-based learning program.

Addressing the arts in the classroom is tied to assuring that children are "learning to learn" — how to find evidence, how to assess the quality of the evidence they discover, how to allow the creative urge to surface and be adequately expressed in word, image, or movement.

5. SECURING A BODY OF EDUCATIONAL RESEARCH EVIDENCE

One of the most disconcerting aspects of work in the field of education is the lack of easily accessible research into the elements of learning. There is a mountain of studies, articles, books, and unpublished theses on virtually every question that haunts the classroom teacher. Yet there is little evidence that any of this scholarly activity has had an impact on the day-to-day practices of teachers. Some of the reasons for this lack of connection between research and practice have been alluded to, for example, the difficulty of securing controlled situations and the frustration of waiting for data to emerge from longitudinal studies. As well, there is the fact that few resources are assigned to the dissemination and promotion of research in education — in sharp contrast to the world of industry, where it is expected that a substantial percentage of profits will go toward the quest for more information and its circulation. Unfortunately, there are few monetary profits to be found in examining the real outcomes of activities taking place in public educational systems.

Another reason for the limited influence of research on classroom practice is that the most effective research can only be carried out either by, or in close association with, the classroom teacher. However, to expect the average teacher with a full load of class time to take on the role of a researcher, as well as prepare lessons, be responsible for a class over several hours, give adequate assignments of work, mark and evaluate every child's efforts, and provide increasingly detailed reports on progress to every parent, is impossible. As a result, the most valuable source of observation, analysis, and reflection is lost.

It is essential that programs designed to establish an integrated arts-based curriculum in a school include a component of hands-on research and evaluation. The same could be said about every innovation that is introduced into the classroom, but it is particularly pertinent in regard to this substantial shift in focus, in purpose, and in method and expectation. In the recent in-service professional development program for teachers organized by the Ontario Arts Education Institute through the Faculty of Education at York University, there was such a component, and the results support the need for increased research and evaluation of the learning experience at every step of its implementation.

6. AN ALLIANCE OF ARTISTS AND TEACHERS

A significant change, even if developed over several years, can only be successfully adopted in a schooling system when the major participants have a unified purpose and commitment. Both teachers and artists must make a commitment to change the perception of the arts to that of a learning tool that will make the full spectrum of knowledge more accessible to young people, and will provide them with the skills and confidence to contribute as neighbours, citizens, workers, and volunteers. The arts, as the basis for an integrated curriculum, will choreograph students' acquisition of knowledge and skill in a way that their intelligences find most effective, will confront them with the most challenging questions about themselves and the world they live in. That is the ideal both teachers and artists must come to espouse as professionals. Faced with a context of hostility to such idealism, the strategy of such an alliance must be obvious. The acceptance of an educational role by arts organizations and the welcoming of artists into the classrooms, gymnasiums, cafeterias, and auditoriums as partners in the learning process will result from this alliance.

Artists are faced with the challenge of seeing themselves as educators — not a role that has been identified as appropriate in the modern world. Indeed, one could argue that the modernist concentration on "product" has tended to isolate the visual and performing artist from a broader recognition of how artistic insights benefit the entire society. In 1997, the Report of the Canadian Conference of the Arts' Arts in Transition Project makes this point about the emphasis on artistic product: "[M]any younger artists find it confining, unable to accommodate their desire to work more closely with communities and incorporate social and ecological issues into their art."[3]

The time has come, then, for a joining of artists and teachers. Such an alliance can assure the sustainability of the arts. As the Arts in Transition Project report clearly states: "The benefits the arts bring to society, to all Canadians, should be central, not peripheral, to the thinking of all those concerned with the arts."[4] The place to start is in the classrooms of the nation.

7. PREPARING BOTH TEACHERS AND ARTISTS

It is not enough to assume that a few days of artists working with teachers and teachers working with artists will arouse the creative urge in both and thereby assure that integrated arts-based programs emerge. Faculties of education, responsible for providing both pre-service and in-service preparation of teachers, must become a part of the web of institutions engaged in shifting the curriculum. Thus, at least one part of the university system becomes attached to the arts organizations and the artists they represent for what is essentially a single mission to prepare teachers and artists for a different curriculum emphasizing the cultural, connected to the concept of the horizontal approach in relation to all discipline areas and committed to creativity as the central goal of what transpires in the classroom.

The only appropriate form of preparation is one that connects both teachers and artists to the great mountaintops of creativity to be found in the literature, music, drama, movement, and film/video that has emerged over the centuries. But such an examination must be accompanied by the hands-on exploration of the creativity of both teacher and artist. Preferably, learning programs that include both should be readily available. It means bringing the Ontario College of Art and Design, along with programs of the community colleges and the faculties of fine arts in the universities, into the mainstream of preparation and development support of both artists and teachers. In Ontario, a new College of Teachers has an opportunity to broaden the ways by which teachers gain information and skills, but even more important will be the path that must be found to assist working professionals to find self-realization, creative inspiration, and enlarged motivation in a learning environment that includes artists and arts organizations. There could be no wiser investment.

8. CREATING INTEGRATED ARTS-BASED SCHOOLS

It will be an evolutionary process, not an overturning of the present program, but it may come with extraordinary speed. The elements are all there — parents who want their children prepared for work and life, teachers who desire a professional experience that has meaning beyond serving out a term of decades in an impossible situation, a community that demands value for its money and wants to hear less of dropouts, an increasing number of thoughtful people who realize that there is little value in a schooling system that does not prepare youth for a sustainable future.

The school councils made up of parents, teachers, administrators, and interested community people now being formed in many jurisdictions are the basic building blocks for a new educational system. Parents will be able to influence the nature and quality of learning their children are receiving. Every council must be confronted with the questions about learning that have come down through the ages and baffled previous generations. Parents need to be encouraged to think about their own learning experience, not as an invitation to base their children's education on a nostalgia for past times, but as an examination of their own feeling about the school's role in modern society. They understand that the world of the workplace has changed beyond recognition, they know their children face questions about lifestyle, values, and priorities, and that the answers they find will be crucial to their well-being. Many have found their own strength and vitality in the creativity they reveal in their work, their hobbies, their contributions to the life of the community. They know that the arts have been the most influential in helping them to discover and release that creativity. It is from the source of the artistic respect for community and love for children that the vitality of the school must spring in the future.

⌘ ⌘ ⌘

There is no silver bullet, no revelation of truth from on high, that will end all the controversy and despair over the education of our young people. Only through a combination of better-prepared teachers, adequate resources, effective interventions by highly qualified artists, and support services from a host of directions — social service offices, research institutes, curriculum experts, indeed the entire spectrum of knowledgeable, sensitive individuals who can make children's learning a community commitment — can the enterprise of learning be substantially changed.

However, there is a need for something more — a curriculum that has direction and unity, that has the capacity to excite and inspire, that accommodates the multi-faceted way children and young people learn. An integrated arts-based curriculum would serve that purpose. As well, it would mine the rich veins of past artistic achievements, and challenge a generation of artists who are aware of the crisis the arts face if there is no change in society's inadequate comprehension of the cultural extension of a life well-lived. Such a curriculum demands an initial societal commitment to the creative impulse in every child, a recognition of a broad spectrum of achievement in learning that has received little attention in the past, and a substantial investment in the artistic potential of teachers of all subjects and disciplines. In the light of the staggering problems that will confront the children of this generation, we must expose them to the intellectual and emotional energy that has produced those ideas and artifacts we value most.

NOTES
1. John Vidal, "The global formula for social dynamite," *The Guardian*, London, reprinted in the *Globe and Mail*, June 15, 1996, p. D4.
2. George Grant, *Philosophy in the Mass Age* (Toronto: University of Toronto Press, 1995; originally published by Copp Clark Publishing Company, 1959), p. 32.
3. Report of the Arts in Transition Project, Canadian Conference of the Arts, October 1997, p. 6.
4. Ibid., p. 14.

Postscript

In the process of composing this volume, the Government of Ontario released its long-awaited curriculum publication: *The Ontario Curriculum, Grades 1-8: The Arts.*

One cannot expect inspiration from such a document. Its purpose is to instruct teachers in the expectations the government wishes to impose, and, in this case, to make clear the fact that local curriculum initiatives have been replaced by this centralized response to what are perceived as the learning needs of the province's students. Surprisingly, there is little indication that the authors have read the latest research on the way the arts have been seen to improve the capacity of students to conquer other areas of the curriculum (science and mathematics), the very areas that appear to be the preoccupation of the Ministry.

Nor does the document contain any compelling argument for a strategy of teaching the arts in any integrated way, though there is some indication that the arts can bring life and relevance to other disciplines such as literature and history.

Most of all, the reader receives not an iota of any of the magic and excitement the arts bring to the learning of children, nor is there any indication that artists might have a role to play in the work of the classroom. Most important, the prominence that the Common Curriculum gave to the arts, indicating that fully 25% of classroom time in the elementary grades should be given over to arts education, has been eliminated.

The connection of the arts and a healthy economy, the linking of arts disciplines and the very skills upon which success in the 21st century can be based, are not recognized in *The Arts*. Nor is there any understanding that cultural considerations will be the basis of unity for planet and nation. Indeed, in the latter case, the music section mentions Tchaikovsky, Saint-Saëns, Rossini, Prokofiev, Dukas, Handel, Mozart, Debussy, Beethoven, Smetana — but not a single Canadian composer.

However, there is an opening for enlightened teachers, parents, and administrators in their desire to provide both inspiration and practical help through the development of an integrated arts-based school for the children they serve. The involvement of parents in the education of their children is recognized and emphasized. As important, the statement "Teachers are responsible for developing appropriate instructional strategies" is one that encourages the professional role of those who work in the classrooms of the province, just as the advice that "Teachers will provide as many hands-on activities as possible" encourages a role for artists in the learning experience of our children.

Epilogue

It was a cool spring evening and the streets close to Sunny View School in North Toronto were solidly lined with cars and vans of every size and description. Inside the brightly lit, single-story building, there was an atmosphere of high excitement. It was a performance of an original musical, *Catch A Dream*.

Every child who attended the school, along with every teacher and assistant had worked for weeks on the songs, the poems, the dramatic action, the staging, the costumes — even the decorating of the performance venue, in this case, the school gymnasium.

Not an unusual event in the lifetime of most schools across the country, but there was a difference in this case. Every child in the cast, some 150 in number, was disabled, physically and, in many cases, mentally. Most were in wheelchairs. The logistics of having every child involved, every wheelchair on the small gymnasium stage, every voice heard, everybody seen, was monumental.

The evening opened with a welcome from Sunny View principal Peg Monk, a legend in the world of serving disabled children. It was her determination that the arts — all of them, not simply a school choir serving the more mobile students — would be celebrated at Sunny View. She was convinced that children learned through the arts — yes, *learned* to sing and draw and speak — but also *learned* about the world by writing, by painting, by dancing. . .by every expression of body and mind. She believed that children confined to wheelchairs needed all that the arts could teach them about their emotions and about their relationships with others. She knew that children with cruelly limited brain functions could be reached by that panoply of creative activity we call the arts.

And she believes it every day of the week, not just on the evening of the annual concert. She and her team of extraordinarily talented teachers perform miracles every day without spotlights and awards, without accolades and prizes. And with unusual commitment, they do it year after year — many of these teachers have spent most of their professional lives in this school. But they do it with the help of the community, with the help of artists, and with the help of arts organizations such as the McMichael Collection, the Art Gallery of Ontario, and the Toronto Symphony. This year, a particularly gifted mime artist and mask maker, Naomi Tyrell, spent hours with these children. Artists are thrilled with the nurturing, inviting climate they experience in this school. The disabilities fade in significance as these children experience glorious moments of triumph as they draw and paint, make music, and engage in drama.

However, this special night was a chance for these young people to show parents and friends what they were capable of doing.

As one looked about, one could sense the deep concern of the parents and guardians pushing wheelchair after wheelchair from crowded corridors to scarcely less turbulent classrooms where each segment of the production was being marshalled. But there was not a sign of nervous unhappiness in the faces of the children. They waited patiently for their entrances, filled with anticipation for their moment onstage. This was their chance to please the hundreds of parents, friends, and relatives who mean so much to them, who sacrifice in ways they could scarcely understand, but of whose love they are assured.

The gymnatorium was an explosion of colour. The children had been encouraged to use their visual arts classes to express their dreams, as well as their nightmares. Magnificent land and water creatures emerged from their imaginations, visibly influenced by the books they had read, by the scientific information that had been gathered, by the history they had imbibed.

The evening kicked off with a spirited rendition of "O Canada" and the musical was under way. It was apparent that *over* achievement was the order of the evening, and every child had his or her triumph. They moved with halting steps that only a paralysis could have inflicted, but what the muscles could not achieve, the voice and gesture, the power of each individual child's self-confidence, accomplished. Every presentation of the theme purveyed personal extensions of power and purpose. Choral ensembles dominated, but there were glorious moments when solos were performed exquisitely.

My wife and I were there as part of a proud family that had anticipated our granddaughter's performance. Zoë had come through a traumatic birth which had left her severely brain-damaged and paralyzed on one side. But the compensation of the gods had given her the most beautiful face and the most angelic disposition, along with a determined, indomitable desire to be heard and understood. She sang with her class and revelled in the applause the presentation returned.

The arts are all that have been described in these pages...and more. They are the ultimate form of equality, of joy and delight. They are of the moment, to be grasped and celebrated. They are a way of knowing what can be shared with children and adults who have very different intellectual and physical capacities. The warmth and uncomplicated happiness on that tiny stage reminded me that the arts are, above all, how we express the finest elements of our humanity — our understanding, our compassion, our caring, and our love.

Appendix A

Not a Frill:
The Centrality of the Arts
in the Education of the Future

Ontario Arts Council Submission
to the Royal Commission on Learning

by Stephen Campbell,
Arts Education Officer, and
Kathryn Townshend,
Manager of Research and Policy
January 1994

EXECUTIVE SUMMARY

Since its inception in 1963, the Ontario Arts Council (OAC) has been engaged in arts education as an essential component of its mandate. During this time OAC has provided support and leadership to arts education which is unique in Canada. Our focus is on supporting and developing links between professional artists and learners.

The Ontario Arts Council's philosophy of arts education is based on two principles:

1. *All* learners benefit from arts education; and
2. Cultural literacy, which is acquired in large part through the arts, is fundamental in today's society.

OAC's submission to the Royal Commission on Learning describes and documents the essential contribution of the arts in three areas of the Commission's mandate: the goals of education in today's society; the program and curriculum needed to achieve this vision; and, lifelong learning and training.

The Ontario Arts Council submits the following recommendations to the Royal Commission on Learning:

RECOMMENDATIONS

- That the Royal Commission on Learning and the Ministry of Education and Training recognize the essential contribution of the arts to the development of the expanded "new basic" skills needed for success in this rapidly changing world.

- That the Ontario Ministry of Education and Training make available resources to improve and expand opportunities for teacher pre-service and in-service training in the arts.

- That the major players within the education system — the Ministry of Education and Training, the boards of education and the teachers' federations, parents' groups, students, and others — recognize the expertise of professional artists and allow them a significant role in artistic instruction.

- That the Ministry of Education and Training establish a joint study group including artists, educators and other key partners to investigate and recommend expanded and new models for the use of the arts across the curriculum.

- That the Ministry of Education and Training involve OAC, artists, business and labour in a joint planning initiative to ensure that the arts are included as part of ongoing skills and training.

- That the education system (through the Ministry of Education and Training and the boards of education) become more involved in supporting arts education outside the classroom, through whatever means are appropriate to meet community needs.

- That the Ministry of Education and Training establish a working group comprising various partners in arts education, including artists and arts educators, to ensure that a continuum of instruction and training in the arts is provided for all types of learners, and across all communities.

- That the Ministry of Education and Training recognize and support centres of excellence for professional arts training in both official languages to serve the various regions of the province.

Keynote Address by Robin Phillips

Ontario Arts Council Professional Development for
Artists Engaged in Art Education Day
Victoria College, University of Toronto
February 17, 1995

with the assistance of John Murell, Liz Nicholls, and David Pelizzaik

L ast July, the Citadel Theatre in Edmonton presented a three-week Festival of the Arts for teenagers: eight years old to 18 years is the Albertan version of teenagers. So I got my squishy, half-eaten Snickers bar presents from the eight-year-olds. Squished into my hand — half-eaten apples. "Would you like a bite, Sir?" And a lot of stroppy kids who invited me to go and have a quiet cigarette on the fire escape. The project was called *The Alberta Quilt*, and for it I directed — well, I drilled, actually I sergeant-majored — 350 teenagers and for those three weeks proved to be a blessed journey. For those young people who travelled with us I know it was a good experience, too. They wrote and performed with tremendous energy, with concentration, and

I was thrilled to discover as the days progressed a deep sense of national pride. We all came together, more than 300 teenagers from Alberta and more than 20 professional artists from around the province, the country, and the world, to create a kaleidoscopic portrait of a unique place from remote prehistoric, pre-human times, through yesterday and tomorrow.

Part I told of Alberta's history before time itself. "Oceans receded, and mountains erupted, and glaciers sculpted the features of the once peaceful plain that Albertans now call home," wrote Liz Nicholls, in the *Edmonton Journal*. "The land and the animals of this glorious province had a long and colourful story of their own long before the first human eyes swept across that land."

"Nobody was there," the narration began. "Nobody to tell us how it looked, how it smelled, how it tasted, how it sounded, how it felt. Nobody was there with a thermometer, or a microphone or a video camera." Another voice took up the story, "But close your eyes now and take a deep breath of silence. Open your eyes again, and your whole mind, and move directly into it." Another narrator joined in, "Look all around you, it looked like this. Take a deep breath, it smelled like this. Let your taste buds use their imagination, it tastes like this. Listen, it sounds like this, it feels like this." And so with nine narrators on stage, our story began.

"What we saw was a time swirl that lingered over the watery expanse of pre-Tory Alberta, when it was warm and quiet, and then erupted into activity," Liz Nicholls wrote. "And I use the word 'erupts' advisedly since we're talking literally about hundreds of bodies. The explosion of sea into land, land into mountains, and pulsing primordial gunk into animals was mostly presented in dance, movement and song. The kids danced, choreographed, composed and sang for Act I. They studied and performed martial arts, modern dance, jazz, tap, ballet, traditional African dance and a thousand expressive movements yet to be given names. The newly minted creatures paired and tested their unfamiliar bodies in a fascinating series of modern dance. The dominant creatures represented by a sequined rock star in white, quivered with the life force. With a backup group of 200, he belted out a teen hit entitled the *Cyclone Circus Band*." The sea washed over us in a wave of turquoise silk. The cast entered from the back of the auditorium. One hundred and fifty from each side of the auditorium, and from side to side held a vast silk cloth stretched tight over the heads of the audience until we were all engulfed beneath the water.

The Rockies erupted in a roar of heavy metal: the same silk stretches high on 30-foot poles, and pulled by yards of guide ropes. There were times when I thought we were going to lose some of the cast. There were those that I wish we had lost. And the pièce de resistance, a battle between the ice floes in a foot-stomping mixture of traditional African dance and martial arts. Microphones hidden in the floor picked up the thunderous rhythm of the feet, and I think may have done some permanent damage to our main stage (again, we're talking about 200 a side). It certainly did damage my eardrums, although possibly that could have been the coffee and pop breaks. New birds, new insects, brought colour and lyricism in two new ballets. Then to the awesome beat of a giant drum, the long procession from the north arrived and humankind found the valley that was to be Alberta. It was the end of Part I and we did not have an interval, but the 300 kids stopped, stared out in amazement at the gawking spectators in the auditorium, and flame burst up from the centre of the stage, and we were into Part II, the First People.

With the arrival of the aboriginal people comes language, and language breeds stories. Stories that identified a people more closely aligned with natural forces than the European immigrants who came after them. Flame leapt up from the centre of the stage, and dressed in their traditional costumes, the actors began to tell the stories of the new life:

> A great circle of grandmothers, grandfathers, mothers, fathers, women, and men and children. They are blessed by the Shaman. The sweet grass is burned and the sweet smell spreads. When the spirit moves you to speak, you take the eagle feather in your right hand. Everyone listens. No one interrupts. You finish speaking, and you move the eagle feather to your left hand so that the next speaker may take it from you, hold it in his or her right hand, and say what needs to be said. Many stories of the earth, and the sky, and the animals, and the people are told.

We told stories of animals and spirits, of water and trees. We saw carving and cooking, hunting and harvesting. A procession of canoes at one point "defied the giddy natural rush," and we sang, we danced, and we celebrated. Every episode had a storyteller. Each story made use of different theatrical disciplines. One story of the beginning of things went like this:

> The very first person and the muskrat were alone on a tiny piece of dry earth. All the rest was water: surrounding them, covering everything. The very first person said to the muskrat, "There must be more land beneath the water. Will you swim down and see if this is true?" The muskrat dived and swam deeper and deeper trying to find what was beneath the world of water, and finally he found it. But his struggle had been great, and he died before he could swim to the surface again. The very first person found the muskrat floating near him dead. But in his claws the muskrat clutched samples of the sticky earth from beneath the waters. The very first person took this new earth from the muskrat's claws and rolled it, and kneaded it, and warmed it. And the dirt began to expand and spread until it because all the land that is in the world today.

> Even then, the very first person had some earth left over from the muskrat's treasure. This was used to shape animals of every kind, and plants of every kind, into which the very first person breathed life.

The boy that told us that story, or the boy that performed that story, was cast, as they all were, for various reasons, such as, it's his turn, he hasn't had enough to do in Act I; he looks bored; all those usual reasons. When I asked him if he'd like to tell that particular story, he paled, and started to shake. Although I didn't know it, he was a Cree. He took me by the hand and he said, "My Cree name is Little Muskrat."

Fifteen kids stood motionless at the very back of the empty stage and on an endless sigh of sea and surf, unfolded a 50-foot muskrat puppet: a skeleton, but with warm dark eyes. It swam, it dived, its huge head lunging out through the proscenium arch for a quizzical look at the audience. "A silent skeleton, moving with grace and effortless agility, manipulated by a whole team of intensely concentrating puppeteers." It was the single most moving experience that I have ever had in the theatre. A young girl, who was interested in ballet, was one of the supporters of the head: a 12-foot pole, and the head twice the size of the chandelier above you. We said at one point perhaps we should change her to a claw. The girl said, "I'll do the HEAD." She did the head. There were many stories in Part II, and the end of Part II, in the middle of a dance of thanksgiving, a single gun shot announced the arrival of the first Europeans, and again the stage fell silent.

Act III, after an interval, Others Arrive, "was a spiky collage of theatrical images and dramatic exchanges about the growing pains of a fractious, multicultural society," wrote Liz Nicholls. "This act of the *Alberta Quilt* presented a picture of a fair province that also has its dark side. Alberta, cold and tough, ugly and beautiful. An Alberta when sometimes the night sky was bright with northern lights; sometimes with the burning crosses of the Ku Klux Klan; sometimes with the flames of a 1947 oil well gusher; and sometimes with show-biz footlights from the Pentages Vaudeville Theatre of 1913." Whatever facts the young Albertans unearthed, they *presented* them with love.

Two days ago, we celebrated Valentine's Day. The original Signor Valentine, an ancient Italian, lived in the time of Claudius II and almost converted this wavering emperor. He cured the blindness of the daughter of one of Claudius' chief officers and was thereafter immediately decapitated for having performed an act of excessive healing. In the busy afterlife that all saints have, Valentine was canonized. Gradually, paradoxically, he was attached as a sponsor to a universal day of love. A one-day antidote to the unconscionable acts of emperors and other brutes.

The *Alberta Quilt* was about love; love of home, love of family, pride of place. Love, how it works, how it fails, what it cannot do, and what it can. You know, when you are a middle-aged man with a varied life experience that comes with all those years of an international career, you have to consider yourself very fortunate indeed to be also an enthusiastic 21-year-old Canadian. You're looking at such a phenomenon. And though I am aware that my ex-British accent probably gets up your nose a little, there is no one more dedicated to the development of the Canadian artist than this young adult. Never in our history has there been a greater need for art. Never has our country needed her artists more. Never has a dialogue, province to province, been more necessary. Never has a celebration of our national culture been more overdue.

The original destination of the Quilt was this: to celebrate and stimulate the young people of Alberta, to encourage them to know their own history so they could begin building a future which is richer in every way, stronger and prouder but also more tolerant, more enlightened, more human. This is, I know, as paradoxical to the times we live in as

Signor Valentine's unhappy life was to the holiday over which he now presides. All of us have in the last year watched with mesmerized anxiety, as the events of Slovakia and the Czech republic, Somalia, Rwanda, and Chechnya, have unfolded. All the thought and talk we devote to these matters have displaced all the thought and talk we were devoting only a few years ago to what finally seemed a world in recuperation after years of self-inflicted wounds. A world of thawing cold wars, tumbling Berlin walls, uniting Europes, fading apartheids, honing constitutions. But now most distressing of all is the real possibility of a nation basically, humanly, fuelled on love and spirituality, shuddering to a halt on suspicion and distrust. The *Alberta Quilt* celebrated the simultaneous coming together of today's young people, and of the rich past of our province: paradoxically, and precisely. Because outside the theatre we seemed to have yielded into a systematic tearing apart.

In the Quilt we told of pre-human times, the arrival of humankind, the arrival of the first Europeans, and we told of today. As you all know, it is not an easy task to teach the young about the past. It's even harder to prepare them for the future. How can we expect them to understand what it is to be Canadian when much of the world seems to have forgotten what it is to be human?

We know that some 500 years ago, Columbus, with wrong geography on his charts and wrong goals on his mind, spotted the terra firma that has become the Americas. We know that in that tiny moment when the first hand on shore waved to the first hand on the ship, the history of the world was utterly changed. And we are deeply aware of who was here long before Columbus arrived, and how the aboriginal people lived harmoniously with this vast land, and of the ways they helped to make us what we are today. And though it was taken us far too long, we are beginning to realize how much they have to teach us about the natural world surrounding us, about each other and about ourselves.

Our instinct to explore is still strong, but now we reach through projects like the *Alberta Quilt* and the many projects in which you are all involved, to learn to understand and to share. The suppression of the communal creative experience, such as the arts provide, in favour of short-term, self-serving, political agendas has helped to engender the terrible isolation, the disconnection which many people feel today. The aloneness which drives them to feel that the impact they can have on society is through violence, through racism, and other forms of bigotry. In a speech given to a group of Montreal businessmen in 1978, I spoke of the importance of Quebec to English Canada and of our support of them, and our admiration for their culture and their beauty. The message seems even more urgent today.

I spoke then of Chekhov's *Uncle Vanya*: a country doctor is reminded by a young woman that he is capable of beauty. A remarkable phrase, a remarkable thought — capable of beauty. Dr. Astrov's medical specialty is assisting women in childbirth. But he cares about renewal and nurturing in all of nature's rich activity. He plants forests where old ones have been cut down, he seeks remedies for diseases which most of his colleagues accepted as epidemic and incurable. And he describes those who continue to fight the good fight, those who have a hands-on relationship with nature and with humanity as being capable of beauty. This very poetic, yet realistic and hard-working definition is the one that I like to apply to artists. In the toughest, most demanding sense, we are all capable of beauty. And, like Astrov, I believe that this blessing brings with it an immense responsibility: that creative people have an obligation to set and monitor standards of integrity, sensitivity and cooperation for all of mankind. And almost everything we do is easier than fulfilling that one blessed capacity.

We must, in our own way, fight until it is achieved, and we must surely strive within our own province, and from province to province, to see that the young people who come after us understand that they are all capable of beauty. As a member of the human family, each of us feels the need to effect the condition of our species. Unfortunately we cannot, or will not, achieve this through nurturing, through the sharing of beauty and ideas, through questioning and refining. Our next impulse may be to attack, to humiliate, to raise our own self-esteem by obliterating others. This is the human equation at its barest and most irrational. But one must not forget that art is a powerful antidote. Creativity is a powerful alternative. Art keeps tearing us away from petty prejudices and minor grievances; turning us back to nature, to our own kind, and to the great triumphs and sorrows which we have in common.

The *Alberta Quilt* embraced our past in as much detail as we could encompass in a two-week period, and the contribution of these young people who reflected all the economic, educational, and cultural diversity of Alberta itself, was immeasurable. They were the principal authors, performers, designers, technicians, and stage managers of virtually everything that the quilt embraced. The teams explored the history of their home province far beyond the boundaries of the regular school curricula while gathering astounding new insights and skills from masters of the theatrical art. Everyone from the most experienced professional to the most wide-eyed beginner gave generously of his or her time, energy, and knowledge. Everyone was required to commit above and beyond the customary commitments to rehearsing a play because we were reinventing our history, our art, and ourselves. There was no guidebook or blueprint for collecting and presenting a project of this size. We were flying by the seat of our collective pants — flying high, and ranging wide, and learning as we went along.

"The kids I met," wrote Liz Nicholls in the *Edmonton Journal*, "couldn't stop talking about the contagious, creative energy, the ingenuity, and the spontaneous invention of their mentors." "Those guys could work with a bunch of us for a couple of hours and ended up with a play," said one kid. "You take 60 dancers, they improvise, and *voilà*, you have a battle of the ice floes as the Rockies erupt." "Hot," he said. "Cool," said another. "You start with an idea," said one diminutive bopper, "you start with an idea," and then in something like awe added, "and you end up with — theatre."

"And indeed by the time the dress rehearsals were happening, the kids were exhausted by the demands on them and continually ecstatic about the practical magic of it all," Miss Nicholls continued. The quality of the work, the immediate correlation between what you learn and what you can make happen, and the excitement discovering that you are creative, was perhaps the most wonderful feature of quilting in every sense of the word. Not far behind was the unexpected revelation that the audience was to share, namely, that Alberta history wasn't a drag. The kids told me that they'd feared the worst, a knee-jerk reaction to school, as they said. They/we were therefore surprised, nay delighted, to appreciate a great sweep of time and the quilt collage of images from pre-human roots 12,000 BC to edgy, wrenching, sometimes hilarious dramatic exchanges in the development of the boisterous, crazy quilt of cultures that is our society of 1995.

Kids wrote the scenes which were written with an economy that is rare in Canadian theatre which tends to the word choked. They erupted in the fluid, nonlinear, cinematic sequences on stage, and they didn't shy away from the dark side of our history. Shrouded with less than glorious moments when persecuting impulses gained the upper hand, the burning KKK crosses, to the taunting of the Mennonite pacifist youth at a Didsbury Farmer's Market, to the internment of Japanese farm workers. Not pretty, but as writer (and colleague) John Murrell put it, "We have to be able to look in the mirror and not squint." It's a story that is close to home as the current Albertan political climate of dissension, deficit obsession, hostility to minorities, official homophobia, etc., etc., will testify.

And it seems important and somehow cheering that kids take a beady-eyed look at what's gone wrong here. Our sense of community has never seemed more fragile and the juxtaposition of scenes from the oil well gush, of the changed life as we knew it in 1947, to a vaudeville show at Edmonton in 1913, to ballet classes in Banff in 1957, took that fragility into account, but had an oddly celebratory spirit too.

From the audience eye view, the *Alberta Quilt* turned out to be a veritable seminar in theatrical possibilities. The production eradicated the frontiers, embracing dance, music, dramatic exchanges, puppetry, and it unfolded on stage in a set of stage pictures that lingered in the mind because of their apparent simplicity. Always a sense of what singles Alberta out, what identifies the province. For that remarkable sense of place alone, something like the quilt is worth doing as an annual event: different every time out. So much ink and angst have been expended on the Canadian identity that the term itself has been bleached into a cliche. Make yourselves a quilt, and explode the cliche into a rich, variegated, tangible experience."

The last scene of our quilt was written by 19-year-old Scott Sharplin. It went like this.

> *The first European on the banks of the North Saskatchewan, November 1754. A letter from Anthony*

*Henday to governor James Sherman at York Fort On
The Bay, dated at Blackfoot Camp, North River, on the
11th of November 1754.*

I have arrived at the camp of the Blackfoot and I have
been received very well. The Chief of the tribe has welcomed me as an honoured guest. I am cheered that the
first meetings have gone so well. As the first man of the
Empire, indeed the first white man at all to traverse
this far west, I considered it my duty to extend favour-
able first impressions to all I encounter. I report with
disappointment that the Blackfoot do not seem interested in trading with us. They will not hazard the canoe
trip back to the Hudson's Bay, as it threatens danger
and starvation. After my travels, I understand their
hesitation. Besides, the Indians seem to want for nothing. There is buffalo and moose in abundance here.
And though the region is harsh, they have thrived for
generations. It is, I confess, not the Blackfoot but the
land which holds me in its thrall. Standing today on the
banks of this mighty river, I looked west and beheld the
shining mountains as I've heard them call. I've never
seen anything so beautiful and majestic in my life. The
wide prairies and rich swelling forest of pines contribute to the region's magic. Perhaps the superstitions of
the Indians have influenced me in some way, for as I
look at this exalted stretch of God's earth, I cannot help
thinking of spirits. It seems the forests and plains are
alive with spirits, or with some equally ineffable energy. The Indians believe that the spirits of their ances-
tors inhabit the landscape. I feel the influences of the
past here, shaping the present, guiding the land and its
inhabitants. But there is more. There is the past, and
then there is the future. This land burgeons with potential. Perhaps it is simply the potential for profits, as we
may yet find a way to trade with the Blackfoot, but to
my humble imagination, it seems as though there is
more. Between the past and the future, this land seems
indeed infinite. You must by now be questioning the
sanity of your explorer. I assure you I am of sound
mind, but I cannot expect you to understand my senti-
ments unless you were here with me, stood up where I
stood, between the shining mountains and the endless

prairies, and felt the spirits of what has been and what is yet to come flow through you. It is a wondrous thrill, an unparalleled joy, and a source of hope which, I pray, will remain for as long as the land is here.

Your obedient servant, Anthony Henday.

Three hundred and fifty figures standing in the darkness watching a display of Northern Lights began to sing:

> Proud, feeling proud, want to shout it right out loud, being proud.
> Young, being young, singing till our song is sung, singing young.
> Free, singing free, that's the best of you and me, feeling free.
> So write a new page, create a new age, create the new land, dream large, understand.
> Remember what's past, good things that must last.
> Be brave, being new, be strong, being true, being proud,
> Proud, feeling proud, want to shout it right out loud, being proud.
> Young, being young, singing till our song is sung, singing young.
> Free, singing free, that's the best of you and me.
> Feeling free, feeling young, feeling proud, proud.

Philadelphia Resolution

MARCH 24, 1986

- Whereas, American Society is deeply concerned with the condition of elementary and secondary education; and

- Whereas, the arts are basic to education and have great value in and of themselves and for the knowledge, skills and values they impart; and

- Whereas, the arts are a widely neglected curriculum and educational resource in American schools; and

- Whereas, numerous national reports have cited the arts as one of the most basic disciplines of the curriculum; and

- Whereas, every American child should have equal educational opportunity to study the arts as representations of the highest intellectual achievements of humankind;

- Therefore, the undersigned individuals, representing a broad cross-section of national arts organizations, agree:

- That every elementary and secondary school should offer a balanced, sequential, and high quality program of instruction in arts disciplines taught by qualified teachers and strengthened by artists and arts organizations as an essential component of the curriculum;

- That we promote public understanding of the connections between the study of the arts disciplines, the creation of art, and the development of a vibrant, productive American civilization.

- That we urge inclusion of support for rigorous, comprehensive arts education in the arts development efforts of each community;

- That we pursue development of local, state and national policies that result in more effective support for arts education and the professional teachers and artists who provide it.

Appendix D

Ontario Arts Education Accord

A Statement on Arts Education to the Royal
Commission on Learning
September 1993

Arts Education Council of Ontario
Council of Drama in Education
Dance/Community of Educators
Ontario Music Educators' Association
Ontario Society for Education through Art

STATEMENT OF INTENTION

Five associations — the Arts Education Council of Ontario, the Council
of Drama in Education, Dance/Community of Educators, the Ontario
Music Educators' Association, and the Ontario Society for Education
through Art — serve as the provincial voice for arts education in the
Province of Ontario. Together we represent all levels and areas of specialization within arts education. Our mandate is to advance and promote education in all the arts.

These five arts associations advocate and promote on behalf of the
arts in education, offer opportunities for professional and leadership
development, communicate information about current trends, develop-

ments, future directions and innovations in arts education. In addition, we provide access to a large network of arts educators and artists, and represent the interests, concerns, values, and priorities of arts educators in the province. We recognize that there are many dimensions to teaching and learning in the visual and performing arts and that other organizations share our concern for the arts in Canadian life.

The following statements represent a summary of the joint beliefs, objectives and positions of the Arts Education Council of Ontario, the Council of Drama in Education, Dance/Community of Educators, the Ontario Music Educators' Association, and the Ontario Society for Education through Art.

LEARNING AND THE ARTS

We as a society will know that education has fulfilled its mandate when our citizens have learned how to:

- create healthy personal lives
- becoming contributing members of their community
- be productive within a global economy
- embrace education as a lifelong quest.

Learning in, through, and about the arts involves:

- using the mind, body, heart, and soul for intellectual, social, emotional, and spiritual well-being
- participating in, and contributing to, the arts life of your community
- knowing how you can earn a living in the arts, and how the arts community contributes to economic productivity
- using creative, critical, and constructive thinking to connect life experiences
- recognizing the role of the artistic community and its contributions to the culture of the province.

DEFINING THE ARTS

Students are engaged in an arts experience when they:

- communicate their own ideas and feelings, and appreciate those of others;
- use the vocabularies and processes of dance, drama, music, and visual arts, as well as creative writing, film and media arts;
- generate ideas and make choices as individuals or in groups; and
- develop the ability to imagine what has been, and what might be.

POSITION STATEMENT FOR LEARNING IN THE ARTS

Program Equity

The arts education associations believe that every school in the Province

of Ontario must:

- provide for all students at every level, a balanced, comprehensive, and sequential arts program;
- have teachers who are qualified, competent, and confident in the arts;
- provide environments which allow for healthy and safe learning in the arts;
- include arts in their core curriculum, and allocate quality classroom time to arts experiences;
- provide significant financial support for arts programs;
- support teachers in their professional growth as educators in the arts.

Program Excellence

The arts education associations believe that the arts programs in every

Ontario school must:

1. develop the capabilities of each student;
2. reflect the cultural diversity of our society;
3. be responsive to the needs of the diverse special populations present in our schools;
4. connect with the content of the wider curriculum;

5. incorporate appropriate and current teaching materials and equipment;

6. use new technologies to enhance the outcomes of teaching and learning in the arts.

Program Accountability

The arts education associations believe that accountability for the arts in education in the Province of Ontario rests with:

1. students who demonstrate artistic competence and understanding, and assess their own and others' work;

2. teachers who model authentic assessment, using both objective and personal criteria;

3. administrators who value process and can assess beyond arts products and performance;

4. an informed and responsive public.

Program Partnerships

The arts education associations believe that in the Province of Ontario:

1. students should be contributors to, and participants in, the cultural life of their community;

2. schools should have the primary responsibility for providing quality instruction in the arts for children and adolescents;

3. professional artists and community arts groups should be used to complement and enrich school-based arts programs;

4. parents should be actively involved in the arts experiences of their children;

5. cultural and business organizations should be invited to become partners with their community schools.